THE HUMAN DIFFERENCE

THE HUMAN DIFFERENCE

Animals, Computers, and the
Necessity of Social Science

ALAN WOLFE

UNIVERSITY OF CALIFORNIA PRESS
BERKELEY   LOS ANGELES   OXFORD

Portions of this book have appeared in somewhat different form in the following articles: "Sociological Theory in the Absence of People: The Limits of Luhmann's Systems Theory," *Cardozo Law Review* 13 (March 1992): 1729–43; "Mind, Self, Society and Computer: Artificial Intelligence and the Sociology of Mind," *American Journal of Sociology* 96 (March 1991): 1073–96; "Social Theory and the Second Biological Revolution," *Social Research* 57 (Fall 1990): 615–48; "Up from Humanism," *The American Prospect*, Winter 1991, pp. 112–27; "Algorithmic Justice," *Cardozo Law Review* 11 (July/August 1990): 1409–34; "Sociology as a Vocation," *American Sociologist* 21 (Summer 1990): 136–48; and "Books vs. Articles: Two Ways of Publishing Sociology," *Sociological Forum* 5 (September 1990): 477–89.

University of California Press
Berkeley and Los Angeles, California

University of California Press, Ltd.
Oxford, England

Library of Congress Cataloging-in-Publication Data

Wolfe, Alan, 1942–
    The Human difference : animals, computers, and the necessity of social science / Alan Wolfe.
        p.   cm.
    Includes bibliographical references and index.
    ISBN 0-520-08013-0 (alk. paper)
        1. Sociology—Methodology.   2. Social sciences—
    Methodology.   3. Sociobiology.   4. Human ecology.
    5. Computers—Social aspects.   I. Title.
    HM24.W64   1993
    301'.01—dc20   92-8355
                                                             CIP

Printed in the United States of America

1   2   3   4   5   6   7   8   9

The paper used in this publication meets the minimum requirements of American National Standard for Information Sciences—Permanence of Paper for Printed Library Materials, ANSI Z39.48-1984. ⊗

The difference between facts which are what they are independent of human desire and endeavor and facts which are to some extent what they are because of human interest and purpose . . . cannot be got rid of by any methodology. The more sincerely we appeal to facts, the greater is the importance of the distinction between facts which condition human activity and facts which are conditioned by human activity.

John Dewey

*This book is dedicated to my children,
Rebekka, Jan, and Andreas.*

Contents

Preface

It is inevitable that those who come late to their passions are more attached to them, and more concerned with how they flourish, than those who develop them early. My concern with sociological theory is relatively recent. Trained as a political scientist, I learned Durkheim and Weber by teaching them to undergraduates when I accidentally found myself employed in a sociology department. It was a case of appreciation at first sight. Sociology, a field with little public respect (and an often all too easy target when administrators eye departments ripe for closing), remains, for me, the best way available to understand what it means to be modern. It is an academic discipline capable of offering lasting insights, not only into how we live but also into how we ought to live.

As a late convert to sociology, I have spent considerable time drawing intellectual maps that locate this discipline in relationship to other ways of inquiry. My previous book, *Whose Keeper? Social Science and Moral Obligation,* was at one level an effort to address the contradictions between modernity and morality. But it was also concerned with the relationship between sociology and the other social sciences, especially economics and political science. Even if this second theme was more important to me than it was to many of the book's readers, I felt a need to say something positive about a discipline that seemed to have lost a sense of purpose. In attempting to map sociology's location among the social sciences, I made three general points.

First, I argued, sociology generally proceeds by moving from
particulars to universals, whereas economics and politics often
go in the other direction. If there is something distinct about
sociology, it is an emphasis on specific places and situations,
based on the belief that knowledge lies in the details. (This
emphasis on location may well be responsible for my concern
with sociology's own location.) Erving Goffman is in this sense
the quintessential sociologist. From a particular encounter,
event, or situation, Goffman would extract more detail than
anyone thought possible. His refusal to generalize, always the
mark against him as a theorist, may have been a silent protest
against other social scientists who were so quick to reach conclusions in the absence of particulars. (To argue, for example,
that all behavior is motivated by self-interest, as many economists do, is to run roughshod over the particulars of time and
place.) Sociology, in making those particulars its major domain,
will always stand in awkward relationship to the modern tendency to universalize. The attention lavished by sociologists
on community, ethnicity, family, and informal networks is at
least to some degree an effort to preserve particulars in the
face of increasing universalization.

Second, I pointed out that sociology's distinct location on
that intellectual map called knowledge was a product of how
it thought about parts and wholes. For economists, whose commitment to methodological individualism is strenuous, individuals and their voluntary choices make up social systems.
For political scientists, concerned with states and (in the contemporary world) even larger entities, individuals disappear
into classes, populations, and vast shifts of power. But sociologists, unable to decide whether the macro or the micro
ought to be their major focus, combine both in ingenious efforts to reconcile positions that other disciplines take more for
granted. This ambivalent location between the macro and the
micro can work to sociology's detriment, as when practitioners
turn with envy to the models generated by other social sciences
for their inspiration. But it can also be a major advantage,
staking out a claim that an adequate theory for real people will
concentrate neither on individual decisions nor on large-scale
structures but will find truth in the interaction between them.

At the heart of the sociological enterprise is a concern with how parts and wholes interrelate.

The third major difference between sociology and the other social sciences, I concluded, lies in the way each discipline approaches the problem of rules. Whatever the differences between theories based on voluntary choice and those that emphasize the coercive capacities of states, both imagine the individual agent as a rule-follower. The rule may be a law codified by a state or an instinct hard-wired into the brain, but in both cases individuals are understood to confront a set of predetermined options and to pick one (or to have one picked for them). The somewhat naïve psychology of both approaches was, I argued, a major flaw in their ability to account for the paradoxes of modernity. Sociology's concern with rule-making—that is, its emphasis on how people construct the world around them—contrasts with the concern with rule-following contained in economics and political science. If we are to understand how people make the rules that in turn rule their behavior, we will need a more sophisticated understanding of how cognition is not universally hard-wired into brains but situated in particular contexts. A sociology influenced by ethnomethodology, like a psychology capable of understanding culture, could supplement and enrich those models of human behavior that are more concerned with predictability and regularity than they are with the messy details of real people acting in real life.

The Human Difference is a sequel to *Whose Keeper?*—not because it directly addresses issues of moral obligation (it does not) but in the sense that it carries forward a concern with the location of the sociological enterprise. This time, however, the map is not confined to the social sciences; rather, it extends the borders to adjacent fields of inquiry. Since at least the middle of the nineteenth century, many practitioners of social science, including sociologists, have assumed that the physical and biological sciences constitute the proper model of how to conduct the search for knowledge. We now may be at the end of a specific period of intellectual history characterized by that faith, for the results produced by the scientific model have been few indeed. Although the scientific model continues to dominate the way social science is carried out in American universities, an earlier optimism that "behavioral science" would both produce uncontestable findings and help us bring order out of modernity's chaos no longer rings true. At a time when the natural sciences themselves are racked with epistemological, political, and gender-sensitive disputes over knowledge, they can only reinforce, rather than solve, dilemmas that have been at the heart of social science since their origins.

But if the social sciences are not "science," what are they? C. P. Snow told us in the 1950s that the intellectual world was characterized by two cultures, the scientific and the literary, and there was regrettably little communication between them. Should social science, in turning away from the natural sciences, turn instead to literature? Historians of sociology, such as Wolf Lepenies and Bruce Mazlish, have begun to uncover the important nineteenth-century relationship between literature and social science, and later in this book I will argue that there are reasons why modern literary forms and modern forms of social science share some of the same assumptions. But whatever the relevance of literature to social science, literary theory, as currently practiced, is another matter entirely. Literature is in fact under attack, and rarely with more vigor than among its own interpreters, especially those influenced by post-modernism. Texts are not written, especially not by authors, we have been told; they write themselves. The study of literature ought really to be understood as the study of rhetoric, it has been argued, and while the laws of rhetoric may be different from those of physics, they are laws and they do have their own logic. It would be odd indeed for the social sciences to turn away from science to literary theory when literary theory is itself turning to information theory and other sciences for models of how texts can organize themselves self-referentially.

I argue in this book that neither science nor literary theory can serve as a proper model for the social sciences. Social science is different from these adjacent fields of inquiry, just as, within the social sciences, sociology has emerged in a form quite different from economics and political science. Specifically, the subjects of the physical sciences play no role in interpreting the rules that govern their behavior, whereas the subjects of the social sciences at least have the potential to do so. We cannot study rocks, plants, and beavers (or computers and other algorithmically driven machines) with the same tools that we use to study modern people, who have capacities of mind, because the tools that offer insights into the former are unlikely to help us predict and understand the behavior of the latter. The social sciences, I will argue, are distinct sciences because the species they presume to understand is a distinct species. To understand the location of the social sciences on contemporary maps of intellectual knowledge, one must return to the emphasis on philosophical anthropology that characterized nineteenth-century efforts at grand social theory. Because humans are different from other animal and mechanical species, our methods of understanding their behavior have to be different as well.

Like *Whose Keeper?* this book argues that there are distinctive ways of understanding the world associated with different academic disciplines. My arguments to some degree go against at least one significant strain in contemporary theorizing, which advocates techniques that cross disciplinary boundaries. Rational choice theory, post-modernism, and hermeneutics, whatever their differences with each other, all see themselves as applying to many disciplines, not just one. I often feel uncomfortable when I argue for one particular discipline, especially when the discipline I advocate has practitioners, including many of the leading voices in the profession, who do a very different kind of sociology than I do. Nonetheless, there is a historical discipline called sociology; it included many of the greatest social thinkers ever to reflect on the modern condition—people such as Emile Durkheim, Max Weber, and George Herbert Mead; and it remains a continuing source of inspiration for late-twentieth-century dilemmas.

Although *The Human Difference* carries forward an argument for sociology, however, it is less confrontational with the other social sciences than was *Whose Keeper?* For this book—in comparing the social sciences to ways of knowing associated with the natural sciences, on the one hand, and rhetoric, on

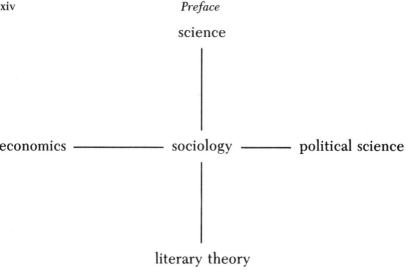

Figure 1

the other—necessarily emphasizes at least one similarity between economics, political science, anthropology, and sociology. All of them presume, at least most of the time, to study human beings. (Each, however, has a few practitioners who want to apply the insights of these disciplines to animal behavior.) Because my concern is with human beings, I hope that what I have to say will be of interest to all social scientists, even though, because my own field is sociology, I will speak disproportionately of it and will, especially in the first and last chapters, argue for its special insights. My objective is not to practice a form of sociological imperialism—I consider myself generally a pluralist in these matters—but simply to use the discipline with which I am most familiar to argue for insights valid to the social sciences as a whole. And if a touch of sociological imperialism remains, it may be because sociology has focused more thoroughly on the question of the human difference, and its implications for how we understand the world, than other intellectual traditions.

Sociology, as a social science, can be located on a "vertical" axis with respect to its adjacent disciplines, just as it can be located on a "horizontal" axis with respect to its sister social sciences. If the arguments of *Whose Keeper?* are linked with those presented in this book, sociology would be located as shown in figure 1—although what is on the top and on the bottom, as well as on the right and on the left, can all change, depending on one's perspective. From this perspective, sociology is in many ways on an equal plane with the other social sciences, while at the same time occupying something of a special location. That captures, as best as I can map it, my own sense that sociology both is and is not a special and unique way of understanding the human world around us.

If there is one conclusion that follows from this mapping, it is that social scientists ought to stop looking around them to decide how to carry out their work. It is time for them to find a way of studying human beings that takes full account of the distinctiveness of the human beings they study. *The Human Difference* is a defense of humanism, not in the sense that the humanities are different from the sciences, although they are, but because humanism is especially concerned with our species and what it does. We are a puzzling species, capable of doing great things while also capable of wreaking great harm. Our fascination with ourselves strikes some of our numbers as arrogant and narcissistic. But for all our concern with ourselves, we have only recently begun to understand some of the most elementary things about us. The more we learn about how we act and think, the less likely we will feel the need to model our understanding of ourselves on the study of other animal species or computers. Humanism is anything but at the end of the road; properly understood, it has only just begun.

Acknowledgments

Colleagues at two institutions provided the critical commentary necessary to a project of this sort. When I was at Queens College, I received sound advice from Charles Smith, Dean Savage, and Melvin Reichler. At the Graduate Faculty of the New School for Social Research, Richard Bernstein gave the entire manuscript the benefit of his careful reading as well as his frank and helpful criticism. Neil Smelser and Howard Becker provided in-depth commentary when asked to do so for the publisher, and I am grateful to both (though neither bears any responsibility for the final product). Abdul Malik helped with the bibliography. Finally, as always, I want to thank my wife, Jytte Klausen, for her confidence in me.

Chapter One

A Distinct Science for a Distinct Species

Sociology's Fragility

Sociology, one of the youngest of the social sciences, may also prove to be one of the most short-lived. The product of a progressive intellectual milieu, sociology announced a faith in the ability of people to control the world they had created. Just as the forces of civilization and culture were beating back the irrationality and wildness of nature, so the forces of reason and science would create order out of what was once a Hobbesian war of all against all. Sociology's optimism stood in sharp contrast to the debunking realism that had prevailed in political thought since Machiavelli and the playful cynicism that Mandeville contributed to the science of economics. To its earlier practitioners, sociology was the queen of the sciences because it was at one and the same time noble, caring, and somewhat imperious.

Begun at a time when the problems of industrialization, urbanization, and bureaucratization raised in compelling form the question of what it means for humans to live together in groups, sociology sought a precarious path between the attractive individuality of liberalism and the equally seductive, but even more dangerous, quest for a return to organic wholeness and unity. Its stance would always be in the middle—not only, in Wolf Lepenies's phrase, between literature and science but also between left and right, realism and romanticism,

1

the sacred and the profane, and the individual and the collectivity.[1] This last ambivalence is worth stressing. Sociology's two
greatest discoveries were the self and society, and neither of
them had much in common with the individual and the state.
Unlike the individual, who in liberal theory was governed by
an unvarying human nature, the self was embedded in culture
and was plastic enough to develop and learn. Unlike the state,
which in theory exercised a monopoly of violence, society was
the product of consensus openly arrived at, ruled by the norms
created out of the behavior of real people in real life. Sociology
was the product of a particular intellectual opening, a period—
no one now knows how brief—when it seemed possible to
maintain order without sacrificing liberty.

This precariousness of sociology gives its subject matter a
temporality, in contrast with the more timeless concerns of
economics and political science. No one doubts that there will
always be money, that some will try to get more of it than
others, and thus that scarcities of valuable things will always
constitute the human condition. Similarly, despite the shock
effect he thought he would have on polite opinion, Gaetano
Mosca's discovery that there will always be some who rule and
others who will be ruled no longer seems especially noteworthy. But that society can continue to exist, that ties of solidarity
will continue to link people together as partners in a common
project—this is a riskier proposition. The rise of totalitarian
states in this century showed that organic unity can destroy
the social self as well as the atomistic individual. The popularity
of laissez-faire conservatism in the late twentieth century, two
hundred years after its significant flaws were exposed, shows
that untrammeled individualism can weaken society as well as
the state. Late in arriving, sociology could be early in leaving.

Its departure would be a tragedy. For the very fragility and
temporality of the social make it worth preserving. If the social
ties that link people together in groups are unappreciated,
there is little need for a discipline emphasizing their continued
importance. And if such ties are universal and permanent, we
need hardly concern ourselves with the ways in which changes
in social and intellectual fashion threaten them. Sociology, un-

like the other social sciences, requires constant rediscovery, taking us by surprise at precisely those moments when we forget about its existence. Always vulnerable, it is always changing, critically reexamining itself to account for rapid social transformation. (In contrast, the very timelessness of the economic contributes to the fact that the discipline of economics has changed so little, in all but technique, since Adam Smith.) The more we take society for granted, the more we need to rethink its importance.

And, it seems, we do take the social very much for granted. Modern societies are composed of dense cities, complex bureaucracies, huge industries—all of which are dependent on fragile social ties to function at all. We rarely understand the importance of these ties until their breakdown results in crime, chaos, or lowered productivity; and we all too often rely on models of human behavior that pay little attention to them. The concerns of sociology—especially ties of trust, caring, and personal knowledge—are in one sense trivial and obvious and in another sense vital and irreplaceable. They are so crucial to our existence as human beings that we can, for long periods of time, forget about them completely.

The classical social theorists of the nineteenth century understood better than we do the potential fragility of the social. For them, the social world was an essential aspect of the human world, and the human world was understood to be a very recent discovery. Indeed, compared to the natural world, which has been with us since the beginning of time, the social world seemed not only miraculous but also improbable. Nineteenth-century sociologists could not take society for granted, because it was all so new to them. Today, surrounded by societies that seem overdeveloped in their density and complexity, we would rather ignore the social than argue for its special role in our existence.

No other aspect of nineteenth-century social theory better captured this sense of society's fragility than the almost automatic anthropocentric assumptions it contained. Sociology was a product of the notion that humans were, and ought to be, at the center of our attention. Its founding thinkers agreed that the line between humans and the worlds surrounding them was dangerously thin and that, therefore, humans and their accomplishments required a special defense. This sense that the social could at any moment be taken back by other worlds recently conquered gave nineteenth-century social theory its predisposition to view our own species as superior to everything else.

From the perspective of nineteenth-century sociology, two worlds surrounded human creations: the supernatural world above them and the animal world below. At one level, sociology's anthropocentrism represented a long struggle on the part of secular thinkers to turn attention away from superhuman entities to human ones. Asserting the centrality of the human was a way of insisting that the products of people's activity, including religion itself, grew out of the capacity of individuals to make the world in which they lived. Because some of its practitioners, especially Durkheim, regarded sociology as a secular religion, they placed humans at the center, just as theologians placed God at the center. As long as sociology and religion were to some degree in competition, many sociological theorists were not prepared to conclude that the social world was safe from the supernatural one. Indeed, Durkheim could ensure the security of the human and the social only by elevating them to the status of the sacred.

The milieu that led sociology to its anthropocentrism was shaped by sociology's relationship not only to the superhuman but also the "subhuman," the world of other animal species. Sociology separated itself from the world of nature just as vigorously as it separated itself from the world of God. Nearly all thinkers in the sociological tradition regarded humans as a special and distinct species capable of taking control over its destiny. No one doubted that humans were driven by biology, or that some aspects of their behavior were similar to the behavior of other animal species. Obviously, humans lived in nature and therefore were to some degree subject to the laws of natural science. But because humans built culture out of nature, their affairs could not be understood on the basis of laws borrowed directly from the study of the nonhuman world. Different from religion, sociology would also be different from science, at least the biological sciences. It would certainly borrow much from science, as indeed it would from religion, but its ultimate calling would be neither prophecy nor taxonomy.

Sociology and religion have settled into a relationship of tolerable coexistence. Since the intellectual turf of both is similar, sociologists soon developed respect for religion, and religious thinkers made their peace with sociology. But if a war ended between the human centeredness of sociology and the God centeredness of religion, no peace exists between the human centeredness of sociology and the challenge to anthropocentrism coming from those who respect nature and other animal species. The contemporary intellectual milieu, which finds little to question in the secularism of sociology, challenges at every turn the sociological separation of culture from nature. It is precisely the commitment to humans and their accomplishments—an outgrowth of the Enlightenment and its faith in powers of mind and reason—that marks the difference between the late-nineteenth-century intellectual environment and the late-twentieth-century milieu. Sociology's fragility, in its latest manifestation, is not the result of controversies over method or theory. The challenge is far more serious than those, for it involves the question of whether the subjects of this new science—human beings themselves—have any distinctive features that require a distinctive science to be understood.

Nature's Revenge

The Enlightenment's greatest discovery was ourselves. In the writings of leading eighteenth-century thinkers—Immanuel Kant comes immediately to mind—this discovery of the human being took two forms. On the one hand, all humans were assigned equal moral worth. In what was surely a radical point of view for his time, Kant refused to accept the notion that servants, peasants, or menial workers ought to be regarded with any less respect than bankers or aristocrats. For Kant, such equality was more than political. Human autonomy—a product of the mind's rationality and universality—linked together everyone as equally capable of engaging in practical reason. Since we all possess potential moral agency, none of us has a right to treat another as a mere thing.

Equality within the human species was, however, accompanied by inequality among the species. Because respect for persons occupied a prominent place in Kant's thought, things lacking autonomy, including other species found in nature, could not exist on the same moral plane. For Kant—as for the sociological thinkers who would come later—the human creature was distinct from all other species. Humanism was literally that. In its strongest form, anthropocentrism was frankly hierarchical: human beings stood at the top, and all other species existed to serve their needs. In its softer forms, disproportionate attention was paid to human beings compared to other living creatures. But in most of these traditions, most fascinatingly in Kant's, people ought to respect nature, not because animals or trees should be treated as moral creatures but, instead, because if we mistreat nature, we are more likely to mistreat one another.[2]

The first of the Enlightenment's discoveries has survived almost intact for two hundred years. One simply cannot find an intellectually credible defense of inherited inequality in the modern world, so strong is the commitment to the notion that all human beings ought to be viewed as having equal moral worth. Inequalities persist, and often worsen, but those defenses of inequality that remain—based on notions of the market or of just deserts—still tend to contain an argument that all humans are *potentially* equal, even if forces in the real world prevent such equality from being realized. Because inequality is now more often understood economically than mentally, one of the Enlightenment's discoveries, at least in theory, is secure. The burden of proof is on those who would argue for inherent inequality, not the other way around.

That same sense of security does not extend to the other of the Enlightenment's great discoveries about humans. Anthropocentrism is embarrassing to contemporary readers. The idea that human creatures ought to be at the center of the world has been challenged by two intellectual awakenings. First, we have come to learn so much about the wonders of the natural world that placing humans at the center seems not only morally crude but also scientifically inaccurate, reflecting what has been called "an outdated metaphysic, an anthropocentric evolutionism that uses humanity as the yardstick by which to measure the rest of the animal world."[3] And second, confidence in the human project has been unable to survive the political and ecological horrors of recent history: how can a species capable of genocide and total war possibly congratulate itself on its special place? From Martin Heidegger to Theodor Adorno and Max Horkheimer, the Enlightenment's Faustian bargain with nature is viewed as problematic. Nature, it would seem, is having its revenge.

In contrast to the eighteenth-century consciousness that inspired thinkers such as Kant, a new cosmology emerging in the late twentieth century challenges the notion that people are, or ought to be, the measure of all things. A recent statement by a leading paleontologist illustrates all the major themes that characterize this new awareness. According to Stephen Jay Gould, nothing less than our understanding of life itself, and how it evolved on our planet, is at stake in the way we interpret the fossils found in the Burgess Shale in British Columbia. Painstaking reconstruction of the animal life revealed by these fossils suggests that an earlier metaphor of a "tree" of life—consisting of a main branch and subsidiary ones leading off from it—ought to be replaced by the metaphor of a bush composed of many growths, all of them of equal importance. "Our origin is the product of a massive historical contingency," Gould writes, "and we would probably never arise again even if life's tape were replayed a thousand times."[4] We who are human are the result of no purpose, divine or otherwise, but instead a consequence of the random operations of chance.

Gould's controversial points are not about fossils—his refutation of Charles D. Walcott's earlier interpretations is convincing—but about cosmology. Who are we, he repeatedly asks, to think that we are special? The lessons Gould learns from his investigation are the direct opposite of the lessons learned by the earlier worldview in which nineteenth-century social theory once flourished. Then the laws of nature or society revealed rational organization, which our minds were capable of understanding. Now the physical world teaches that, being lucky, we ought to be humble. It is, from Gould's perspective, hubris on a grand scale to put humans in the center, no different in principle from Europeans' putting Europe in the center. Such imperialism has no place in science. Evolution is not a progress report. It says nothing about worth. There are no moral lessons in nature. Its laws reveal no teleology. Evolution just is.

Implicit in this new cosmology is a reversal of the dualism between nature and culture that formed the core of late-nineteenth-century sociological theory. "It is civilization that has made man what he is," Emile Durkheim once wrote. "It is what distinguishes him from the animals: man is man only because he is civilized."[5] Durkheim's frank preference for civilization reads, in the context of today's cosmological assumptions, quaint at best, colonialist at worst. That human beings tear apart nature in order to build cultures capable of satisfying their needs is viewed as a flaw, not an accomplishment. Barry Commoner's "Third Law of Ecology"—Nature knows best—expresses in succinct form the idea that humans are no longer to be trusted.[6] From every corner of academic and intellectual life—the sciences, the humanities, and the social sciences—the human and the cultural are on the defense.

As Commoner's law suggests, ecology is one of the main ingredients in reinforcing the new antihumanistic cosmology. Ecology developed as the study of how organisms interact with each other and with their environment. What made ecology a powerful way of understanding the natural world was the notion that nature generally finds ways to work things out without human intervention. Disturb the food chain, alter the pattern of predator and prey, relocate a species from one habitat to another—and the whole intricate chain will be broken, with consequences no one can predict. Respect for nature, from an ecological perspective, is premised upon avoiding the Faustian temptation to alter what is found. Although ecology originally concerned itself primarily with nonhuman organisms, such as plants and animals, it was not long before moral lessons dealing with the human world were drawn from its premises. Deeply impressed by the self-regulating character of the natural world, many ecologists began to look with dismay upon the clumsy, awkward, and unplanned character of human affairs. It was a short step from that conclusion to one that reversed the distinction between nature and culture by assigning a privileged status to the former rather than the latter.

The revolution in ecological consciousness that occurred in the 1970s took place simultaneously with a revolution in feminist consciousness, and it was not long before scholars such as Carolyn Merchant began to point out the similarities.[7] The concept of nature as a caring and nurturing mother—central to an earlier, more organic theory about the world—gave way to the notion of nature as unpredictable and occasionally nasty; and this notion prepared the way for a rationalized, scientific intervention into natural processes. Science emerged in the seventeenth century not only as a set of techniques but also as an ideological system in which "science was a purely male and chaste venture, seeking domination over, rather than commingling with, a female nature; it promised, and indeed helped promote, the simultaneous vanquishing of nature and of female voracity."[8]

That the scientific quest proceeds by metaphor, and that metaphors can take on a life of their own and affect the results of scientific investigation, seems beyond doubt. But for some writers, the relationship between gender and science is understood more than metaphorically. In their view, the entire process of forcing secrets out of nature and calling the results science produces bad knowledge.[9] Science, this way of thinking continues, is a form of narrative, and, once it is understood as such, the subjects of scientific investigation have as much right to have their story told as those who carry out the investigations. Primates, for example, are "active participants in primatology," and the scientist's obligation is "to listen to the practices of interpretation of the primate order in which primates themselves—monkeys, apes, and people—all have some kind of 'authorship.' "[10] There is no fixed line between our world and that of the other primates, and our understanding of their world is subject to all the limitations of historical knowledge and struggles over power. Therefore, according to these writers, women must be suspicious of any attempt to separate nature from culture. They need to challenge every aspect of the modern, scientific, rational worldview, listening to suppressed voices buried inside themselves or going "deeper" than deep ecology in rejecting instrumental reason.[11] The dualism between nature and culture ought to take its place as one of many dualisms to be rejected or transcended: male/female to begin with, but also subject/object, fact/value, text/reader, being/knowing, presence/absence, noise/silence.

From the perspective of many of the writers just discussed, whether feminist or environmentalist, the evils against nature have been perpetuated by a scientific *Weltanschauung* containing inherent Faustian proclivities. It is therefore noteworthy that some thinkers working in scientific fields also share the assumptions of this new cosmology. One such field, somewhat ironic given its general opposition to feminism, is sociobiology.[12] Impressed by ethological studies of animal behavior, at least some sociobiologists imagine no fundamental break between nature and culture. In their view, humans are driven to a considerable degree by their genetic structures and are limited in their ability to make many of the choices that their excessive pride leads them to believe they can make. At the same time, other animal species possess culture. They are able to reproduce themselves not only through DNA but also by developing tools, communicating, and living in groups. All evolution is a product of both cultural and genetic factors, and the only difference between the human and other species is a matter of degree. What Carl Degler calls the "revival" of Darwinism in American thought, inspired in large part by sociobiology, has altered the intellectual landscape; an earlier belief in the power of culture to explain the world has had to share the stage with theories less certain that culture stands autonomous and distinct from the realm of nature.[13]

Whatever position one may take on the difference between nature and culture, both biology and sociology deal with living creatures. Imagine, therefore, the importance of the discovery of a brand-new species—a nonliving creature endowed with intelligence. A once-firm duality between the world of nature and the world of culture has become a trinity with the invention of the computer, and respect for machines has become as important an item in the antihumanist cosmology as respect for animals. There is an irony in this development as well, for few intellectual trends in the contemporary world seem further removed from the antirationalistic strains of deep ecology and eco-feminism than developments in cognitive psychology, linguistics, and artificial intelligence; Merchant—as well as other feminists, such as Susan Bardo—points to Descartes as a central figure in the mechanical view of the world, while the current wave of interest in artificial intelligence is invariably Cartesian in inspiration.[14] Yet on one point many of those who work with artificial intelligence agree with those who seem to prefer the ethics and morality of nature: both groups do not join Descartes in believing that humans are a superior species. Artificial intelligence elevates the human over the animal only to turn around and elevate the machine over the human. The computer is one more nail in the coffin of anthropocentrism, an additional discovery that makes it impossible for humans to congratulate themselves on their allegedly special powers. And since the powers in question are powers of mind rather than physical strength, the challenge may well prove the most important to date.

If the times were more sympathetic to humans than they are, one would expect a defense of anthropocentrism from the humanities. After all, the very name by which we describe the study of literature and philosophy indicates a proclivity to put humans at the center of the cosmos. Moreover, the challenge to the centrality of humans has come from such scientific fields as ecology, sociobiology, and artificial intelligence—fields that have little in common with aesthetics, poetry, art, and other humanistic disciplines. Yet recent intellectual trends in the study of philosophy and literature strengthen rather than weaken the case that human subjects are disappearing from an emerging contemporary cosmology.

Two philosophers in particular have had an inordinate influence over the way contemporary literary theorists think. Nietzsche, the greatest misogynist of modern times, is the inspiration for those post-modern and post-structuralist sentiments that culminated in Michel Foucault's famous image of man as a figure in the sand about to be washed away by the next severe wave.[15] Meanwhile, Heidegger, who has served as a source of ideas for those involved in the deep ecology movement as well as for many who work in artificial intelligence, has also exerted strong influence over recent movements in literary theory that question humanistic premises about the use of texts to reinforce moral meanings.[16] Deconstruction in particular strives, as Luc Ferry and Alain Renaut put it, "to be fundamentally more Heideggerian than Heidegger himself,"[17] rooting out whatever last vestiges of humanism it can find in Heidegger's thought.

Some of the more extreme versions of the antihumanist cosmology that has assumed such importance in this century consequently come from post-modern professors of literature. Representative of at least one version of this strain of thought are the ideas of Barbara Herrnstein Smith. Like many natural scientists, Herrnstein Smith believes that the distinction between nature and culture ought to be disarmed of its ideological power. There is, she claims, no particular value to the notion that culture gives humans the ability to attribute some permanence to the world. Humans live instead in a natural state of perpetual flux: "With respect to human preferences," she writes, "nothing is uniform, universal, natural, fixed, or determined in advance, either for the species generally, or for any specific individual, or for any portion or fraction of the species, by whatever principle, sociological or other, it is segmented and classified."[18] Because nothing is fixed, the value of a work of literature is functionally equivalent to the evolution of life in Gould's account. In both cases, contingency and randomness, rather than inherent worth or special abilities, dictate the survival of cultural products: humans on the one hand; their creative masterpieces on the other. Herrnstein Smith, of course, speaks only for herself and not for any intellectual movement, but the ideas she expresses indicate that at least one important thinker in the humanities is no longer convinced that there is anything inherently of value in things human.

Finally, despite their origins as a specific science of the human, the social sciences have also felt the impact of an emerging cosmology skeptical of the liberating potential of human efforts. In the years after World War II, American social science in particular was based on premises originally developed by behavioral psychology. If the tools of the natural sciences could not be used to study such slippery matters as consciousness and intention, they could be used for such uncontested actions as how people voted or what groups they joined. The fact that the statistics measuring behavior were generated by human activities rather than the behavior of any other species was viewed as simply part of an intellectual division of labor and involved no sense that the behavior of humans might possess features making rigorous and predictable study of them impossible. Like the founder of behaviorism, John B. Watson, much of behavioral social science recognized "no dividing line between man and brute."[19]

Even though behaviorism is in eclipse, human beings still have not found their way back into social science. Instead, the replacement of behaviorism in psychology by a cognitive science modeled on the computer is premised on the unimportance of the dividing line between man and his machines. One approach to the science of human behavior takes center stage for a short time, and is immediately followed by another, but all with a shared understanding that a science of human society can be modeled on the study of other than human organisms. This failure to develop a human science based on models appropriate to humans is especially evident in the most contentious debate currently taking place in social science theorizing. In nearly all fields of social science inquiry, approaches tend to be divided into two camps: on the one hand, a structuralism that ignores individuals; on the other hand, an emphasis on rational choice that neglects social forces. Yet whatever their other differences, both have a tendency to believe that insights into human behavior can be gleaned by references to the nonhuman world.

Durkheim's unfortunate comment that "the division of labor does not present individuals to one another, but social functions" is still alive in contemporary social science theorizing.[20] Many structuralists, for example, believe that the nonhuman world, with its order and systemic regularity, provides a model for well-functioning, integrated, complexity-reducing human activities. In highly structuralist accounts of social organization, system logic is what counts; specific human characteristics matter little. Echoing Durkheim, Niklas Luhmann argues that "society is not composed of human beings, it is composed of the communication among human beings."[21] What is required, once we grasp this truth, is a "conceptual revolution within sociology."[22] That revolution would turn to cybernetics, biology, and other disciplines concerned with the processing and transmission of information rather than to the humanistic disciplines. In the world as imagined by Niklas Luhmann and other hyperstructuralists, systems are all and people merely contingent.

The situation, however, is not all that different among those who begin with the individual and downplay the importance of systems. Rational choice theory stands worlds apart from Luhmann in its emphasis on the voluntary character of individual decisions, but the question of whether it is *human* individuals who make such decisions is generally answered in the negative. For economists such as Gary Becker, the intellectual overlaps between an economic theory based on self-interest and the Darwinian emphasis on the efficiency and long-term gain of selective evolutionary mechanisms are too powerful to ignore.[23] Indeed, so great is the affinity between rational choice theory and the study of evolutionary mechanisms developed to account for species other than the human that even the critics of the theory rarely argue from specifically human premises. Jon Elster has many critical things to say about the limits of rational choice. He suggests, for example, that natural selection, when applied to specifically human affairs, is a more powerful theory than rational choice. But Elster peppers his examples with references to nonhuman choices and concludes that sociobiology offers a "supplementary" rather than a "rival" theory to his own work.[24] Robert Frank, an economist even more critical of rational choice theory, and one who emphasizes the importance of altruism and sympathy as fundamental passions, nonetheless relies on experiments with nonhuman animals to make many of his points, as if their social behavior could act as a model for understanding ours.[25] It does not seem to matter whether the principles of methodological individualism or its opposite are chosen; in both cases, relatively little emphasis is placed on specifically human ways of constituting the self and society.

There is, then, a set of ideas that can be found in all fields of contemporary intellectual endeavor, whether viewed as part of the sciences, the humanities, or a mixture of both. These ideas transcend any political identification, sometimes appearing among those on the left, such as Steven Jay Gould, Barry Commoner, and the post-modernists; at other times among those on the right, especially some sociobiologists and rational choice theorists. Some versions are sympathetic to modern rationality; others are critical of it. Some are structuralist; other are individualistic. The contours of this emerging cosmology are anything but fixed, and borrowings across disciplines have recently been noticed. Yet when all the strands are added together, a fundamental challenge to one of the two principles that shaped Enlightenment thought about humanism can be discovered. It is not equality within the human species that is being challenged. It is instead the notion that we ought to accept inequality between the human and nonhuman species. Humans have no special qualities and deserve no special place. Our ideas have finally developed to the point where we can stop assigning fundamental qualities to ourselves. It is time to take our place as one of nature's minor miracles, no different in degree from all the other minor miracles found therein. Any intellectual enterprise premised on the assumption that humans occupy a privileged place in the world begins, these days, with the burden of doubt. Enlightenment thought, with respect to its favorite subject, seems to have come full circle. The intellectual conditions that gave rise to a belief in the special and distinct characteristics of the human self and human society are weaker than at any point in the past century.

Equality at What Price?

Increasing respect for nature is surely one of the most positive developments in societies that are increasingly polluted, disrespectful of the natural environment in which they exist, and unable to sustain themselves in a sensible manner. For this reason alone, the discovery that other species besides our own merit respect carries forward the Enlightenment trajectory. Although there does exist, among those who reject the anthropocentrism essential to nineteenth-century social thought, a preference for premodern, antirational consciousness (embodied in respect for tribal rituals and organic religions), at least some of the thinkers associated with the defense of nature posit an image of progress, in which rights previously assigned only to white male elites are extended to all white males, to former slaves, to women, and finally to all other species found in nature.[26] For anyone whose political principles include both a respect for rights and a belief that they should be spread throughout the population, the notion of an expanding circle of rights seems fully within the progressive traditions of eighteenth-century rationalism. No wonder that the fastest-growing political movements in Western societies are those stressing ecological issues and animal rights.

A certain skepticism toward the special claims made for the human species seems appropriate. Humans can behave arrogantly toward other species and have done so repeatedly. The development of computers has to be viewed as a challenge to the idea that we are masters of computation, or even of chess playing. Ideological, and not purely scientific or humanistic, considerations underlie both epistemological assumptions about the natural world and the definitions of what ought to be included in literary canons. Yet all these points can be accepted and certain questions can nonetheless be raised: Ought we to be so willing to dispense with a sense of ourselves as especially important in the cosmic scheme of things? Do we lose something when we do so, something so important that we ought to continue to hold fast to anthropocentric assumptions, even if in chastened form? If there is no dividing line between ourselves and other animals and machines, can we properly understand our affairs by simply adopting the models and scientific techniques that best explain the evolution of fish or the calculating abilities of computers?

One can, of course, claim that even though humans may possess special or distinct characteristics, these characteristics are not necessarily superior. Humans can be appreciated for what they are, other animal species can be respected for themselves, and even enough sympathy can be left over for computers. What Christopher Stone calls a moral pluralism that spreads across species is not only possible but probably necessary.[27] In theory, we ought to be able to appreciate others even while liking ourselves, but the matter turns out to be far more complex. It was, after all, a major advance in the history of Western thought to discover that humans were capable of reason, that they could join with others to create societies that protected them against the caprice and brutality of living under the sway of forces beyond their control. If we could protect that vision while at the same time appreciating all other species, both living and artificial, there would be no problem. But one major difficulty stands in the way of cross-species pluralism. Those who imagine equality between the species usually do so by lowering the human level to that of all others, not by elevating others to the level of humans. To illustrate why too easy an acceptance of the claims of other species can result in a depreciation of humans and the societies they create, consider three issues raised by the challenges to anthropocentrism we have been discussing: rights, intelligence, and language.

That animals have rights—or, for that matter, that trees can have legal standing—seems, at first glance, a notion worth defending.[28] (It has also been suggested that computers have rights, that we ought to reverse Isaac Asimov's "Law of Robotics" and protect machines against us rather than the other way around.)[29] Yet to accept such notions uncritically is to redefine what a right means. From one point of view, humans possess inalienable rights because they are humans; that is, they are capable of thinking and reflecting about their own nature. This conception of a right is closely connected to a conception of a self. Rights may be out there somewhere in the world, to be asserted and claimed, but they do not mean anything until acted upon. Indeed, it is not the right itself that is, finally, important, but the political and social awakening that emerges out of the efforts of an individual self to discover his or her rights and to act upon them. Rights are not given; they are taken.

Things found in nature are not acting selves, possessing the capacity to understand the meaning of their acts. To assign rights to animals (or computers) is to say that a being is entitled to rights without understanding what rights are. A right thus becomes a passive thing to be delivered to an object, not part of a subject's self-expression. Some of the same reasoning applies to the notion that a fetus has rights, when the fetus has simply been an unconscious and unthinking product of the sexual activity of its makers. (Of course, the fetus is also a potential human.) In short, from this perspective, I have rights not because I understand the consequences of my actions for the fate of others but because I stand there like a tree. Moreover, not being able to understand myself as a rights-bearing creature, I am totally dependent on a guardian to exercise my rights for me, guaranteeing work for lawyers and judges, but hardly guaranteeing a society in which rights are linked to self-understanding.

Self-understanding is important in the context of rights, because rights have been traditionally linked to obligations: we owe something to society in return for the rights we have won. Yet if humans can extend rights to nonhumans, the latter cannot return the favor. Only members of an understanding species cognizant of its environment and able to take into account situation and context can choose *not* to exercise a right for the sake of group or communal solidarity. To extend rights to nature is to reproduce a state of nature, in which rights given without corresponding responsibilities eventually create a Hobbesian struggle over claims. Abstract rights for all creatures, in that sense, can easily lead to fewer practical rights for most. Obviously, one might sometimes wish to extend rights to those unable to claim them by their own efforts, such as children or the mentally retarded. But when exceptions multiply to cover creatures who possess neither agency nor understanding, the concept of a *human* right is cheapened.

Similar issues are at stake in the debate over whether computers, because they can compute, are capable of manifesting intelligence. Obviously, they are, if intelligence is defined as the ability to compute. Long before computers, some philosophers and psychologists believed that human minds worked essentially by reasoning syllogistically. Such perspectives continue to attract students of the mind.[30] Cognitive abilities, such as thinking and speaking, are understood as the result of the logical ordering of internal representations of the world. Indeed, everything the mind does, even its ability to dream, could, in theory, be broken down into a series of calculations. With the development of machines that can process information logically, one of two conclusions about human intelligence can be reached: either such a computational theory of mind must be rejected as an adequate theory of what human intelligence is or computers ought to be viewed as a thinking species.

The latter conclusion is reached by those who celebrate the achievements of machines over humans, believing that robots will usher in a new era in which machines will do most of our thinking for us.[31] But in the process they give priority to only one definition of intelligence, just as a theory of animal rights redefines what a right is. There are, in fact, many kinds of intelligence; some apply better to machines, others to humans.[32] One particular kind of intelligence—the ability to recognize realities outside the brain by relying on contexts, cues, ambiguities, and conversations to supply what brains themselves cannot generate—is specific to humans. It is this kind of intelligence that enables human selves to form societies with richly textured levels of meaning. To downplay its significance in order to elevate the mental power of machines is to achieve equality between our species and computers on terms established by the latter. If that is equality, it hardly seems worth the trouble.[33]

Language, finally, provides a third illustration of why it makes sense to emphasize the meaning-producing aspects of human selfhood. Some ethologists and linguists have argued that humans have no monopoly on either language or communication, as we shall see in the following chapter. There was a time when enthusiasts for artificial intelligence believed that only technical obstacles prevented the development of computers that could translate from one human language to another, although in more recent years this belief has begun to fade. In short, language can be understood as possessing formal properties and grammars, as structured by the rules that make it possible to speak (or to think). Speakers do not make language; language makes speakers. When we speak, we rely on rules that are already there. Indeed, in the view of contemporary thinkers such as Jacques Lacan, we speak words that are already there.

If the rules that govern the use of language are hard-wired in the brain, then it is possible to imagine that other animal species or computers can have linguistic abilities. But, as with the question of rights or intelligence, we achieve such correspondence between different species by adopting a very specific definition of what language is. Focusing on the universals underlying communication, we ignore the particulars of specific conversations: the "noise" of real human speech, including mutually understood gestures, irony, definitions of the situation, and other conventions used by human selves to construct the meaning of the words they hear. The languages of all species, including our own, may be structured algorithmically in the most basic sense, but only one species is capable of bringing meaning to words in the real world. Since the meaning of words lies not in the rules that govern their usage but, instead, in the real-world activities of acting human selves, to argue for cross-species equality with respect to linguistic ability is inevitably to undervalue the significance of meaning.

For all these reasons, it is worthwhile stressing that the human self is not the same as any other body or machine. Our specifically human capabilities enable us to claim rights, exercise our intelligence, and enrich our language. Obviously, we can appreciate our special qualities while appreciating those of other species as well. But we need not turn on ourselves with disgust, as some adherents to the emerging anti-human-centered cosmology do from time to time. Moreover, there is also reason to question the claim that we can imagine nonhumans as rights-bearing creatures equal to us in their capacities and still appreciate our own capacities to possess rights and utilize our cognitive powers. Without an appreciation of our special capacities, the equality we achieve with other species is of the most primitive kind: we have rights simply because we exist; we are intelligent merely because we can count; the words we speak do not belong to us; the rules that govern our affairs are as automatic and self-generating as those that govern the affairs of other species; our motivations are the same as those of rats and pigeons; the morality and justice that exist in human society are not the product of our minds but a by-product—an unanticipated consequence, to use one of the most popular terms in functional sociology—of behavior intended for other purposes. We are equal without being autonomous, without exercising judgment, and without governing our own affairs. We exist, but we have no self-identity. If, in the face of this risk, the price we pay for respecting and enhancing our special capacities is a certain immodesty about our species, that price may not be especially high, especially when compared to what we lose by denying those skills and therefore refusing to cultivate them.

The Interpreting Self and the Meaningful Society

However awkard they may seem from a late-twentieth-century vantage point, reflections on the uniqueness of the human species were not just *obiter dicta* in the writings of nineteenth-century social theorists. Marx and Engels built their entire theory on the assumption that "men . . . begin to distinguish themselves from animals as soon as they begin to *produce* their means of subsistence."[34] Max Weber regarded culture as "man's emancipation from the organically prescribed cycle of natural life."[35] For Durkheim, as we have seen, civilization constituted the fundamental difference between the human and the animal world, while George Herbert Mead's reflections on mind and self began with a distinction between the gestures of other animal species and the "significant symbols" used by humans.[36] What the Germans call philosophical anthropology—the effort to deal with fundamental ontological questions not by arguing from first premises but by empirically contrasting the responses of human and nonhuman species to different environmental challenges—was crucial to the development of all modern social thought.[37] So close is the link between the classical tradition in sociology and philosophical anthropology that one perhaps could not exist without the other.

But it is not just the classical tradition in sociology that premises its investigations on a distinction between the world of nature and the world of culture. The same distinction has been made by leading anthropologists, such as A. L. Kroeber ("The essential difference between animal and man . . . is not that the latter has finer grain or the chaster quality of material; it is that his structure and nature and texture are such that he is inscribable, and that the animal is not"); Leslie White ("Without the symbol there would be no culture, and man would be merely an animal, not a human being"); and Marshall Sahlins ("The 'distinctive quality of man' is not that he must live in a material world, circumstances he shares with all organisms, but that he does so according to a meaningful scheme of his own devising, in which capacity mankind is unique").[38] Contemporary sociological theory has also insisted on a certain anthropocentrism: "We can call men and women, children and adults, ministers and bus conductors 'rational,' but not animals or lilac bushes, mountains, streets, or chairs," Jürgen Habermas has written; "Man occupies a peculiar position in the animal kingdom. Unlike the other higher mammals, he has no species-specific environment, no environment firmly structured by his own instinctual organization," argue Peter Berger and Thomas Luckmann; "Human beings make their own history in cognizance of that history, that is, as reflexive beings cognitively appropriating time rather than merely 'living' it," suggests Anthony Giddens.[39] Assumptions about special and distinct human characteristics are not, in short, a nineteenth-century artifact.

Even those who seem to reject the notion of human distinctiveness in favor of functionalism and structuralism—theorists such as Talcott Parsons, Robert Merton, and Niklas Luhmann—argue at times for such distinctiveness. The inspiration for much of Parsons's theorizing came not only from Durkheim and Weber but also from biologists like L. T. Henderson, who had published important work in physiology and biology before reading Pareto's *General Sociology* in the late 1920s. (The book was recommended by William Morton

Wheeler, who would become a leading American exponent of Herbert Spencer's theories and whose own work on insect societies would later be revamped by Edward O. Wilson.)[40] Yet although Parsons recognized the importance of biology, he also noted "the much discussed 'plasticity' of the human organism, its capacity to learn any one of a large number of alternative patterns of behavior instead of being bound by its generic constitution to a very limited range of alternatives," as well as "the accessibility of the human individual to influence by the attitudes of others in the social interaction process, and the resulting dependence on receiving relatively particular and specific reactions."[41] Merton's functionalism, also inspired by his wide reading in biology, was influenced as well by the love of irony and paradox associated with literary critics (and humanists) such as Lionel Trilling and historians like Richard Hofstadter.[42] In more recent years, Parsons's structuralism has undergone a rebirth in the theories of Niklas Luhmann, this time aided by developments in ecology, cybernetics, and computers unknown to Parsons.[43] Yet although Luhmann's work is premised on a frank antihumanism and a search for self-reproducing models—indeed, as we shall see in chapter 5, he presents an exemplary version of antihumanistic social science—he too notes at one point that "the decisive advantage of human interaction over animal interaction stems from this elemental achievement of language."[44] Macro or micro, classical or contemporary, structuralist or functionalist, humanistic or scientific, American or European, social theory without some element of anthropocentrism seems to be impossible.[45]

Although reflections on the distinctiveness of the human species are a constant in the history of sociological (and anthropological) thought, the features believed to constitute the human difference have varied. Some theorists—including not only Marx but also eighteenth-century political economists and the early Durkheim, in his analysis of the division of labor—regarded the human difference as a producing difference: we are what we make, and what we usually make is culture. Yet these notions of *homo faber* no longer seem to provide the best way to understand the potential, as opposed to the actuality, of the human condition. Other animal species make tools. They also, depending on how the term is defined, possess culture. As I will argue in the next chapter, a recent revolution in ethology—which provides far more closely grained accounts of how animals actually live in the world—renders a good deal of nineteenth-century philosophical anthropology obsolete. We share more with the world of nature than we were once prepared to admit.

Even Marx recognized that an emphasis on *homo faber* was not enough. "A spider conducts operations that resemble those of a weaver, and a bee puts to shame many an architect in the construction of her cells," he wrote in *Capital*. "But what distinguishes the worst architect from the best of the bees is this, that the architect raises his structure in imagination before he erects it in reality."[46] Although this passage introduces qualities of mind and anticipates a good deal of twentieth-century social theory, Hannah Arendt is correct to point out that "the apparently all-important element of 'imagination' plays no role whatsoever in [Marx's] labor theory."[47] What was left out can, however, be put in. Nineteenth-century social theory, in seeking the features of human distinctiveness, added culture to nature. The twentieth-century version of the same quest will have to add mind to culture. For human thought processes are different not only from those of other animal species, which lack powers of interpretation and imagination, but also from the minds—if minds they be—of computers, which, for all their powers of calculation, also cannot imagine worlds other than the ones for which they have been programmed. Contemporary theories of human distinctiveness, in short, ought to stress interpretation rather than production: we are what we imagine ourselves capable of being. As Charles Taylor's work in particular demonstrates, any contemporary theory of the human difference is much more likely to emphasize our narrative capacities, our abilities to tell stories that make sense out of the situations in which we find ourselves.[48] We are, in Taylor's phrase, "self-interpreting animals," in the sense that what we are is indistinguishable from how we understand ourselves.[49]

Once the focus shifts to interpretation, social psychology, and not economics, becomes the grounding for social theory. Whether imagined as structured by social class, embedded in materialist realities, governed by laws, obligated by morality, enlightened by literary texts, or made sacred by religion, interpreting selves possess the capability of self-understanding. Yet this shift from production to interpretation in no way stands in conflict with the principle that distinct human features of the self make necessary a distinct social science. From the interpretative point of view, human beings are different from other species not just because their culture is more complex but because their development is not preprogrammed by their genetic structures. They can bend the instructions given to them in ways that the giver of instructions could not have anticipated; therefore, the rules they follow and the programs that guide their actions are their own. They can alter and shape the rules that govern them because they add mind to culture, in addition to adding culture to nature. Self-understanding makes self-governance possible.

Interpreting selves can create meaningful societies. That is, a species capable of understanding the rules that govern its behavior can direct its social organization to the accomplishment of goals defined by the members of that species as meaningful. As long as sociologists focused disproportionately on the technical skill with which vast forms of social cooperation are organized, as Durkheim did in his *Division of Labor in Society*, they developed a remarkably coherent theory—for ants. Indeed, if we examine Edward O. Wilson's later work on ant societies, we might conclude that Durkheim's awareness of social complexity and interdependence was insufficient for ants, whatever its relevance to humans.[50] But Durkheim's relevance for ants extends only up to a point. For he was not only interested in understanding the dynamics of social organization; he was also a moralist with a vision of the good.[51] In his *Elementary Forms of Religious Life*, Durkheim turned away from a mechanistic theory of the division of labor in favor of a perspective emphasizing the cognitive and symbolic powers of human beings. That change in perspective marks a crucial moment in the intellectual history of sociology, linking, as it does, a theory of the distinctiveness of the human self to a theory of the meaningfulness of human society.

Humans add to the profane worlds they share with other

animal species a sacred world in which meaning, and not just behavior, becomes emblematic. Human society is distinct from all other forms of social organization because, in the well-known words of Clifford Geertz, "man is an animal suspended in webs of significance he himself has spun."[52] An interpreting self imagines possibilities beyond the sensate world. A meaningful society realizes such possibilities. Drop the anthropocentrism of social theory, and one can still discuss individuals and groups. But having dropped it, one can no longer discuss who we are, how we came to be that way, and how we might be in the future. Durkheim called sociology a moral science, and that is why it was different from biology.

Sociology, for all these reasons, remains a distinct science for a distinct subject. In positing sociology as a science, its founders were distinguishing it from literature and the humanities. But in asserting the existence of a unique human self that made possible a meaningful form of human society, they were also distinguishing it from the existing natural sciences, such as biology. Sociology was *Geisteswissenschaft*, not *Naturwissenschaft*. It required a methodology that stressed the need to enter into the minds of its subjects, and this alone made it different from biology; for, as Isaiah Berlin has commented, "one cannot enter into the hopes and fears of bees and beavers."[53] Although sociological theorists borrowed Darwin's concept of evolution, they did not borrow his belief that the evolution of man is continuous with that of other animals species. To be sure, there were exceptions, from Herbert Spencer to contemporary sociologists influenced by sociobiology, as Degler's recent account emphasizes.[54] But the creed of the field could be summarized in one fairly typical account, from Charles W. Ellwood in 1918: "If we follow the clue which modern anthropologists are giving us," he wrote, "we shall reach a 'human'—one might also say a 'humanistic'—sociology rather than the biological or mechanistic one which obtains among some social thinkers."[55] Distinctive subject suggested distinctive method: if there were nothing unique called the social, biology would be a perfectly appropriate science of human affairs. Because there is, sociology had to be invented.

Despite an emerging cosmology that questions any account

which privileges human beings and their affairs, this is no time to give up the quest for a special and unique social science. It is not because we have liberated ourselves completely from biology that we need special tools to understand and realize our potential; we remain biological beings, we live in nature, and some aspects of what we do (although increasingly fewer and fewer) can be understood on the basis of biological laws. Nor is it because—as nineteenth-century social theorists believed—we have added the realm of culture to the realm of nature that a distinct social science is justified. To be sure, we *have* added a realm of culture, one that has dynamics that are different from biological imperatives and that consequently demand a different science. The classic thinkers in the tradition of social theory were trying to develop that science, proposing theories—often highly structural theories—that sought laws of the cultural realm to supplement the laws of the biological realm.

The more modern people become, the more their affairs are governed by something other than both biology and culture. That something else is mind. Unlike our biological destiny, it enables us to have a say in the rules that govern how we reproduce ourselves. Unlike our cultural destiny, it confronts the way we usually have done things with an imagined capacity to do things in other ways. We cannot, nor should we ever, rule out the biological and cultural sciences as ways of understanding some of what we do. But if we want to understand some of the most interesting things about us, we need to add the interpretative sciences to them. Most animal species are governed only by their genes. Some, at least according to contemporary ethologists, have the rudiments of culture. But only one is subject to the dynamics of three different imperatives— nature, culture, and mind. And that species requires a specific social science that can elevate mind to the status of nature and culture.

Chapter Two

Other Animal Species and Us

Social Theory and the
Second Biological Revolution

There seems no end to the number of books about gorillas living in the wild that will sell in large numbers in American metropolitan areas.[1] Surely this fascination with the natural world of animals reflects the ambivalence that modern individuals show toward the artificial world of culture. No matter how dense and concentrated our social environments, we seem to want to believe that, like the other primates, we are still an animal species, even if we remain unsure how different we are from them.

Because the world of nature remains close to us, if often more in fantasy than in actuality, social theory and biology are fated to be linked.[2] Sociology is a youthful social science in comparison to the other social sciences; similarly, biology is a relatively youthful natural science in comparison to physics or chemistry. (Indeed, social theory is to some degree older than biology; Marx and Engels wrote *The German Ideology* twelve years before Pasteur convincingly disproved the notion of spontaneous generation.) Both social theory and biology discovered their subjects within the past century; our knowledge of the animal world is as young as our knowledge of ourselves. The rate at which our knowledge of each has expanded, however, is so different as to belie common origins in the same historical period.

Sociology has not developed especially fast; few would claim

28

that there are any contemporary sociologists as widely read and theoretically sophisticated as Durkheim and Weber, and much of what sociology does these days bears little relationship to its founders in any case.[3] But if sociology's evolution has been slow, biology's has been extremely rapid. In the last thirty years alone, a veritable revolution in biological thought has taken place, represented by such developments as the discovery of DNA and its structure, the cracking of the genetic code, neurophysiological and molecular insights into brain functioning, animal ethology, population genetics, theoretical ecology, notions about evolutionary stable strategies, theories of inclusive fitness, and sociobiology. Darwin would no longer recognize Darwinism for different reasons than Durkheim would no longer recognize Durkheimianism.

Animal ethologists and sociobiologists have learned so much more about the natural world and its laws than sociologists have of the cultural world and its laws that the two disciplines can barely hold a conversation. Still, it makes sense to return to the impact of sociology and biology upon each other, because, with this recent revolution in biology, the natural world is better understood than ever before. How do animals behave? Do they think? Are they conscious? Are they social? Can they communicate? What governs their evolution? Is there something to be learned about humans in all this—not only how we think and behave but also how we have evolved? Questions like these, which formed the intellectual framework at the time that social theory began, are once again on the intellectual agenda, only this time with answers more rooted in the actual study of species other than our own.

There is bound to be resistance within the social sciences to the discoveries furnished by biology. Because some of those associated with the revolution in biological thought, especially sociobiologists, conclude that human behavior is just one more form of animal behavior, social scientists are quick to criticize their approach.[4] Yet one must in this context make a distinction between the scientific claims and the political controversies surrounding them.[5] In their opposition to the political positions taken by some leading sociobiologists, social scientists were quick to dismiss their science as well. But if we instead examine the actual findings of this recent revolution in biological thought, there is not much ground for hostility. Observation of animals in their natural habitat, experiments in animal psychology with possible relevance to humans, and the lessons learned from sociobiology about species variations lead to two conclusions concerning other animal species and ourselves. The first is that many of the nineteenth-century social theorists, in assuming little or no relationship between animal and human behavior, got it wrong; other animal species can do a surprising number of things that we can do. But the second conclusion is that they do them quite differently. As I will try to show in this chapter, even when animals communicate, use tools, or reproduce themselves, they do so in ways quite distinct from the human ability to recognize context; consequently, there is little to be gained by modeling human behavior on the study of nonhuman species. Far from challenging the notion that the uniqueness of human beings lies in interpretative capacities of mind, the recent revolution in biology thought provides strong support for it. Few, if any, of the antihumanistic political conclusions drawn by sociobiologists follow from their own scientific observations of how human beings reproduce themselves.

The Case for Other Animals

For many students of animal behavior, any statement about human uniqueness constitutes a challenge to be met. (For the sake of linguistic facility, the term *animal behavior,* in what follows, will refer to nonhuman animals.) Acting as if they were advocates for animals in a lawsuit brought against humans, ethologists have questioned nearly all existing claims about human uniqueness. At least nine such claims have been advanced by social theorists since the nineteenth century; humans, it has been said, possess a monopoly of (1) communication, (2) metacommunication, or talk about talk, (3) the capacity for thought, (4) symbolization, (5) toolmaking, (6) culture, (7) self-reflection, (8) the division of labor, and (9) morality. In each area, ethological research has demonstrated that nonhuman species have capacities that are far more developed than most nineteenth-century anthropocentric social theories were willing to admit. But in every area, what constitutes the human difference remains a unique ability to interpret and provide meaning.

It is obvious that animals communicate.[6] What is surprising is that the ways in which they communicate involve more than programmed instructions established by their genes to produce unvarying behavior. Birds, for example, sing certain notes, receive "answers" from other birds, and then alter their own songs accordingly—a process similar to what George Herbert Mead called the "triadic" relationship, by which the self modifies its behavior after ascertaining a reaction from another.[7] Birds also sing in duets, developing joint repertoires in the process.[8] Chimpanzees, furthermore, have been discovered to have communicative ability. To examine this phenomenon, researchers ingeniously devised substitutes for spoken language, such as the use of American Sign Language, plastic shapes, and languages based on computer keyboards.[9] Such experiments demonstrated that, when language is distinguished from the ability to make sounds, chimpanzees possess language. Lest all this seem that humans, at least, have a monopoly on vocalization, apes can utter sounds that indicate the existence of some phonetic ability.[10]

Yet to pronounce an end to the monopoly that humans were believed to possess over communication skills is actually less radical than it sounds. What matters is not the ability to communicate but the ways in which different species communicate. Humans, in this respect, possess special features that make their ability to communicate unique. In part, these features are biological; the structure of the human tongue, lips, and lung are more fully developed to make speech possible than those of any other species. In part, these features are mental; human brains have evolved from those of other primates, and indeed from those of previous hominids, in ways that permit syntactical abilities. And finally, human communication is facilitated by social and cultural factors, ones that make possible communication through symbols, texts, and ways of recording and transmitting memory. In short, even when one acknowledges that other species possess communication skills, the nearly infinite plasticity of human communication stands in sharp contrast to the limited and inflexible skills of the most advanced other species.[11]

According to some theorists, it is the ability to communicate about communication, rather than communication itself, that is a uniquely human attribute. Although other animal species cannot incorporate into their communications a sense of context, they do possess skills that approximate metacommunicative ones.[12] Altmann argues that primates not only give to-whom-it-may-concern messages; they also engage in three types of metacommunication: cues that distinguish between play and serious situations; metamessages, which direct messages to specific individuals; and claims about status, signaled in the way they walk.[13] In so doing, such species, in Wilson's words, "evaluate the general 'attitude' of the other members of the society."[14]

Many activities believed to be exclusively human are premised upon metacommunication more than they are upon communication per se. Metacommunication makes possible a far richer social life than the simple transmission of messages; if other animal species can communicate about their communication, they ought to be understood as social creatures as well. And, according to Dorothy Cheney and Robert Seyfarth, at least one other species—the East African vervet monkey—does have remarkable cognitive and social skills. Mental states, such as an ability to understand relations among kin, can be attributed to these monkeys. They have language and even understanding. But most important of all, their intelligence is social, different in the laboratory from the way it exists in "real life" among group members. Although they cannot attribute motives and beliefs to species other than their own, they can, through their group memberships, figure out what others within their species are asking of them. Yet, for all the impressive social qualities of these monkeys, their social life, the authors conclude, is like "a puzzle that has not been assembled correctly," when compared to the social life of humans.[15] Cheney and Seyfarth have made the most vigorous case yet made for the similarity between monkeys and humans, but it is a hypothetical and conjectural case that, by their own admission, does not prove anything.[16]

Some primatologists conclude that, along with their possession of social skills, other animal species engage in more complex behaviors—such as love, hate, hypocrisy, and diplomacy—that are strikingly human. In one of the boldest assertions of this idea, it has been argued that primates strategize and attempt to deceive, thereby making politics among them possible.[17] But we ought not to take such claims too far. The human ability to deceive others, as Cheney and Seyfarth point out, "rests on the assumption that other individuals have mental states, that these mental states affect behavior, and that other individuals' mental states can be manipulated to one's own benefit." Because monkeys cannot do these things, "each species can provide us with one or two examples of 'deceptive' behavior but no one species, except possibly chimpanzees, exhibits the flexibility, modifiability, and variety of lies, deceit, and half-truths that are so easy to find among humans."[18] And even the exception of the chimpanzees is not as significant as it sounds. On the surface, chimpanzees appear capable of pursuing objectives, just as a chess program has the objective of winning a chess match. But human activities include not only choosing from a set of objectives but blending objectives in unexpected ways. Our politics and strategy, for example, involve winning over someone else, but also allowing the other to save face, finding ambiguous language that enables both sides to a dispute to claim victory, rationalizing a defeat, and applying the lessons of one political context to another. The kind of politics in which chimpanzees engage, even assuming it can be called politics, involves no such orders of complexity.

If, as some philosophers argue, thought has its own language, then species that can both communicate and communicate about communication ought surely to be viewed as possessing the capacity to think.[19] Ethologists have been reluctant to reach such a conclusion, in part because behavioralism affected the study of animal behavior as much as it did the study of human behavior. From a behavioral perspective, it was possible to argue that animals store information and, on the basis of previous experience, learn to adapt their behavior when presented with new situations, since none of these activities necessarily presupposes the existence of mind. Behaviorists could therefore resolve the question of whether animals "think" by defining thinking in terms of learning, making the question of how that learning took place unnecessary.

As the behavioral consensus broke down, ethologists aware of post-behavioral developments in cognitive psychology and the theory of mind were no longer content with answers that avoided difficult questions involving animal awareness and consciousness.[20] They became increasingly impressed by the abilities of certain species of animals to engage in activities that indicated abilities hard to explain by notions of direct reinforcement. The macaque monkeys on Koshima, a Japanese island, furnish a dramatic illustration. After scientists buried sweet potatoes in the sand, one monkey dug them up and washed the dirt from them before eating them, a practice that all the others eventually adopted. In an even more complicated experiment, the scientists put rice in the sand, and the monkeys learned to throw both rice and sand in the ocean and watch the latter sink—a complex process that, according to Donald Griffin, might indicate the possession of consciousness and thinking ability. Griffin finds other evidence for animal thought as well. Foraging, he argues, can be examined not just as an efficiency-optimizing strategy but as behavior requiring planning and adaptability, such as in the stocking and refurbishing of food caches. The predator-prey relationship, furthermore, turns out to be a complicated affair, with both sides to the relationship engaging in deceptive and strategic tactics. Animals also engage in construction activities—the building of nests, for example—that reveal significant architectural skill.[21]

Although these abilities are impressive, whether they constitute consciousness is another matter. Griffin defines awareness as "versatile adaptability of behavior to changing circumstances and challenges," a definition that speaks far more to adaptability and flexibility than to consciousness per se.[22] And even such versatility may be limited. Human investigators' efforts to tamper with animal procedures cause great bewilderment among the animals—a reaction suggesting that other species do not possess qualities of mind but tend instead to respond to preprogrammed genetic rules, which are of little help when, so to speak, the rules change. (There are, however, examples in nature of an ability to adapt to such interventions; when an experimenter holds food within the reach of orb-weaving spiders, they will shortcut regular procedures and simply grab the food.)[23] Griffin concludes that some animals ought to be viewed as possessing templates in their brains, which enable them to choose among possible options when faced with unusual circumstances. But even Griffin's strong case for animal thought gives no evidence that animals approximate human abilities to make choices about choices, to alter the structure of their templates.

Cognition is generally linked to the capacity to engage in symbolization. Not surprisingly, therefore, the idea that only humans have developed the capacity to symbolize has been questioned. Duane M. Rumbaugh, for example, has written that "chimpanzees share with other apes the ability to learn both to comprehend and to produce symbols, which can function as representations of referents that are not necessarily present."[24] Rumbaugh is in good company here; Claude Lévi-Strauss, although (in his earlier work) trying to maintain the hypothesis of human distinctiveness, nonetheless pointed out that "recent experiments have established the existence, among chimpanzees, of certain rudimentary forms of symbolic thought. What is remarkable is that it is especially feelings, such as religious fear and the ambiguity of the sacred, normally associated with the noblest part of human nature, that are most easily identified among the anthropoids."[25]

Symbolic abilities are not limited to the higher species of animal. Consider what we now know about the waggle dance of honeybees, who are capable of indicating to others that it is time to move to a new source of food and of giving directions for finding those new sources.[26] By one definition of symbolization closely related to sociological thought—Charles Sanders Peirce's theory of meaning, which, through Charles Morris, strongly influenced Mead—the waggle dance of the honeybees would qualify as symbolic.[27] It is, first of all, habitual, which for Peirce constituted an essential feature of symbols.[28] It is, in line with the understanding of pragmatism shared by Peirce and William James, effectual, in the sense that one can assign meaning to the action based on the effects it produces. It is finally, as Griffin points out, in accord with Morris's definition of a symbol as "a sign produced by its interpreter which acts as a substitute for some other sign with which it is synonymous," in the sense that the dance of the honeybees replaces the act of directly leading others to a source of food.[29] All this suggests that either we ought to give up the notion that humans possess a monopoly of symbolization skills or that the way earlier philosophers thought of symbolization needs to be reconceptualized.

Work with computers and artificial intelligence can come to our aid on this point. As Pagels has argued, one can make a distinction between signs and symbols: the former work "bottom up," combining small bits into a whole; the latter work "top down," with a whole that can be broken into understandable parts.[30] Animals, like computers, may be able to use signs, but whether they interpret symbols is another matter entirely. Signs make substitution possible; they do not make meaning possible. As with communication skills, the representational capacity of animals is more analogous to the way computers use signs than to the way humans use symbols. Developments in both animal ethology and artificial intelligence, in short, suggest that reliance on the Peircian conception of meaning is insufficient for understanding why symbolization is important for humans. Symbolization achieves its power for human cognition not by enabling one thing to stand for another but, instead, by creating frameworks into which human minds can read significance.

Another hypothesis about human distinctiveness concerns the use of tools. There is considerable evidence that animals are both tool makers and tool users. Jane Goodall's work with wild chimpanzees in Tanzania demonstrated this capacity, such as an ape's ability to incorporate empty kerosene cans into its protective strategies.[31] Thanks to the work of Benjamin Beck, we now know that tool behavior is found in many more species than chimpanzees. Polar bears use pieces of ice to kill seals. Sea otters use small stones to open shellfish. Green herons, instead of eating a piece of bread they find, drop it in the water and use it as bait to catch fish.[32] Beck is careful to state that he undertook his studies "without consideration of purposiveness, symbolic mediation, or cognitive understanding of causal relationships."[33] Still, as Griffin argues, these examples do involve something more than "directly seizing, battering apart, and eating the food."[34] Of all the hypotheses of human uniqueness, the notion of *homo faber* may be the weakest. Granted that humans make far more complicated and impressive tools than other species, one could still argue that this is a difference of degree rather than kind. Here is one area where our species has much in common with other animals. If we are to look for what makes us unique, it ought not to be along the lines of our ability to make and use tools.

The capacity to make and use tools is generally understood by sociologists and anthropologists to be part of a more general process of possessing culture. Since some animal species can symbolize as well as use material objects, do they therefore possess culture? John Tyler Bonner, for one, finds many examples of culture in animal behavior—again striking at the heart of a theory of human uniqueness. (Bonner, a naturalist, developed his ideas about animal culture in part out of a seminar organized by Talcott Parsons and attended by a significant number of contemporary sociologists.) Bonner relies on many of the examples already cited in this chapter and then adds more, such as Goodall's discovery that chimpanzees used sophisticated tools to "fish" for termites, the learning of tameness, the ability of birds to use "maps" in planning their migrating routes, and the capacity of titmice to open milk bottles in order to drink the cream at the top. "One can," he concludes, "think of the appearance of culture as a new niche that arose from the experimentation of animals with multiple choice behavior. And as a macroevolutionary step, it is undoubtedly among the biggest of them all."[35]

The link from tool use to culture, however, is also a big step. Bonner can reach his conclusions about animal culture only by defining culture as all nongenetic means of transmission— a definition so broad as to preclude the issue of human uniqueness. The biologist's definition of culture, in other words, leaves out any consideration of mind. Culture is out there in the world affecting behavior, but it is not understood as part of an interactive process between an individual self and the cultural world he or she inhabits. Such a way of thinking about culture may be compatible with certain forms of structuralist social science, but, like them, it tends to ignore or downplay human agency as a force in making and transforming culture. When culture is viewed as both a microphenomenon, involving agency and choice, and a macrophenomenon, involving history and evolution, the links between animal and human culture break down.

Still another version of the human-uniqueness argument involves the Meadian emphasis on self-awareness. Considering the importance placed by early theorists of the self on reflection—illustrated by Cooley's notion of the "looking-glass self " or Mead's comment that we cannot visually see every part of our body[36]—the work of Gordon Gallup is especially interesting. By exposing chimpanzees to mirrors for long periods of time, Gallup demonstrated that they were able to recognize that they were watching an image of themselves, not another chimpanzee. When painted with a nonsmelling dye while unconscious and then placed before the mirror, they immediately tried to wipe the dye off. Moreover, they used mirrors for grooming purposes, including parts of their bodies that they would not be able to see without the aid of the mirror.[37] He further demonstrated that chimpanzees raised in isolation were less likely to recognize themselves in the mirror than those who were raised in social groups. He concluded that their way of gaining awareness of the self evidently met the Meadian criterion of viewing the self from outside the self. Indeed, he wrote, "better quantitative evidence of self-recognition exists for chimpanzees than for man."[38]

At their strongest, Gallup's experiments demonstrate self-recognition, not self-awareness. But even that conclusion is questionable, since—by strictly Meadian criteria—Gallup's chimps have no self that they can recognize. What Gallup's chimps see in the mirror is their bodies, not their selves. Animals and humans share the possession of bodies. Both species can use their bodies to signal behavior that enables others to alter their behavior; this is, Mead argues, what dogs do when they engage in play (or fighting). But only humans can interact with other human selves to take into account the specifics of the time and place within which they interact.[39] Since no self can exist unless another self is present, even a human talking to a chimp would not possess selfhood, let alone a chimp looking into a mirror. (In a similar way, neither a human talking to a computer nor a computer interacting with a human would possess a self, as I will argue in the following chapter.)

Social theorists also have emphasized the importance of the division of labor in human affairs. Here, as with the concept of *homo faber*, animals possess abilities that do not seem fundamentally dissimilar from human ones. Wilson's work on insect societies demonstrates extraordinary degrees of task differentiation among other species. As is well known, ants in particular have exceptionally complicated divisions of labor, or what Wilson calls polyethisms. Their tasks can be broken down in two ways: by caste and by age. Ant tasks are divided, of course, between male and female, with the former doing remarkably little and the latter responsible for the reproduction and maintenance of the species. Among soldier ants, numerous activities exist, including shearing, piercing, and blocking. Worker ants also differentiate tasks, the complexity varying from one kind of ant to another. In the Surinam colony, to take one illustration, tasks include the disposing of corpses and refuse, dismembering and feeding, foraging, attending eggs, and feeding larvae. Young ants and older ants also have different tasks: young ants work inside the nest, whereas older ants engage in activities outside the nest, such as care of brood, care of queen, cleaning, and handling of the dead.[40] So extraordinary are the capacities of ants in this regard that, as I argued in the previous chapter, it makes little sense to search for the uniqueness of the human along this avenue, as Durkheim realized when he shifted his attention from the division of labor to human cognitive and symbolic powers.

Finally, for many philosophers and for the social theorists influenced by them, one particular mental quality is usually viewed as the single most important unique characteristic of the human species: the ability to act according to a moral sense of right and wrong. As in many other areas under discussion here, some forms of animal behavior approximate human moral capacities. Reciprocal altruism exists in numerous animal species; even if one accepts Richard Dawkins's reformulation that it is genes that are selfish, not the organisms that carry them, one is left with many examples of animals that sacrifice themselves for the sake of others.[41] Similarly, Maynard Smith's concept of "evolutionary stable strategies" helps explain why one finds numerous instances of cooperation in nature and, in turn, why among higher primates, in de Waal's words, "making peace is as natural as making war."[42] In its reformulation by Hamilton, moreover, the notion of evolutionary stable strategies has been used to explain the possibilities of human cooperative behavior.[43] The picture of animal aggressiveness inherited from Konrad Lorenz and Robert Ardrey is no longer generally accepted; animals follow rules that make their mutual coexistence possible.

Yet Gunther Stent is surely correct in arguing that animals do not have a specific moral sense, because they are incapable of taking universal positions organized in conformity to agreed-upon moral imperatives.[44] Animals cannot be regarded as Kantian agents, capable of distinguishing right from wrong. Even a strong advocate for animal rights along roughly Kantian lines, Tom Regan, concludes that animals ought to be respected because they are moral patients rather than moral agents.[45] Autonomy, which makes morality possible, is a capacity that remains uniquely human. Animals, in other words, can act in ways that resemble duty to the species over interest of the individual; but missing from such "moral" behavior is the element of responsibility for one's choices, which makes morality a worthwhile possession for human beings.

The second biological revolution of recent years obviously changes the picture of human uniqueness from the more naïve days when social theory first began to separate culture from nature. Unlike the founders of the sociological tradition, who speculated abstractly about these matters, we have accumulated valuable, and extensive, information about the behavior of species other than our own. Impressed by the accomplishments of other species, some see a fundamental challenge to humanism and thereby to the notion that humans ought to have their own science. "The boundary between human and animal is thoroughly breached," Donna Haraway has written. "The last beachheads of uniqueness have been polluted if not turned into amusement parks—language, tool use, social behavior, mental events. Nothing really convincingly settles the separation of human and animal."[46] As impressive as animal accomplishments are, however, there is still one essential difference between the worlds of nature and culture: other animal species cannot attach meaning to a context by recognizing its uniqueness. Animals lack the capacity for interpretation. There are at least preliminary grounds for concluding that human distinctiveness might be found in the area of meaning production: the ability not merely to follow rules but to "read" a situation in order to define for oneself what a rule might mean.

What Sociobiology Teaches Us

Further support for the notion that interpretative abilities divide humans from animals comes from those who attempt to address the question of human uniqueness by examining why different species evolve at different rates. Sociobiologists in particular begin by assuming that evolution is governed by genetic coding. Such an assumption, if true, would lead to the conclusion that all species are, at root, similar and would also downplay the importance of specific abilities to interpret the meaning of rules. But even those sociobiologists generally viewed as the most committed to a genetic explanation of human behavior, such as Edward O. Wilson and Richard Dawkins, do not take such a position but argue instead for the importance of culture. In so doing, they shift the debate on human evolution into a field where sociologists have been more comfortable. Once culture is admitted to play a role, the question becomes "What makes culture possible?" Inevitably, and uncomfortably, sociobiologists are led into the territory of mind, where the human capacity to supply meaning takes on important significance.

Sociobiologists argue, no doubt correctly, that long ago in historical time—very long ago by most people's standards—

genetic transmission was the only form that evolution took in all species. Under such conditions, species developed in accordance with what Lumsden and Wilson call primary epigenetic rules, which are genetically determined and do not vary, at least not much.[47] As Dawkins puts it, DNA reproduces itself through imitation and does so with astonishing accuracy, rarely making a single mistake. But when even a slight imperfection in the imitation process takes place, species evolution becomes possible.[48] The key to the whole process is time; given enough time, the mathematics of population genetics guarantees that even the slightest change at point A can have significant long-term effects at point B. Time itself therefore becomes the independent variable in the explanation, since the matter which is changing does so imperceptibly and without any consciousness that it is contributing to important results millions of years in the future.

Primary epigenetic rules, governed by the dynamics of population genetics, enable sociobiologists to meet one of the first requirements of science, explaining as much as possible with as few simple rules as possible. The same goal could be reached in other ways as well. One could, for instance, imagine the human mind as a computer; for if all the information needed to adapt to the environment is stored in the brain, then relatively simple search rules, such as those associated with computer software, can organize a rapid search through a stock of data and find the appropriate response. Such rules rely on a stochastic notion of decision-making: predetermined rules give shape to a decision tree in such a way that any decision along that tree leads to another set of choices, eventually producing enormous variation. Time is similarly not a problem for such stochastic theories of evolutionary variation when computers model them; for rapid calculation permits the generation of new decision trees over short periods of time. It is therefore possible to develop a computer program which, using the superior speed of calculation, can essentially replicate an evolutionary process that took place over millennia, as Dawkins has shown.[49]

As we move closer to the present, however, we begin to run out of time. A biological explanation of evolutionary variation based solely on population genetics faces the following difficulty: the closer we come to the present day, the less variation we can have; yet it seems obvious to any observer of human evolution that the speed at which we develop and change has increased the closer we get to the present time. Moreover, it is extremely doubtful that any model of rule-governed evolutionary dynamics based on the computer can explain human variation; for, as Lumsden and Wilson emphasize, the hardware necessary to store all the information about possible changes would require a brain far larger than the ones we actually have.[50] Clearly, then, to explain the unique features of human evolution, we need something more than a purely genetic theory.

Both Wilson and Dawkins accept the notion that human evolutionary patterns are unique because, in addition to the genetic transfer of information, humans also rely on culture. (Wilson and Dawkins define culture, as did John Bonner, as all nongenetic forms of informational transmittal.) In his empirical work with ants, for example, Wilson notes that ant colonies, even though they have divisions of labor, act "in a way that causes them to respond with certain behaviors, in accord with certain probabilities, to the stimuli normally present in the colonial environment. If the single social insect does not comprehend the environment in which it lives, at least it is able to make, on the average, the correct contribution to colony activity."[51] Humans, by contrast, are "eucultural" and therefore able to engage in reification, defined as those aspects of the human mind that incorporate "(1) the production of concepts and (2) the continuously shifting classification of the world." Hence, "there is . . . a unique activity that fully separates mankind from the most advanced protocultural animal species."[52]

Although the key to human evolution is therefore found in our possession of culture, Wilson does not believe that evolutionary dynamics are determined entirely by culture. Lumsden and Wilson argue for a middle position between a genetic and a cultural explanation, one in which mind is

driven by a *selectional*, rather than an *instructional*, mechanism. This procedure, which can be called a *schema activating system*, is still genetically fixed but permits a flexibility of response to the environment. The brain develops a large but finite number of neural assemblies that have the capacity to develop into cognitive schemata. When such a system operates in the gene-culture mode, a particular culturgen or class of culturgens triggers the maturation of one of the assemblies into its predestined schema, by means of cell growth and differentiation, synapse formation and modification, or the establishment of fields of electrogenic activity.[53]

As we get closer to the present time, in other words, primary epigenetic rules are supplemented by secondary ones; these latter are particularly important in explaining such human variations as "facial recognition, visual complexity preference, nonverbal communication, mother-infant bonding, fears and phobias, incest avoidance, and other behaviors."[54] In cultural evolution, "the summed decisions and innovations of all the members of the society" interact with information already presented in the brain's hard wiring, enabling new variations to take place.[55] Cultural forms, even highly developed rituals, do not in this sense exist independently of epigenetic rules, but tend instead "to reenforce them."[56]

Richard Dawkins, who is best known for his theory of the "selfish gene," goes even further than Lumsden and Wilson in the role he assigns to culture. Dawkins concludes with an argument that he admits will be "surprising" to readers of the earlier chapters of his book: "for an understanding of the evolution of modern man, we must begin by throwing out the gene as the sole basis of our ideas on evolution." Memes, his term for the units of cultural evolution, "propagate themselves in the meme pool by leaping from brain to brain via a process that, in the broad sense, can be called imitation." This imitative process will constitute new replicators, which have the potential to "start a new kind of evolution of their own."[57] Culture will, in fact, take over from genetic transmission entirely, since more efficient replicators always drive out less efficient ones.

That humans—and, depending on how it is defined, perhaps a few other species as well—developed culture, which altered the pace of their evolutionary development, does not seem a particularly controversial point. What is controversial is the timing of the process. Culture is a relatively recent innovation, by evolutionary standards at least. In contrast to the primary epigenetic rules associated with DNA replication, cultural forms of transmission have had far less time in which the rules governing their dynamics could have been worked out. In the absence of enormously long stretches of time almost impossible to imagine—a precondition, as we have seen, for the dynamics of evolution to be understood through the mathematical techniques associated with population genetics—the question that emerges when cultural evolution becomes part of the explanation is whether the dynamics of cultural change can be modeled in a way similar to the dynamics of genetic change. Specifically, can we still find relatively simple mathematical algorithms that, when applied at point A, will produce considerable variation at point B? If we cannot, then the dynamics of population genetics will not be helpful to us in explaining the evolution of culture.

One possible way to deal with this problem—suggested by the fantastic computational power of computers—is to argue that the speed by which cultural variation occurs can act as a substitute for vast amounts of time—that the change produced by cultural evolution is, in a sense, qualitative rather than quantitative. This is how Lumsden and Wilson deal with the problem, for, as Wilson has noted, "cultural evolution is Lamarckian and very fast, whereas biological evolution is Darwinian and very slow."[58] (Wilson clearly means "fast" in this context in contrast to evolutionary time; if he were comparing his theory of gene-culture coevolution to the theories of a cultural determinist, what appeared fast would be viewed as very slow indeed.) Genes are, to use the metaphor supplied by Barash, the tortoise, while culture is the hare.[59] Yet no matter how fast cultural evolution takes place, does it take place so fast that alterations in cultural habits—say, the kinds of changes in table manners studied by Norbert Elias[60]—can be explained mathematically? The key question facing a theory of gene-culture coevolution is how fast is fast. If fast is fast enough, sociobiologists can add culture to what was formerly a purely genetic explanation of evolution and still retain models based on the mathematics of population genetics. If fast is too slow, they will be forced to choose between adding culture to the explanation and dropping the models or keeping the models and dropping a cultural explanation.

Many efforts are now being made to link genetic factors to cultural ones in the explanation of social change.[61] The amounts of time under consideration are instructive. In their study of the emergence of human agriculture, Ammerman and Cavalli-Sforza discuss a period of approximately 10,000 years. Around 6000 B.C., both the domestication of cereals and the domestication of animals emerged in Southwest Asia. Whether these innovations spread to Europe by purely cultural means or by "demic" spread—the migration of the farmers rather than the migration of farming methods—it took roughly 2,000 years for farming to move from Greece to Britain.[62] The resulting pace of 25 kilometers per generation may be fast in genetic terms, but in human terms it seems remarkably slow.

Nonetheless, Lumsden and Wilson are impatient with a time period even as "short" (in genetic terms) as 10,000 years. In recent work, they suggest a "thousand year rule": as few as fifty generations are necessary even for significant *genetic* changes to manifest themselves.[63] Since genetic changes take place at a slower pace than cultural ones, the application of this rule would enable us to explain differences between classical Athens and ourselves through a theory of gene-culture evolution. But it is precisely at this point that any claim to hard science breaks down, for although we cannot with any precision decide whether genes or culture has played the largest part in human variation since Socrates drank his hemlock, most interpretations would note rather minimal genetic changes and rather major cultural ones during those years. In other words, it makes perfect sense for evolutionary theories of human variation to add the dimension of culture; culture is crucial for understanding how our own species has evolved in the way it has. But the moment that culture is introduced, we can no longer rely as much on the "hard," mathematical, and less controversial rules of science; we will have to rely more on "soft" forms of explanation associated with history and the social sciences. Wilson, wishing to preserve the hard sciences, advances a conception of culture that, in Kaye's words, is "genetically controlled in its form and function" and therefore "in no way distinct from biology."[64] But, at least for humans, culture is not only something more than biology; it is also barely understood. Whereas the structure and dynamics of genes are relatively well understood, there is little agreement surrounding the agents of cultural transmission. (There is even less agreement on what they ought to be called, since Dawkins does not wish to surrender the term *memes* and Lumsden and Wilson insist on the term *culturgens*.) Once we introduce culture, we are on the turf of the social, not the natural, sciences, and on that turf one plays with rules that are more than algorithmic.

Although the introduction of culture shifts explanations of human evolution away from the hard sciences, it does not, by itself, shift them far enough. To account for the speed and relative recency of human social change, we need something besides genetic and cultural explanations. The most likely candidate is mind. As François Jacob has pointed out, "the very nature of the genetic code prevents any deliberate change in programme whether through its own action or as an effect of its environment. It prohibits any influence on the message by the products of its expression. The programme does not learn from experience."[65] Mind, by contrast, suggests the incorporation of experience into the rules by which a species is governed. What enables culture to exist, in short, is not the mere transmittal of information; DNA and computers can both transmit information. Cultural evolution is so speedy, and can therefore account for variation over shorter periods of time than purely biological evolution, because the agents affected by the changes have certain mental capacities that enable them to understand (and thereby alter) the speed at which variation occurs.

Once mind replaces time and supplements culture as the most important explanatory variable in human evolution the closer we get to the present, the question becomes whether sociobiology offers a sufficient theory of mind. At this point, nearly all sociobiologists back off. The essence of their science lies in mathematical dynamics, and—as they would be the first to admit—such an approach can only be used with confidence when one is attempting to explain what happened very long ago. Even Richard Dawkins, who understands that at some point in the development of humans culture took over from genes, is unwilling to develop a theory of mind. He recognizes that culture developed "at a rate which is orders of magnitude faster than genetic evolution"[66] but refuses to give up the idea that replicators replicate through imitation—an idea that he obtained from his genetic theory. Indeed, he coins the term *meme* precisely because of its similarity to "mimesis."[67] But this emphasis on imitation is revealing, for it takes very little cognitive activity just to do the same thing over and over again. Dawkins reminds one of the nineteenth-century social theorist Gabriel de Tarde, who never achieved significant influence in this century because his emphasis on imitation ran contrary to a more modern concern with meaning, representation, and cognition.[68]

Dawkins's approach is not sufficient for Lumsden and Wilson. Unlike Dawkins—indeed, unlike most sociobiologists—they want to work with relatively recent evolutionary patterns. Having entered the forbidden territory of very recent transformations in human behavior, Lumsden and Wilson have no choice but to enter as well the forbidding territory of thinking about the human mind. "No longer do the genes dictate one or a very few behaviors—instead the mind intervenes decisively. Ranging widely, it creates a much greater array of actions. It permits each combination of genes to have multiple expressions and offers alternative solutions to most problems *within a single lifetime.*"[69] Because of mind, the thousand-year rule is shortened to a seventy-five-year rule. We are down to very short periods of time indeed.

Not all species, of course, possess such powers of mind. Rejecting the notion that pure replication is responsible for variation in the species that resemble ours, Lumsden and Wilson argue instead there are about a million species that neither learn nor imitate, another ten thousand that learn and can imitate, a further fifteen that can imitate and teach offspring, but only one that can both imitate and teach through reification.[70] (They may have to add another, since, by their definition of reification, computers would have to be included.) Mind, therefore, which explains how human variation could have occurred so dramatically in so short a period of time, is presumed to exist in the capacity to symbolize. Yet, as we have seen, a case can be made that more than one species can engage in reification and symbolization, if these processes are defined as simply the substitution of one thing by another without the things themselves having any meaning. The question that remains is whether this minimal capacity to symbolize, which we may well share with other species, is enough of a theory of mind to explain what it is being called upon to explain: the distinctive variation of the *human* species.

Lumsden and Wilson at first seem to be leaning toward a strong theory of mind. They reject the point of view of their critics that "meaning is beyond the reach of evolutionary models." To the contrary, they argue, work in computer science and cognitive psychology demonstrates that "the human mind can conceive of a biological device that creates purpose— and from purpose, meaning."[71] The problem, however, is that there is an inverse relationship between a strong theory of mind and the degree to which one can rely on an algorithmic understanding of rule-governed variation. Agents possessing qualities of mind decide for themselves what to do. Yet the moment that agents begin to make decisions for themselves, the possibility of modeling decisions through algorithmic rule-following begins to atrophy. Population genetics is a method best applied to beings that follow rules. It is barely applicable, and may be irrelevant, to those who make the rules they will then follow. If qualities of mind enable people to alter the rules that govern their development, then a science based on rule-following will have to be replaced by a specifically human science that understands its subjects as rule-creating as well.

Furthermore, the laws of population genetics concern the dynamics of an entire species, whereas minds are possessed by individual members of the species. To shift to an explanation of human evolution emphasizing mind is therefore to alter what one is trying to explain. The concept of mind, as George Herbert Mead was the first to point out, inevitably leads to a concept of the self. Minds are not the same as brains, as will be discussed in the next chapter. Qualities of mind have something, but not everything, to do with computational powers of

cognition and logic. But the social mind, Mead argued, supplements the biological brain by recognizing social realities
lying outside the brain. Once we move into the terrain of mind,
we require a theory that explains not what makes whole species
evolve but, instead, how individuals make choices that are not
determined by their genes or even by their culture.

For obvious reasons, then, a turn toward mind and meaning
puts Lumsden and Wilson in an awkward position. To rely on
an explanation in which culture and mind play a role, they
must drop their stress on population genetics and become social scientists with a different, and distinct, methodology. To
maintain their faith in mathematically governed evolutionary
rules, by contrast, they have to reemphasize cultural determinism as well as genetic determinism. Recognizing this di-
lemma, they introduce considerations of mind only to turn and
argue against the autonomy of mind, viewing change as lying
in rules themselves, rather than in those governed by them.
From this perspective, an emphasis on reification constitutes
a minimal theory of mind: cognitive abilities are defined as the
relative efficiency to be gained by substituting shorter symbols
for longer instructions, not as the ability to grasp meaning and
interpret situations.

Sociobiology's concession to a theory of mind, in short, is a
reluctant one. Adhering to a weak theory of mind, sociobiology
is unable to explain in any convincing way—certainly not in a
way more convincing than sociologists and anthropologists do
in emphasizing culture—why humans dress differently, speak
differently, and act differently now in the United States than
they did a couple of thousand years ago in the Middle East. If
we are to develop an adequate explanation of how the human
species evolved as it did, we will require an explanation that
allows greater scope for the mental capacities of its individual
members. Such an explanation will take us away from the study
of whole species and toward the analysis of individual minds.
It will use the tools of a different kind of science, one that,
instead of copying the rules of biology, will be cognizant of
the specific and unique human powers of mind. What we gain
by moving in that direction is an explanation of human evolution more powerful than such passive ones as time in itself,

the sheer speed of change, or a minimal theory of mind. What we have to give up is the precision gained by models that operate by fixed mathematical laws borrowed from the sciences concerned with other than human species.

Tertiary Rules and Human Choice

Given the origins of social theory in a milieu dominated by Darwinian themes, it is not surprising that sociobiology should have its advocates among contemporary sociologists and anthropologists.[72] Political scientists as well have turned to sociobiology to understand such practices as leadership and war.[73] Legal theorists have on occasion been attracted to sociobiology, both as a way of dealing with specific courtroom issues and as a way of understanding the evolution of legal systems.[74] The popularity of sociobiology has led to a number of efforts to link biology with sociology.[75] At least one historian, impressed by these examples, has shifted his own focus away from culture and more toward biology.[76] The idea that human behavior, however complex, is at root a form of animal behavior is too powerful an idea ever to disappear.

At the same time, given the popularity of the notion that human practices and institutions are "socially constructed" by people themselves, it is also not surprising that sociobiological assumptions are routinely criticized by contemporary sociologists. When sociologists speak of the social construction of identity, they are arguing that practices once believed to be biological, such as gender or homosexuality, are the products of history and politics.[77] As Joan Scott puts it, "nothing about the body, including women's reproductive organs, determines univocally how social divisions will be shaped."[78] When it comes to the differences between men and women, Cynthia Fuchs Epstein has argued, "social factors can account for most of the variation."[79]

This shift from biology to sociology as a way of explaining the speed and variation of human distinctiveness is clearly appropriate, but it is especially appropriate for people who have added culture to nature and then added mind to culture. The biological, the cultural, and the interpretative sciences are all relevant for human beings, but each under conditions and circumstances different from the others. If we want to understand how we emerged from our ancestors who lacked the advantages of both mind and culture, sociobiology would be of great help to us. If we are trying to explain the lives of people who lived in different conditions some time ago, or who are so governed by tradition that they do not use the powers of mind they possess, we would focus more on culture and less on both nature and mind. But if we value what modernity has given us, especially the capacity first to shape nature by culture and then to shape culture by mind, we will look more to sociology as a distinct science for a distinct subject. The most important socially constructed subject, in short, is mind itself.[80]

If we are to develop a science that accounts for the powerful capacities of mind developed by human beings, a science that assumes weak powers of mind will not be very helpful. No doubt, some of what human beings do is determined by what Lumsden and Wilson call primary and secondary epigenetic rules. But the accomplishments of human beings in recent times require something in addition: a new set of rules, which we might call tertiary or epicultural rules. Such rules are possessed by members of a species that have capabilities of mind. They are the opposite of primary epigenetic rules, in the sense that, instead of being fixed by genetic criteria, they would be the most free to vary, even if they are constrained at the outer margins by biological factors. These tertiary rules, moreover, are also quite different from what sociobiologists mean by culture. They are not the product of an evolutionary process governing our species as a whole. They are, rather, a reflection of the choices made by individuals within the species. Tertiary rules are those created by members of a species themselves, through their capacity to use their minds to attribute meaning to their experiences; these rules thereby affect the choices facing those who come later in time. The existence of tertiary rules explains why human evolution has followed a path that is different from the evolutionary paths of other species: the capacities of mind that distinguish us from other species make it possible for us to discover the self and thereby to attribute meaning to our biological bodies. Unlike all other rules, these rules are the result of individual agents making choices that are determined neither by their genetic structures nor by their inherited cultural patterns.

What makes sociology a distinct science for a distinct subject is its awareness of the importance of such tertiary rules. Tertiary rules do not substitute for nature and culture, both of which still play a role in human affairs. They are, rather, the direct result of situations in which people can use their powers of imagining alternative worlds in order to change the rules that govern what they do. Consider childbirth patterns, a subject that sociobiologists and sociologists often debate. Primary epigenetic rules create fundamentally different genetic structures for women and men, which allow the former to develop a uterus, breasts, and other specifically female anatomical parts; in that sense, nature is determinant. Secondary epigenetic rules have a cultural flavor, in the sense that in most societies women have been understood to have primary responsibility for children, but in other societies, with contrasting cultural patterns, men share some of that responsibility. But in very modern societies, under the influence of a movement such as feminism—women using their minds to change the world around them—a new balance is established. Tertiary rules explain how many children a woman will have, how work and domestic obligations are balanced, who will provide primary care for the children, how long infants suckle, what children are taught, and other such behaviors that do vary greatly from one place to another.

Because so much of what they do is governed by their ability to make sense of the world around them, modern human beings have nothing to fear by comparing themselves to other animal species. It is not our strength, or our complexity, that makes us distinct but our power to use mind to alter the rules that govern us. In teaching us about other animal species—how they communicate, whether they think, whether they make tools, and, most important of all, how their evolution is governed— the second biological revolution undergirds the belief that what is distinctive about humans is their capacity to add mind to culture as well as culture to nature. Sociobiology, a very modern science, *is* appropriate for humans—but only for humans who lived in premodern times, before qualities of culture and mind became important. For very modern people, whose minds determine the rules that create their culture, only an old-fashioned science—one rooted in the increasingly distrusted anthropocentrism of the Enlightenment—seems appropriate.

Chapter Three

Mind, Self, Society, and Computer

Respect for Machines

For those who work with them, computers can teach the same sense of humility toward human endeavors as work with animals has done for ethologists. Carried away by the extraordinary ability of machines to process information—especially in contrast to the sloppy, irrational, and trial-and-error methods used by humans—researchers in the fields of artificial intelligence (AI), cognitive science, and robotics have, like students of animal behavior, been questioning the hypothesis that there is something special or unique about human abilities.

If anything, the vehemence with which the hypothesis of human distinctiveness is rejected is stronger among those fascinated with the properties of machines than it is among those fascinated with the properties of nonhuman animals. Although the invention of the computer could be taken as a further manifestation of human ingenuity, almost simultaneously with its development has arisen the hypothesis that artificial intelligence will eventually prove itself superior to human intelligence. As two writers in the artificial intelligence tradition have written:

And in all humility, we really must ask: How smart are the humans who've taught these machines? On the evolutionary time scale, thinking animals are relatively recent arrivals. Evolution hasn't had a great deal of time to work on the perfection of human cognition.[1]

55

Reflecting that notion, some envision a "post-biological" world, in which machines will carry out most of the work that we used to do.[2] If indeed "these artificial intelligences will help run society and relieve mankind of the burden of being the leading species," we would be guilty of what Edward Fredkin calls misplaced human vanity to think we occupy a privileged position over other species, including *machina sapiens*.[3] The computer surpasses us at precisely the moment that non-human animals have caught up to us.

When research in artificial intelligence is linked to research in sociobiology, as it often is, the resulting perspective on humans is, literally, mind-boggling. The notion that "a body is really a machine blindly programmed by its selfish genes" seems to lead to the notion that machine programming can become the unifying element of all scientific understanding.[4] The information sciences have become the basis for what its advocates call a unified theory of cognition, linking DNA reproductive codes to animal cognition to human decision-making and finally to machine calculation.[5] When such a theory is developed, if it ever is, any notion that there is a specifically humanistic dimension to the study of human behavior would become obsolete, for its laws would be reduced by the mathematics of information transmission. The proper study of man, as Herbert Simon puts it, would no longer be man but "the science of decision."[6]

Humans now have a new challenge to their view of themselves as unique. And so, therefore, do social theorists. For if machines can be developed and programmed in such a way as to emulate, or surpass, human intelligence and dexterity, then not only, *pace* Simon, would there be no basis for a specific human science; there would also be no basis for assigning any special importance to our cognitive powers. Sherry Turkle describes the computer as an "evocative . . . object that fascinates, disturbs equanimity, and precipitates thought."[7] One of the thoughts it stimulates is that human selves have no special and distinct features worth singling out for special respect or special study.

As it happens, however, the claims of many enthusiasts for artificial intelligence are now generally viewed as exaggerated.

Computers have accomplished many wonderful things, but they have not yet replaced human intelligence. The question is not really which "machine" plays better chess: the Cartesian or the computer. The claims made on behalf of AI need to be examined, not so that we can praise its possibilities or gloat over its failures but, instead, so that we can learn about ourselves by contrasting the way we think and act to the way machines do. AI is a vast *Gedenkenexperiment,* a stimulus to reflections about what makes people human. As such, it is fully as important for the last half of this century as Darwinism was for the last half of the previous one. And the experiment appears to show that human thinking differs from machine calculation precisely because humans have interpretative capabilities.

The Human Essence Test

Let us, in the spirit of a thought experiment, accept for the moment the working hypothesis that there are no essential differences between computers and humans. (Reversing what appears to be common sense in order to test common sense is a crucial aspect of the way theorists in artificial intelligence think.) In order to confirm such a point of view, we need to return to questions of philosophical anthropology. We need to ask whether humans are different from any other species and, if they are, what makes them different. Unlike classical social theorists, however, who compared humans with other animals, we need to make comparisons with machines.

Researchers in AI have a test of machine intelligence, called the Turing test (though, it should be added, their version of the test is often different from the version originally proposed by Alan Turing).[8] To determine whether a machine is intelligent, the Turing test suggests that we imagine a person being given instructions by both a machine and another person. When the person can no longer tell which of them is giving the instructions, intelligence has been modeled by the machine. How, in the same spirit, do we know we are in the presence of a human, rather than machine, intelligence? I propose that in thinking about a "human essence test," we turn to the one sociological theorist who most addressed questions of mind and intelligent behavior: George Herbert Mead.

Mead's argument is that the difference between human and nonhuman species involves two further distinctions: all animal species have brains, but only humans have minds; and all other species have bodies, whereas only the human has a self. Brains, to take the first distinction, are physiological organs composed of material properties and represented by what in Mead's day was called the central nervous system.[9] But in contrast to the study of the brain, Mead wrote, "it is absurd to look at the mind simply from the standpoint of the individual human organism." Because "we must regard mind . . . as arising and developing within the social process," in human forms of cognition the social mind complements the biological brain: "The subjective experience of the individual must be brought into relation with the natural, sociobiological activities of the brain in order to render an acceptable account of mind possible at all; and this can be done only if the social nature of mind is recognized."[10] Mind, therefore, presupposes at least two brains. Mind supplements brain to the degree that an individual incorporates into his or her actions the point of view of another.

Can communication between a human and a machine therefore be considered mindful? Humans can, of course, put themselves in the place of a machine and identify with it, as was the case with Joseph Weizenbaum's ELIZA. Although a very early program, and offered more as a practical joke than an experiment in artificial intelligence, ELIZA is nonetheless helpful in understanding Mead's distinction between mind and brain. ELIZA prompts the respondent to answer the question,

How do you do? Please tell me your problem.

ELIZA will recognize certain key words in the responses given to the question and transform those words into another question. If the response, for example, is

I hate my father,

ELIZA will prompt,

Tell me more about your family,

and so on. One of the questions posed by such a program is not whether ELIZA possesses the Meadian quality of mind—clearly, it does not—but whether the human being interacting with ELIZA does.[11]

If we take a human individual as the focus of our concern, and ask whether he or she has undergone a transformation in the process of talking with ELIZA, the answer would seem, at first glance, to be yes. After all, the person did exist in what Mead viewed as a triadic relationship: gestures elicited responses, which, in turn, elicited new gestures. Moreover, all this activity took place in the form of language, signs that were recognized by both parties. If our test for the possession of intelligence is the capacity to incorporate into our actions the responses of others as determined by some form of symbolic communication, the human subject interacting with ELIZA exercised qualities of mind. (For similar reasons, the triadic form of communication among birds, discussed in the previous chapter, would also appear, at first, to constitute communication in this sense.) Even more impressively, the human talking to ELIZA experienced growth; Weizenbaum, discussing what he learned from his experience, notes that many people were moved by their interaction with ELIZA, writing to him about how much they learned about themselves—all of which indicates that some people very definitely put themselves in ELIZA's place.[12] If emotion, transference, catharsis, identification, growth, and transformation can all be experienced by a person through interaction with an artificial other, all the ingredients for mind would seem to be present.

Other programs direct our attention to the question of whether a machine talking to a person displays qualities of mind. Intelligent tutoring systems (ITS) are designed to flag down inappropriate questions from student programmers and check whether the programmer really meant to ask them.[13] Possibly the machine has assumed too much knowledge (or too little) on the part of the student programmer, or perhaps the options presented to the programmer are too restricted. Under such conditions, ITS systems are capable of spotting errors by, in a sense, substituting themselves for the questioner. GUIDON, for example, was designed to supplement the medical diagnosis program MYCIN. By comparing a student's questions to those asked by MYCIN, the program can determine when the diagnosis being followed by the student is off-track. GUIDON is also capable of analyzing the discourse patterns of the questions posed of it, to see whether they are consistent with earlier questions.[14] And, as the limits of GUIDON are reached, other programs—such as NEOMYCIN, HERCULES, IMAGE, and ODYSSEUS—have been developed to refine its possibilities further.[15] If the Meadian concept of mind is based solely on the ability to take the point of view of another, including another program, these programs would also, like the person communicating with ELIZA, appear to possess mind.

But there is more to the Meadian analysis than reflection by putting oneself in the place of another. The second Meadian distinction is between the body and the self. A physical body becomes a social self when an interaction with another social self has taken place. Since "selves can only exist in definite relationships to other selves," qualities of mind exist when a gesture "has the same effect on the individual making it that it has on the individual to whom it is addressed."[16] No individual can therefore possess reflective intelligence—that is, be viewed as having a mind—without another individual who also possesses a mind. Mead's formulation is the converse of the Turing test: the other must itself be a self before a self can communicate with it. Human cognition, because it requires that we modify our thoughts by the ways we expect others to react to them, is therefore distinct from any other kind of cognition. By this definition, neither ELIZA nor intelligent tutoring systems would thus qualify.

Here, then, is a relatively parsimonious statement of the argument in favor of human uniqueness: Because we are biological creatures, we possess brains, but because we are social creatures as well, we also possess minds. This distinction between mind and brain is somewhat arbitrary. There are neurobiologists who argue for the existence of a "social brain," in the sense that many activities studied by sociologists, such as religious belief, can be explained by pure neurological functioning.[17] On the other hand, there are theorists in cognitive science who argue that we have a "cognitive mind," that thought has its own language, so that qualities of mind do not lie, as Mead argued, in things external to it.[18] Some work in AI even suggests that there is no distinction between mind and brain at all, but only something called "mind-brain," combining elements of both.[19] Still, if we accept Mead's distinctions for purposes of analysis, the questions we want to ask are (1) What would a machine need to do to approximate the qualities of the human brain? and (2) What would a machine need to do to approximate qualities of the human mind?

The question of what a machine would have to do to approximate the human brain is technological and biological in nature. Since the brain is composed of a series of neural nets, we should, in principle, be able to develop a machine capable of equaling, or surpassing, the information-processing capacity of human brains (although scientists who have tried to do so generally come away impressed by the information-processing capacities of human brains). If a machine or series of machines were capable of processing information faster and more efficiently than a human, we would have to reject the hypothesis that the brains of humans are superior to those of all other species.

The second question—What would a machine have to do to approximate qualities of mind?—poses a different set of considerations. If we follow Mead's conception of mind, we already have an answer by definition: no machine could ever approximate qualities of mind in interacting with a human, nor could a human show qualities of mind in communicating with a machine, since mind always implies the presence of at least two individuals. Yet, although the "human essence test" is in that sense rigged, it nonetheless helps us understand the importance of social context in the way any particular self understands the world. Real human beings do not make sense out of the world by searching through memory in an application of algorithmic rules. Instead, individuals rely on the social world around them to supply the contexts within which communication takes on meaning. To approximate qualities of mind, then, a machine would have to approximate the social environment that enables human minds to function. The question, in that sense, is not whether machine brains are superior to human minds or vice versa. Rather, the biological brain and the social mind work in radically different ways: one seeks information as complete and precise as possible; the other does not need hard-wired and preprogrammed instructions—or even trial-and-error learning through the strengthening of neural nets—because it can supply meaning from outside itself. As with the study of animal behavior, we learn from AI that the unique properties of human beings are their interpretative and meaning-producing capacities—this time defined by the presence of other minds, since interpretation and reflection are possible only in a social context.

Software Intelligence

Work in artificial intelligence is generally divided into two kinds: software and hardware approaches. By a software approach is meant one that tries to model what the brain does without entering into the question of how the brain does it. Hardware approaches to AI reject an analogy with the computer and try to model intelligence and learning in machines upon a direct analogy with the neurological structure of the brain.

Early work in AI proceeded along both approaches, but it was not long before the hardware efforts, represented by Frank Rosenblatt and his ideas about perceptrons, gave way to software approaches, which seemed to offer more promising payoffs.[20] These approaches assumed, as a thought experiment, that the brain resembles the Von Neumann architecture of a digital computer. Somewhere in the brain, according to this point of view, a central processing unit (CPU) stores information in the form of memory. Access to it could be made through instructions causing a search through memory in order to find the correct response. The beauty of this approach was that the human brain did not have to resemble a computer in a physiological sense. If a program could be written that could represent reality, then intelligence lay in the application of instructions or algorithms.[21] Only one assumption was necessary for this procedure to work, and that was that a complete set of instructions could be provided. As Von Neumann put it,

"Anything that can be exhaustively and unambiguously described . . . is . . . realizable by a suitable finite neural network."[22] Many researchers in AI are convinced that even the world of everyday life—of metaphor and ambiguity, for example—can be programmed into formal rules that a machine can understand, if only we specify them in all their complexity.[23]

If memory were infinite, as it could be imagined in the purely abstract theories of Alan Turing and Alonzo Church, machines would simply take as much time as they needed to find the information relevant to an instruction, even if the time to do so was, say, the equivalent of three human lifetimes. But in the real world, researchers designing software approaches to AI soon discovered that the reality outside the computer was more complicated than anyone had realized. They therefore attempted to devise some indirect way of representing reality. One product of these attempts was the creation of "expert systems," programs based on a model of how experts in various areas make decisions.[24] As long as they confined themselves to relatively limited domains of rule application, expert systems were a success, especially in medical diagnosis with the creation of DENDRAL and MYCIN. Such successes have led researchers within this tradition back to efforts to create more general programs, such as a unified theory of cognition, discussed above; but although such efforts have generated a good deal of excitement, their potential lies in the future.

Another way to get around the problem of representing reality was to take certain shortcuts—to assume that the reality outside the machine could be broken down into smaller and less complicated categories, which then could be combined. Minsky, for example, argued for "frames," while Roger Schank talked about the existence of scripts.[25] Unwilling to reject the CPU metaphor—but recognizing that to hold information about everything that ever happened to us throughout our lives, such a human CPU would be unwieldy—these researchers assumed that memory is stored by humans in the form of episodes. Each set of generalized episodes could be called a script. In Schank's famous example of a restaurant script, a set of associations is presumed to exist in the brain about what happens to an individual upon entering a restaurant; within this set of associations, any particular experience in a real-world restaurant can be framed. We may not, the argument ran, be able to represent the whole of reality at any one time, but we can break reality up into all its possible components and represent it that way.

Schank's ideas about scripts were subject to one of the most searing critiques in the literature generated by AI, Searle's effort to prove that machines cannot "understand" the instructions given to them.[26] The implication of Searle's "Chinese room" critique was that there cannot be any artificial functional equivalent, not of human intelligence, but of human understanding. In the absence of the human capacity to understand, not even frames and scripts can avoid the problem that to know anything, the machine must first know everything.[27] No wonder that many of the early criticisms of work in the area were directed primarily against software approaches.[28] Even AI researchers themselves began to look for another approach, one based more directly on the hardware of the human brain.

Yet software efforts to create artificial intelligence did raise one fascinating question. If machines have trouble representing reality outside themselves, how do human brains do it? Humans, like machines, can also be given rules that they are expected to follow. But since our memories are imperfect, it would be difficult to conclude that our rules can also be programmed in detailed specificity if the same technique did not work for computers. Work in AI stimulated neuroscientists to take a closer look at the *human* brain, and some of them—especially those associated with Gerald M. Edelman—discovered that the whole idea of a CPU in the brain had to be rejected.[29] The scientists who have taken this position offer instead what Edelman calls a nonalgorithmic understanding of the brain, or, more accurately, of brains; for he argues that different brains develop differently in the form of a selective system, just as certain species are understood by Darwinian theory to evolve in response to new challenges.[30] Humans have, in other words, what Edelman and Mountcastle called a "mindful brain," which software approaches, because they are dependent purely on algorithms, could not have.[31]

But if human memory is not stored somewhere, how do we, in any particular circumstance, know what to do? Putting the question in another form, if it is true, as one neuroscientist argues, that "we are probably much better at recognition than we are at recollection," what we need to understand, in dealing with humans, is not how memory is stored but how it is activated.[32] The answer may very well lie in what I have been calling the "human essence test" associated with the Meadian distinction between mind and brain. In contrast to the ideas about brains contained in software approaches to AI—ideas emphasizing the brain as a CPU, which, it turns out, may not have been an adequate model of the brain after all—humans have minds, which are capable of interpreting rules and instructions. We do not just search through memories to match a representation to a reality; instead, we fill in the frames or interpret the scripts, because our minds recognize the external reality that our brains cannot.

If this line of reasoning is correct, it would follow that the human brain, unlike machine brains, can be incomplete, that the brain does not need to understand everything with which it is presented, because we also have minds that make sense of the world to our brains. Work in AI unintentionally seems to show that humans are distinct not because their brains store *more* information than machines but because they can store *less* and get away with it. Our distinctiveness, in short, lies in the *unknowability* of the world around us. We gain access to knowledge by interacting with other minds, reflecting on what we learn from that interaction and experiencing growth as a result.

The role played by unknowability in the social world can be illustrated by theorists such as Harold Garfinkel. Although ethnomethodology was formulated in response to Parsonian structural-functionalism, it is highly relevant to the debates about brain and mind stimulated by AI research. For Garfinkel, conversations are interesting not for what is said but for what is not said. Thus, the words

Dana succeeded in putting a penny in a parking meter today without being picked up

might be difficult for a computer to process, because it would not know whether Dana was being lifted up to the parking meter or had not yet been met by his parents in their car. But even if a "natural" language program had anticipated this problem and could reject the incorrect meaning of "pick up" in favor of the correct one, would it be able to interpret the sentence to mean what one of Garfinkel's students assumed it to mean: "This afternoon as I was bringing Dana, our four-year-old son, home from the nursery school, he succeeded in reaching high enough to put a penny in a parking meter when we parked in a meter parking zone, whereas before he has always had to be picked up to reach that high"?[33]

Research into human conversations stimulated by Garfinkel illustrates the difference between how human minds and machine brains talk. Although some researchers use conversational analysis as a method for understanding breakdowns in communication between machines and humans, the whole point of ethnomethodology is to analyze how people themselves develop the rules that structure what they do, including how they talk.[34] Thus, to take only one example, Schegloff and Sacks showed that something as seemingly obvious as the closing of a conversation is a socially negotiated process between the speakers. If "there are possibilities throughout a closing, including the moments after a 'final' good-bye, for reopening the conversation," then human agency is always a third party to conversation between two human beings.[35] Because human conversation is indexical (the meaning of words depends on the context in which they are uttered), computers have shown a remarkable inability to translate from one natural language to another.[36]

John Bateman has pointed out that nearly all of Alfred Schutz's concepts can be translated into AI language; Schutz's "stock of knowledge," for example, is the same as Minsky's frames or Schank's scripts.[37] Yet despite this similarity, ethnomethodology seems to lead to an appreciation of how plastic our tacit understandings of the world tend to be. Schutzian phenomenology fills in the gaps that a formal analysis of grammatical rules can never fill: the everyday world provides the background or tacit knowledge that enables us to act in a contingent world—to act, as Dreyfus puts it, without a theory of how we act. Tacit knowledge, background assumptions, and practical reasoning are all features of mind that enable individuals to be rule-governed creatures, even if they do not know all the possible rules. The Wittgensteinian regress (the notion that the specification of any set of rules always contains a *ceteris paribus* condition that cannot be understood within the terms of the rules specified), while always a logical problem, rarely becomes a practical human problem.[38] We can define the situation because the situation is not defined. We can construct meaning because the meaning is not known. Having gone through a period in which they tried to escape from ambiguity, sociological theorists are coming to appreciate it—in part, as Donald Levine states, because of "the recent ascendancy of computerized thoughtways."[39] Ambiguity is essential to human communication. Because the world is infinite in its possibilities, we will never be able to capture it perfectly in the way we represent it to ourselves. This impossibility forces us to turn to others to share meanings, a social act that binds us together in human communities.

The differences between the knowing brain and the unknowing mind are illustrated by one of the activities that both machines and humans periodically undertake: the playing of games such as chess. As Georg Simmel once pointed out, in a metaphor exceptionally appropriate to the age of artificial intelligence, there are two conditions that would inhibit an individual from playing a game of chess. One is not knowing any moves. The other is knowing all the moves.[40] Chess-playing programs developed by AI researchers cannot specify all moves; that is why heuristic rules were developed that eliminate nonsensical moves, making it possible for computer programs in the real world to play exceptionally expert chess. Yet let us grant one assumption of science: that if something is theoretically possible, we can imagine it to be practically possible. When the perfect chess program is developed, the result is to stop "playing" chess: when all moves are known, it can no longer be a game. A minimal condition for gaming, as Erving

Goffman once pointed out, is that "a prior knowledge of the players will not render the outcome a foregone conclusion." What makes a game a game is that interaction has taken place: "The developing line built up by the alternating, interlocking moves of the players can thus maintain sole claim upon the attention of the participants, thereby facilitating the game's power to constitute the current reality of its players and to engross them."[41] Winning games is something our brains do; playing them is something our minds do. (That people both play and play to win only means that they have both minds and brains.)

There would be no need for mind if—not only in the playing of chess but in all other human activities as well—human agents acted with complete knowledge of the consequences of their acts. If the self knows the consequences that will follow from any gesture, speech, act, or form of behavior, it will no longer be a self. Human selves are distinctive not because they are "smarter" than machines but because they are "dumber." Not knowing everything there is to know in advance, they have to rely on social practices, the cues of others, experience, definitions of the situation, encounters, norms, and other ways of dealing with uncertainty that enable mind to develop. One of the leading German philosophical anthropologists, Arnold Gehlen, argues that because humans remain infants far longer than other creatures do, their specific traits develop out of their need to compensate for the lack of what nature has given them.[42] The same can be said for their brains. Imperfect, trial-and-error, hesitant—the human brain is incomplete in the absence of a social mind. Even if a computer someday surpasses the human brain in its intelligence, it is unlikely to surpass the collective power of assembled minds. It is because humans have minds that we can speak of artificial intelligence, but almost never of artificial wisdom or judgment.

If the human brain and the Von Neumann architecture of the computer cannot model each other, software approaches to AI will never meet the first stage of the "human essence" test necessary to reject the hypothesis of human uniqueness: modeling the brain. It seems virtually impossible, therefore, that these approaches can ever reach the second state: modeling the human mind. We are not sure how we comprehend the world outside our brains; but we are fairly certain that we do not do it through a detailed set of algorithms, specified in software or its functional equivalent, that model reality outside the brain in exact equivalence.

Hardware Intelligence

In part because of the kinds of problems just discussed, the software approach to AI is generally considered to have met a dead end. Indeed, some of the strongest criticisms of efforts to represent reality outside the brain have come not from those hostile to AI itself but from those committed to the kind of "hardware" approach with which AI began—an approach based on the work of Frank Rosenblatt and his notions about perceptrons.[43] These approaches have been revived, but under a new name, generally called neural networks, parallel distributive processing (PDP), or connectionism.[44] They represent the latest effort to prove that machines are capable of engaging in humanlike intelligence, thereby disproving the notion that any special characteristics are unique to us.[45]

Rather than modeling how a brain decides without entering into the way it decides, hardware efforts to model intelligence use certain understandings of neurological behavior to develop analogous data-processing systems. Because the brain works much faster than computers, these thinkers argue, it must be composed of many computational devices working in parallel fashion. And because the brain does not necessarily store its memory in specific locations, waiting to be activated by signals that enter the system, its architecture is better viewed as a series of nets activated by the connections between them. In that sense, PDP approaches circumvent the most conspicuous flaws of earlier efforts: using a Von Neumann machine instead of the brain itself as a model for human intelligence:

One important difference between our interpretation of schemata and the more conventional one is that in the conventional story, schemata are stored in memory. Indeed, they are the major *content of memory*. In our case, *nothing stored corresponds very closely to* a schema. What is stored is a set of connection strengths which, when activated, have implicitly in them the ability to generate states that correspond to instantiated schemata.[46]

Two important considerations follow from this major shift in emphasis. One concerns rules and scripts. Researchers in the PDP tradition "do not assume that the goal of learning is the formation of explicit rules. Rather, we assume it is the acquisition of connection strengths which allow a network of simple units to act *as though* it knew the rules."[47] It follows that the machine—more accurately, in this kind of work, a set of parallel machines—can learn, because it can react to ambiguous or incomplete instructions and furnish the context that can make sense out of them. While researchers in this tradition are cautious about making large claims for their work, they are convinced that machines can reproduce the human capacity to act in particular ways based on past experience.

One example provided by researchers in this tradition helps illustrate what is new about this approach when compared to older forms of AI work. Suppose that a child is in the process of learning the past tense of verbs. The general rule is that we take the present tense and add "ed." Following this rule, a naïve subject would reason as follows:

jump	jumped
walk	walked
swim	swimed

To respond to such a difficulty, earlier research in AI would have begun a search for all exceptions to the general rule, specifying them as precisely as possible, so that a machine would know how to respond if asked to give the past tense of a verb. PDP works in the opposite way. It begins with what the naïve subject would do, makes a mistake, corrects the mistake, and accumulates in the process enough associations that it eventually comes to learn when an "ed" ought to be added and when some other form of indicating the past tense is correct.[48] In short, the reasoning here is trial-and-error reasoning, and is in that sense similar to the way humans think.

If software approaches to AI located intelligence in a set of instructions to a CPU, hardware approaches locate intelligence in a set of procedures that can activate connections. "Under this new view, processing is done by PDP networks that configure themselves to match the arriving data with minimum conflict or discrepancy. The systems are always taming themselves (adjusting their weights). Learning is continuous, natural, and fundamental to the operations" of a system.[49]

At issue is the way that "learning" organisms relate parts to wholes. One of the root assumptions of work in AI is that intelligence is manifested when enough very small bits of information are assembled together into something called knowledge. Working within a particular philosophical tradition inspired by Descartes and Hume, AI researchers believe that understanding how machines process information enables us to solve what Hume called the problem of the homunculi: that we cannot understand what takes place in the brain by imagining that a little man exists inside of it, giving it instructions; for then we would have to posit a little man inside the brain of the little man, etc.[50] Their response to the Humean problem is to try to fashion a small machine out of exceptionally dumb components—indeed, the dumber the better. Although writing about AI in general, and not hardware approaches specifically, Daniel Dennett illustrates AI's response to the Humean problem:

Homunculi are *bogeymen* only if they duplicate *entirely* the talents they are rung in to explain. . . . If one can get a team or committee of *relatively* ignorant, narrow-minded, blind homunculi to produce the intelligent behavior of the whole, this is progress. . . . Eventually this nesting of boxes within boxes lands you with homunculi so stupid (all they have to do is remember whether to say yes or no when asked) that they can be, as one says, "replaced by a machine." One *discharges* fancy homunculi from one's scheme by organizing armies of such idiots to do the work.[51]

As Douglas Hofstader has put it, the paradox of AI is that "the most inflexible, desireless, rule-following of beasts" can produce intelligence.[52] But how, exactly, do they do it? Connectionist advocates of AI feel that they have a major advantage over software approaches in the way they produce intelligence. The human mind, they claim, does not work by accumulating small bits of information, but instead works more holistically. Their approach (involving neural nets), they say, enables them to bypass the problem of dumb components by designing machines that can make associations. Yet the units of such systems are still electrical charges, and it is by no means clear that the associations made by such charges are in any way similar to the ability of human minds to incorporate realities outside the brain into the thinking process.

Even at their most sophisticated, parallel data-processing machines still think of intelligence as parts that somehow add up to a whole. In that sense, some of the problems facing workers in the field of AI are similar to problems that have plagued sociological theory. Durkheim's notion about the division of labor—where each human agent, generally acting in ways unknown to other human agents, nonetheless contributes to the effective overall functional performance of the society— is but one formulation of an age-old problem of how parts and wholes interrelate. Durkheim's division of labor, or any strong form of functionalist sociology, is an effort to understand how a smart organism—civilization or social structure—could emerge out of somewhat limited if not necessarily dumb components—people. In relying on a biological metaphor as the basis for his functionalism, Durkheim envisioned society as composed of hearts, muscles, heads, and other organs—all of them with tasks to perform, but none, save perhaps the head, with much consciousness or awareness of why it is doing what it is doing. It was precisely this sense of homeostatic structures and functions (inherited by Parsons from Durkheim) that led microsociologists, especially Garfinkel and Goffman, to pay more attention to individual human minds.

Just as sociological theorists were led to a greater appreciation of how micro and macro interrelate, researchers in AI are recognizing the limitations of the notion that a focus on the smallest possible parts will tell us something about the behavior of the whole. Marvin Minsky, for example, although once associated with software approaches to AI, has, like his colleague Seymour Papert, become sympathetic to the new approaches associated with PDP and connectionism. Confronting the question of how dumb components can make a smart machine, he asks us to imagine that intelligence is a "society" composed of agents—such as the comparing agent, the adding agent, the seeing agent—each of which is ignorant of what the other agents are doing: "Each mental agent by itself can only do some simple thing that needs no mind or thought at all. Yet because we join these agents in societies—in certain very special ways—this leads to true intelligence."[53] The overlap with Durkheim here is striking, and, also as with Durkheim, the question becomes whether PDP approaches can enable us to focus on aggregates—what Minsky calls "societies"—without attributing significant intellectual qualities to the parts that compose those societies.

It is worth noting in this context that Minsky reaches for the metaphor of "society" to talk about the whole, and he also uses the term *agent* to describe the part. The interaction between parts and whole seems to work for human societies because—among other reasons—human beings clearly possess agency: they can shift their attention back and forth from parts to wholes because they are autonomous agents capable of thinking for themselves. (It is the recognition of the power of human agency that led sociological theory away from an overdetermining structuralism.) Can a machine premised upon parts that are dumb replicate the way real human agents operate in the world? Just as software approaches could have manifested intelligence resembling human intelligence if they could have overcome one fatal flaw—the need to specify descriptions of the real world as thoroughly and unambiguously as possible—the ability of the hardware approach to approximate human learning hinges on one point as well: does it make sense to apply the term *agency* to whatever is operating through a set of essentially dumb microprocedures that activate its states?

The role that agency plays in human intelligence is underscored by the same neuroscientists who reject the CPU model of the human brain. True, they admit, the PDP approach is closer in spirit to what we know about how human brains work; yet they are by no means convinced that these new approaches will enable machines to model the brain either.[54] The reason has again to do with the social nature of the human mind.

Rosenfield has written that "the world around us is constantly changing, and we must be able to react to it . . . in a way that will take account of the new and unexpected, as well as our past individual experiences." The question, then, is how we come to "take account" of unexpected events. Rosenfield's view is in accord with the Meadian notion that human intelligence is manifested in the ability to interpret the meaning of stimuli outside the self: "Fixed memory stores, we have already seen, cannot accommodate the factors of context and history. Computations—the use of procedures in a limited way—bring us closer to a better solution but still fail to explain a crucial aspect of our perceptual capabilities: how our past affects our present view of the world, and how our coordinated movements, our past and present explorations of the world, influence our perceptions."[55]

The clear implication of the work described by Rosenfield is that human brains work the way they do because the signs they recognize are not merely representations of parts but also interact with larger wholes in the culture outside of the brain. Human agency, in other words, is a central feature of human intelligence. The unit doing the thinking and learning must be capable of taking in the context of the whole if the parts are going to fit together in any coherent way. If this point of view is correct, then PDP and connectionist approaches to AI cannot reach even the first step of developing an engineering replica of the human brain unless they can demonstrate that their machines in some way model the human agent's capacity to understand the meaning of wholes. Yet it is precisely meaning which, in the PDP view of things, is sacrificed in order to specify microprocedures. As D. A. Norman puts it, "I believe the point is that PDP mechanisms can set up almost any arbitrary relationships. Hence, to the expert, once a skill has been acquired, meaningfulness of the relationships is irrelevant." Because "the interpretation of the process is *not* in terms of the messages being sent but rather by what states are active," it follows that "in general, *there is no single reason why any given cognitive state occurs.*"[56]

PDP approaches, in short, attempt to solve the sociological problem of mind as a problem of engineering. What we get by using them, even under the best of circumstances, is a machine that may resemble the human brain in an architectural sense, but one still without the capacity of the human brain to rely on mind to supply meaning. These approaches come somewhat closer than purely algorithmic AI methods to what would be needed to reject the hypothesis of human distinctiveness, but are still far from having done so. The hypothesis that what makes humans distinctive is the existence of an interpretative self, still safe from animals, would seem to be safe from computers as well. Humans are distinct because they can, together with those around them, rely on their ability to interpret social contexts, so that what they do not know does not become a hindrance in their ability to negotiate their way through the world. Recent work in artificial intelligence, like the second biological revolution, ought to give social theorists a renewed appreciation of how unique the human mind really is.

Computers, Humans, and Rules

The founders of modern social theory were stimulated to think about the specifically human features of their societies because they shared the intellectual air of the nineteenth century with Darwinian theories of evolution. Contemporary social theorizing, in a similar way, will inevitably be affected by the revolution in computing that marks our own age. As two writers have put it, "artificial intelligence . . . is beginning to tread in waters very familiar to sociologists, while sociologists could soon find [that] some of the methods and concepts of AI provide a novel, but reliable approach to their subject."[57] Artificial intelligence promises to have the same relationship to social science as sociobiology has. Many argue for its irrelevance.[58] At the same time, others try to apply its methodologies and principles to such classic sociological topics as Goffmanesque dramatological models, ethnomethodology, sociolinguistics and social cognition, and the sociology of medicine.[59] And in the work of Niklas Luhmann, which will be discussed in greater detail in chapter 5, we have nothing less than a theory that

TABLE 1. *Artificial and Human Forms of Cognition*

	Artificial Intelligence		
	Software	*Hardware*	*Human Intelligence*
Locus	CPU	Neural nets	Mind
Relation to rules	Rule-following (algorithmic)	Rule-excepting	Rule-making
Language	Signs	Subsigns	Symbols
Meaning	Formal/notational	Procedural	Supplied

uses an analogy with the computer to explain how all systems, including social systems, operate.[60]

But, as with sociobiology, the question is not whether artificial intelligence constitutes an adequate scientific framework for the study of human beings but, instead, whether the subjects of each science are intelligent in the same way at all times. At the core of the Meadian distinction between brain and mind are two different ways of thinking about intelligence. Brains, understood neurologically, can be imagined as information-processing mechanisms that work by following preprogrammed rules. But minds do not. Powers of mind enable people to incorporate information from social contexts and situations, thereby rendering huge stocks of stored memory unnecessary. What I called in the previous chapter tertiary rules—which enable humans to use their mental powers to alter the rules that govern them—are precisely the kinds of rules that are inappropriate to machines, even the most sophisticated of them. Because human beings have brains, some of the intelligent behavior they display is similar to that of machines (or other animals). But human beings also have minds, which require a unique science for a unique subject.

A summary of the different ways in which computers and real people think is presented in table 1. Each of the two approaches to artificial intelligence discussed in this chapter conceptualizes the problem of intelligence in a different way; and both types of intelligence are in turn different from human intelligence, which is at least partly the product of qualities of mind. Specifically, these three forms of intelligence relate to rules, communicate, and conceptualize meaning in different ways.

The differences between computer and human intelligence in relation to rules could be illustrated in various ways, but one realm—that of play—is particularly appropriate for questions involving mind and the nature of the self. Charles Horton Cooley's work on the looking-glass self was stimulated by his observations of his own children at play.[61] Similarly, observations of children playing computer games should indicate how they and their computers develop the rules by which this play takes place.

Sherry Turkle has given a succinct account of children's ordinary play: "In this kind of play children have to learn to put themselves in the place of another person, to imagine what is going on inside someone else's head. There are no rules, there is empathy. There are no dice to roll, there is understanding, recognition, negotiation, and confrontation with others." In computer games, by contrast, precisely defined rule structures make empathy and role playing unnecessary. "You can postulate anything, but once the rules of the system have been defined they must be adhered to scrupulously. Such are the rules for creating 'rule-governed worlds.' They are known to every computer programmer and are now being passed on as cultural knowledge to a generation of children. The aesthetic of rule-governed worlds is passed on through Dungeons and Dragons and science fiction before most children ever meet a computer."[62] It is as if the rigidity of the rules in the computer compensates for the absence of predetermined rules that marks human play.

These ethnographic observations sharpen our understanding of how machines and human minds relate to rules. The most extreme form of rule adherence is contained in the software approaches to AI, for there the rules are everything. The failure of such programs—or, more precisely, their success only on condition that heuristics, efforts to generalize about rules rather than to specify them, become the dominant way to run them—indicates that concepts of agency based on the notion that the agent is a rule-follower and nothing else are inappropriate to human beings. Software approaches, being the most rule-bound, are like sociobiology at its most deterministic. Such ways of following rules may be appropriate to some kinds of software programs. But because human beings do not govern their affairs algorithmically, we must, if we are to model how they relate to rules, introduce the possibility that rules can be changed.

It is clearly possible, as hardware approaches have demonstrated, to make machines that will follow rules even when the rules are ambiguous. PDP and connectionist approaches are similar in that sense to sociobiological understandings of culture: they add new elements to a scientific understanding of how organisms behave. By introducing these new elements—elements of mind (or learning)—they avoid purely algorithmic reductionism and take a step closer to approximating how humans think. But the theory of mind that they introduce is minimal. They postulate qualities of mind that allow flexibility in rule-following but not qualities of rule interpretation. PDP and similar approaches remain strongly rule-driven; in the words of Terry Sejnowski, a leading connectionist researcher: "It's not like we're throwing rules away. This is a rule-*following* system, rather than a rule-*based* system. It's incorporating the regularities in the English language, but without our having to put in rules."[63]

If, in contrast to both approaches in AI, we understand the powers of human minds to lie not in how we follow rules, however creatively, but also in how we make them, we need a model of mind capable of interpreting reality outside itself. No machine yet developed is capable of taking the outside world into context, so that it can make the rules it will then follow. A science that is so algorithmic in structure as to negate the possibility of agents following their own rules will not be an especially successful science for mindful human beings.

An emphasis on rules, in turn, raises the question of how they are transmitted. If—following Pagels's terminology[64]—we distinguish between signs (representations that have only one meaning) and symbols (representations into which other meanings can be read), then machines can manipulate signs, whereas minds can interpret symbols. Thus, a Turing machine recognizes a string of 1s and 0s as a set of instructions indicating whether any given switch should be on and off and as an instruction to the next switch; and this property makes possible an extremely impressive set of computations, including those computations that are translated into the signs constituting the letters of this text (and making it possible for me to move portions of this text from one place in the manuscript to another). But no machine, and certainly not the one upon which the signs in this book are being processed, understands what the combinations of signs that form the words I write mean to the reader who is trying to determine whether my argument makes sense or not. In other words, like certain other species found in nature (about fifteen, according to Lumsden and Wilson), computers are capable of reification, of substituting shorter signs for longer signs. But they are not capable of turning signs into symbols.

As long as the instructions given to computers are understood to be signs (and in the PDP version of AI they may not even be signs, but an even smaller electrical charge that can only be called subsigns), little confusion results. But much of the AI literature does refer to machine instructions instead as symbols, thereby forcing some definitional clarity. One way to think about the matter is suggested by Pagels when he notes that symbols are "top down" whereas signs are "bottom up."[65] That is to say, humans recognize symbols as whole configurations and can disassemble them to account for their parts, while signs are the individual elements that together form a symbol. Given the complexity of their parts, symbols are open to interpretation; given the simplicity of their parts, signs are not. Brains, including artificially created ones as well as complex ones found among primates, can manipulate signs; reification is a purely self-referential process. But because the meaning of a symbol does not exist within the symbol but has to be interpreted by a mind, only a species capable of interpretation can attribute meaning to a symbol. A science of mindful human behavior requires that attention be paid to the ways in which symbols help individual minds make sense out of the world, whereas a science of machines (like a science of primates) need only consider the ability of one sign to substitute for another.

Because of the difference between signs and symbols, machines and humans respond differently to questions of meaning. Meaning is formal and notational in some kinds of AI research, especially those based on the software model. In such a model, formal modes of expression enable thoughts to be represented by means of syntactical rules (or grammars) that can be rendered into computations. For this very reason, as Jerry Fodor writes, "the machine lives in an entirely notational world; all its beliefs are false."[66] That is, machines practice "methodological solipsism"; they process data *as if* there were referents in the real world to be interpreted, without, of course, ever interpreting them. (This feature of AI research is elevated into a methodological principle by Dennett, who argues that we can take an "intentional" stance toward machines, ascribing to them certain features without necessarily making an argument that they possess those features in reality.)[67] The development of PDP models reinforces the point, for these versions of AI do not, as the software versions sometimes did, claim that they are representing the real world—except the neural structure of the human brain. For them, meaning lies in the strengths of connections between nets and nowhere else. Meaning is always internal to the dynamics of a system.

The notion that meaning is internal to any system has become increasingly popular—for example, among literary critics reluctant to consider anything outside the text (chapter 5 will examine such self-referential theories). In sociology as well, meaning has been redefined to refer only to the ways in which communication takes place, rather than to the message being communicated.[68] Since some aspects of human behavior are algorithmic, AI research has some, probably minor, direct applicability to the human sciences. But the unique features of human intelligence exist outside the brain; and to grasp those features, we need a science that can add the study of minds to the study of brains. Compared to computers, humans have one minor disadvantage: they calculate more slowly. But they also have one tremendous advantage: they can bring the whole world into their minds.

The reliance on the computer as a model for the operations of the human mind may well prove to be as limited as an earlier fascination with behaviorism. Psychologists have already begun to recognize the flaws of the mind-as-computer metaphor. Some have turned to cultural anthropology as a way of understanding the factors outside any particular individual's brain that help the individual make sense out of the world.[69] Others, such as Jerome Bruner, one of the founders of cognitive psychology, find that the computer analogy carries with it an unfortunate shift "from the *constuction* of meaning to the *processing* of information."[70] Bruner's reflections on the limits of the machine model lead him back to a humanistic emphasis on narrative and story-telling as essential ingredients in understanding human cognition, a fascinating intellectual journey that reveals both the power and the limits of computers as guides to the way we think.

Rather than challenging the anthropocentrism with which sociology began, in short, the development of machines that think actually reinforces it. What research into AI seems to show is very similar to what sociobiology inadvertently demonstrates: both fields, originally perceived as a challenge to the notion of a humanistic subject, strengthen the notion that humans require a distinct science because they are a distinct subject. And in looking at what makes them distinct, sociobiology and artificial intelligence lead to a similar conclusion: humans not only add culture to nature, as important as that is; they also add mind to culture. One best appreciates the powers of imagination and interpretation when confronted with a thinking machine that possesses neither.

Chapter Four

Putting Nature First

The Environmental Impulse

Perhaps the most striking political development of the latter half of the twentieth century has been a surge of concern for the natural environment. The environmental and ecological movements of this period seem to constitute a permanent watershed in the history of industrial societies. No longer will governments, of any political persuasion, be able to take the natural environment for granted. After at least two centuries of unregulated exploitation of nature, nature has begun to receive the benefit of the doubt.

Accompanying this concern with the environment are a number of worldviews, ideologies, and philosophies—all seeking to put nature first. Many of them try to find some balance between the human and natural worlds, whereby humans will treat nature with greater respect but still will be able to enjoy and make use of it. But some of these movements and philosophies are based on a more radical premise—namely, the premise that humans do not occupy a privileged place in nature. Other animal species not only have the moral benefit of the doubt, but all aspects of the natural world—landscapes, oceans, plants, and the earth itself—were here before we were, will be here after we are gone, and consequently have claims more important than our own. Such philosophies radically challenge the anthropocentrism that has been a core component of the Western intellectual heritage since the Enlightenment—and a core component of modern social theory as well.

It is because they attached so much importance to meaning that the founders of social theory—Weber, Durkheim, Mead—made anthropocentric assumptions. Human beings, and only human beings, from their perspective, realize objectives of their own choosing and organize themselves into collectivities as a result of their capacity to make sense of the world around them. If, in our zeal to protect nature, we reject as well the premises that undergird efforts to understand and appreciate our meaning-producing abilities, human affairs become not especially noteworthy, their patterns and activities a by-product of majestic ecological laws, in comparison to which our own fears, desires, and needs seem puny. That is not a conclusion that most of us would want to reach, including those who want to protect the natural environment itself. For without the specifically human capacity to imagine alternative worlds and to guide our destiny to achieve evaluative objectives of our own choosing, we would have no basis for claiming that anything, including nature, is worthwhile and ought to be preserved.

I will in this chapter concentrate on three of the more radical attempts to put nature first: animal rights, deep ecology, and Gaia. As befits any vibrant political and intellectual movement, these ways of thinking differ greatly—sometimes, it seems, more with each other than with the engines of economic growth and natural exploitation they oppose. The animal rights movement has had perhaps the largest impact on popular consciousness, but its concern for the rights of individual members of a species rather than the stability of species in themselves has led some deep ecologists to be deeply suspicious of its ethical stance.[1] Similar disagreements appear between those who respect the creatures who live on the earth and those who respect the earth itself. Yet, in spite of their differences, these three perspectives are similar in their virtual disregard of human selves capable of interpreting the world around them. To live by their moral precepts is to downgrade those capacities of mind that constitute a significant portion of the modern human identity.

Animal Rights and Human Imagination

A debate exists among animal rights philosophers as to whether utilitarianism or some version of rights-based theorizing ought to be used as the criterion for justifying better treatment of other animal species. The justification for animal rights provided by Tom Regan belongs to the latter category.[2] Regan argues that most people are capable of distinguishing right from wrong and are therefore moral agents. Animals, by contrast, cannot make such distinctions and must be viewed as moral "patients." But this does not mean that humans can treat animals any way they choose. Both possess life, which is something that has intrinsic value. Moreover, animals, especially of the "higher" variety, are aware of the world and have interests. If a just act is one that respects the intrinsic value of life—as opposed to the notion that justice as a concept applies only to those who have moral agency—we have a direct duty not to harm animals. There are, however, occasions when it is justifiable to inflict harm; if, for example, the rights of many innocents and a few innocents force a choice, we ought to respect the former. It is morally permissible to kill a rabid fox that is threatening human children, but not to engage in fox hunting for sheer sport.

Peter Singer's defense of animal rights, by contrast, is explicitly Benthamite in outlook, although, at one point, he finds Bentham insufficiently Benthamite.[3] For Bentham, the capacity to experience pain is necessary for any being to experience pleasure. It was as clear in his day as it is in ours that animals know what pain is. One can hear the cries of anguish that come from them as they are mutilated or destroyed. While Cartesians may be right in the purely abstract sense that one can never know whether another being is really in pain, the evidence presented to our senses is enough for any commonsense judgment to be made. It is cruel to inflict pain on any sentient being. Animals are sentient beings. Being cruel to them is morally wrong. The pain we inflict on animals must always be part of any calculus we make involving human benefits.

Both utilitarianism and Regan's modified Kantianism uphold

strong moral principles and expect all individuals to live up to them. There is, consequently, something of an air of disapproval when people do not. This sense of human failure is most explicit in Singer's account. It takes many forms: a lack of respect for the anonymity of those who do scientific research on animals, since any such scientist is not a complex person driven by conflicting motives but a morally insensitive person who deserves exposure; a proposal to subject (older) children to watching pictures of the way animals are killed; a lack of appreciation for the higher prices that many will have to pay for their food if Singer's moral point of view became the law; the assurance that "anyone with the capacity to look beyond considerations of narrow self-interest" will refuse to buy or eat animal flesh produced under modern factory conditions, which implies that anyone who does is guided by "narrow self-interest"; an insistence that any complications or even, in some cases, poor health that might follow from vegetarianism ought to be of little concern to us; and, most seriously, the equation of "speciesm" with racism and sexism, let alone Nazism, as if anyone who likes chicken with broccoli or wears leather shoes harbors fascist tendencies.[4]

Yet it is not, finally, the rhetorical asides of Singer's polemical writings that ought to concern us, or the often-noted point that those who love animals have problems with humans.[5] Rather, the question to be asked is whether the moral principles by which we are expected to treat animals properly lead to conclusions that allow us to treat other humans properly. Both utilitarianism and rights-based philosophies seek to evaluate human practices against the cruelty they inflict on other species. If there are, as in Regan's account, occasions where causing harm is morally justified—or if, from Singer's perspective, certain benefits to humans may outweigh the costs in cruelty to animals—then the question becomes one of finding criteria by which those practices can be judged. The human practice that has received most attention in the animal rights controversy is scientific experimentation. For opponents of animal rights, the attitude of animal rights activists toward scientific experimentation serves as an example of the failures of the entire philosophy; for its defendants, opposition to animal experimentation is the hard case that proves the validity of the entire doctrine.[6] Obviously, the matter of animal experimentation is of central importance; for if humans cannot live, they cannot do anything else. Yet we experiment on animals to keep humans alive, but what do we keep them alive for? The question ultimately posed by the animal rights movement is the question of what value can be attached to life.

Singer raises this question when he argues, mostly as a counter to those who do not appreciate animal life, that not all forms of human life necessarily deserve respect. (On this point I have no complaint with him; since the capacity to make sense out of the world is what makes us unique, a human lacking that sense—say, a brain-dead individual kept alive on a respirator—may be living a life not worth living.) Similarly, Regan, who argues that life has intrinsic value, does not believe that *human* life has some special and unique value. Indeed, Regan dismisses any reference to "human, recreational, gustatory, aesthetic, social, and other interests" in judging the legitimacy of our treatment of animals.[7]

While no one can ultimately answer for anyone else what value life should or does have, one answer to the meaning or purpose of life is implicit in much social theory, especially to the degree that it concentrates on powers of mind and interpretation. Ever since Durkheim, social theorists have understood the human species as one capable of using mind to create richly endowed systems of symbolic representations. Any species capable of attaching meaning to events in the world lives for something more than its own reproduction. "The reality of the human world," Hannah Arendt has written, rests "primarily on the fact that we are surrounded by things more permanent than the activity by which they were produced, and potentially even more permanent than the lives of their authors." It is these artifacts of human creativity that give meaning to human life; without them, Arendt continues, "there would be nothing but changeless eternal recurrence, the deathless everlastingness of the human as of all other animal species."[8] As Keith Thomas, John Berger, and Mary Douglas have shown, for most civilizations the appropriate place to turn to develop a symbolic life was to natural imagery, including images inspired by the human body.[9] The distinction between nature and civilization leads to a host of dichotomies that structure the way humans think about the world: purity and danger, the raw and the cooked, clean and dirty, and sacred and profane.

If humans use their imaginative powers to create monuments of lasting meaning out of the raw materials given to them by nature, there will often be a conflict between living by the principle of doing no harm to animals and the principle of living an imaginative and richly meaningful life. The capacity to create meaning does not come without unfairness. Because making something a symbol involves objectifying it, treating it as something other than it is, interpretation is never innocent; some will be treated instrumentally so that others will live in a richer and more imaginative world. Animal rights theorists are thus correct to detect certain patterns of cruelty in the way we use other species to make our own lives more rich with meaning. At the same time, if we were to revise the ways in which humans make meaning out of the natural world in such a way as never to be cruel to other animal species, we would live in a world without fantasy, excitement, and creativity. A number of the most important human practices—religion, art, sport, and cultural expression—illustrate the tension between the injunction to avoid cruelty and the injunction to live a meaningful life with rich interpretative possibilities.

Religion is one place to start. To this day, some contemporary religions, especially Islam and Judaism, engage in the ritual slaughter of animal species. Singer would prohibit such practices: "If, to preserve religious laws intact, a choice must be made between the taste for meat and the agony of millions of animals, surely it is justifiable to ask those who follow the religious laws to do without meat."[10] At least one country, Sweden, has taken steps toward the eventual elimination of Jewish and Moslem ritual slaughter in the name of animal rights. Although it may seem relatively easy to suggest that it is not worth killing animals so that humans can go on with what, to some, are archaic and barbaric practices, the loss to the human capacity for living meaningful lives is great when, in the name of protecting other species, humans are asked to do without the symbolic richness that follows from ritual and tradition.

It is not religion per se to which animal rights advocates object, but the specific practices of some religions. Obviously, there is a point somewhere here; it is difficult to imagine any society not condemning the ritual slaughter of human beings. But in the real world of human action, banning some religious practices while allowing others would not only lead to underground and illegal activity—rites, as well as rights, are anything but a matter of "taste"—but would also, if successful, result in a more homogeneous, and therefore less meaningful, society. The whole point about religious traditions is that one cannot easily pick and choose among them on the basis of utilitarian considerations. The banning of ritual slaughter is a step—given the importance of animal symbolization, a relatively big step—from the sacred to the profane.[11]

Another example of the use of animals for human symbolic purposes involves zoos and circuses. The city of Denver recently stopped the practice of allowing children to ride on elephants, and not because the practice was a danger to the children. Should we, in the name of animal rights, abolish zoos altogether? In the utilitarian calculus he develops to answer this question affirmatively, Dale Jamieson balances the functions of zoos, including enjoyment, education, and scientific value, against the cruelty through confinement they inflict. Jamieson argues as follows:

Zoos teach us a false sense of our place in the natural order. . . . Morality and perhaps our very survival require that we learn to live as one species among many rather than as one over many. To do this, we must forget what we learn at zoos. Because what zoos teach us is false and dangerous, both humans and animals will be better off when they are abolished.[12]

One could, of course, ban zoos from one's republic, just as Plato would ban poets. Whether we would be a less cruel species if we did so, however, is most debatable. Children learn to use their powers of fantasy and imagination by going to the zoo. Strip them of one of the major symbols of the interpretative life that children have always experienced, and the likelihood is that, as adults, they will be more unfeeling rather than less.

Sport provides a third illustration of the conflict between respect for animals and the human capacity to interpret. Hunting is no doubt cruel. But here, too, animal rights advocates lack appreciation for the symbolic meaning of human practices such as hunting. Just as in the case of religion—where Singer would allow only those practices that conform to his standards of humane conduct, irrespective of the history and symbolic background of those traditions—Regan asks us to alter the very way in which sport is understood:

Standard justifications of the "sport" of hunting—that those who engage in it get exercise, take pleasure in communion with nature, enjoy the camaraderie of their friends, or take satisfaction in a shot well aimed—are lame, given the rights view. All these pleasures are obtainable by engaging in activities that do not result in killing any animal (walking through the woods with friends and a camera substitute nicely).[13]

There are obvious sensual and other pleasures inherent in cruel sport, not all of them admirable. In the name of sportsmanship, humans are equally willing to inflict considerable pain on each other—in sports such as boxing or professional football—as they are to inflict suffering on other species. Reformers have rallied against cruelty in sports for centuries, and with some success, but the sensual pleasures of violent sport endure. No one knows exactly why they endure; but the anthropologist Clifford Geertz—studying what, following Bentham, he calls "deep play"—has come closest to an explanation. Because, in Geertz's words, "the imposition of meaning on life is the major and primary condition of human existence," danger beyond the point of rationality creates moments of intensity so excruciating as to convey truths about self and society, even by testing the limits of civilization itself.[14] It is difficult to imagine that Regan's advice to walk through the woods with a camera will have quite the same effect.

Animal rights theorists are not impressed by the fact that humans are producers of great works of art, music, and literature. When Peter Singer chastises the Renaissance for "its insistence on the value and dignity of human beings, and on man's central place in the universe," his remark ought to give one pause.[15] The Renaissance and the Enlightenment were indeed humanistic in the double sense of encouraging great works of human expression and putting human beings in the center of the world. Singer would like to break that link. It is not clear that he, or anyone else, can. What made the Renaissance and the Enlightenment great were their artistic expression; and the works that we now regard as masterpieces of aesthetic value did not shy away from the depiction of cruelty. Had the artists in question reined in their imaginations out of a sense of fairness to other species—or even to members of our own—the Quatrocento never would have taken place.

In the kind of moral accounting favored by the animal rights challenge to human practices, the question becomes: Is it preferable to live life without religion, sport, and creativity and at the same time not be cruel or to accept at least some cruelty for the sake of a greater richness of meaning? When such cruelty is directed against others of our own species—in the way that the Greek *polis* assumed slavery or much of nineteenth-century fiction was premised on the exclusion of women from politics—we may (or may not) be willing to sacrifice some creativity for the sake of greater equality; debates over the conflict between artistic expression and the offensive portrayal of other humans—such as the way women are depicted in the work of de Sade—continue to this day.[16] But the further our concern with the moral worth of others extends outward into nature, the more we will have to restrict our own imaginative lives in order to be sensitive to the claims of others; it is a short step from prohibiting children from riding elephants to banning elephants from public productions of *Aida.* And if our obligations are extended to an infinite point—if, for example, we ought to consider ourselves obligated to whatever creatures may someday be found in outer space, even if we do not think there are likely ever to be creatures found in outer space— our moral sense may expand, but it is likely that our capacity to create meaning will disappear.[17]

This is obviously not an argument that every human pleasure is justified, no matter what the cost to nature and other animal species. But it is an argument that a simple edict to avoid cruelty—the heart of modern liberal theory, as Richard Rorty and Judith Shklar have argued—loses much of its force if applied to all species at all times.[18] Just as we experiment on animals to keep humans alive, we are sometimes cruel to animals in order to give our lives meaning. The one may be just as justifiable as the other, if not more so; for to be modern is not just to live, but to live for a purpose. Without the capacity to make stories about the world from the raw materials provided by nature—or even the capacity to participate in practices, such as religion and sport, that are often cruel to other species—we cannot have such a purpose.

Animal rights advocates would like us to believe that if we treat other species with more respect, we will be more likely to treat members of our species with more respect. Yet the opposite may well be true. To be fair to them, we must be unfair to one important aspect of ourselves: our freedom to use our minds to create a richly endowed symbolic life. It is appropriate that utilitarianism is the philosophical basis of most animal rights activists, for their outlook on the world does not allow any special recognition of expressive, and thereby not necessarily useful, needs. Accepting the sensations as what defines life, utilitarians are unable to rise above the sensations and to recognize that many species experience pain but only one can transform pain into a story about the world.

There are attractive features of the animal rights movement: fairness, justice, respect toward others, egalitarianism. Yet a society organized in accordance with animal rights would also be poor in imagination, imprisoned by logic, censorial toward evil, puritanical in outlook, and populated by those as lacking in appreciation of themselves as they are sensitive to the pains of others. Most important, however, to live by the tenets of animal rights is to bring about equality between the human and other animal species not by elevating the latter but by lowering the former. The meaning of our lives would be the same as the meaning of theirs: to be born, to develop, to reproduce, and to die, without stopping along the way to reflect on why any of these things happen. If we accept animal rights as a set of moral principles by which our choices ought to be guided—instead of as one set of general injunctions among other objectives—we run the risk of losing sight of why we live on the planet in the first place.

Deep Ecology

Animal rights activists are actually quite moderate when compared to others who have taken the side of nature against humans in recent years. Singer, after all, does not extend the capacity to experience pain to plants, as well as to some creatures whose neural development is so primitive that they have no capacity to feel. It is, he argues, perfectly appropriate to eat creatures that have no sentient capacities; "somewhere between a shrimp and an oyster," as he puts it, "seems as good a place to draw the line as any, and better than most."[19] But oysters are an integral part of that complex ecosystem known as the natural world. From the perspective of those who argue that every system found in nature, down to sand and water, ought to be respected, the animal rights movement does not go far enough. We need, they would argue, a way to appreciate the dynamics by which all things in the natural world reproduce themselves.

The obvious place to turn for an understanding of the natural world is to the science of ecology. In 1866, Ernst Haeckel, the leading German disciple of Darwin, coined the term *Oecologie*, understood as the science of how living organisms relate to each other and to their environment.[20] As its similarity to the term *Oeconomie* implies, ecology was premised upon the ancient Greek understanding of household management. From its early origins, ecology understood the natural world with a language borrowed from the study of the social world. It would be a long time before this overlap between the social and the natural worlds would disappear, if, indeed, it ever has.

Although most earlier ecologists, such as Henry C. Cowles and Frederic Clements, left man out of their models, they were nonetheless groping toward a unified understanding of ecological processes, one that would link all living species into what, in 1939, Clements called the "biotic community," or "biota." The analogy between nature and society was even more pronounced in the work of the British zoologist Charles

Elton, who used the social structure of European feudalism to describe how nature functions. Animals were classified into different orders or ranks—Elton sometimes called them "roles" or "professions"—each with its own proper niche.[21] (Darwin had used terms such as *place* or *office* to describe the same thing.) Various species, within their respective niches, were described as essentially producers or consumers, depending on the workings of the food chain. It therefore became appropriate, from Elton's perspective, to speak of a biotic "community," since nature, like the *Gemeinschaft* societies of Ferdinand Toennies, created an order in which every organism held its proper place. As a way of understanding nature, economics had evolved, rather naturally, into sociology.

The question raised by this correspondence was not whether nature functions by self-regulating laws. The question, rather, was whether there were lessons for human society in what we could learn about nature. If the two worlds of human society and nature could be described by the same language, then either nature could be understood in terms of human capacities or society could be explained by natural processes. Herbert Spencer's ideas loom large over those who opted for the second of these alternatives. For Spencer, all complex ecological systems evolve according to self-regulating laws. Interference in social evolution is as disastrous as interference in biological evolution. The earth, in short, has its own economy, one in which species evolve by adopting the most efficient strategies for survival. This Spencerian understanding of how nature and society are linked would eventually become the dominant one. On the one hand, Spencer's principles became embedded in conservative doctrine, influencing both elite opinion and U.S. Supreme Court decisions.[22] On the other hand, Spencer's influence on such scientists as Clements and William Morton Wheeler was pronounced. Ecology was used to demonstrate that human society owes more to nature than the other way around.

That Spencer's ideas were used for reactionary political purposes in the human world is an embarrassing legacy for contemporary ecologists, many of whom consider themselves on the political left. But that embarrassment abated somewhat when a major change in the science of ecology took place under the inspiration of the Oxford botanist A. G. Tansley (who had once worked with Spencer in revising the 1899 edition of *Principles of Biology*). Tansley presided over a shift from biology to the physical and information sciences as a way of understanding what happens in nature. Objecting strongly to any discussion of communities in nature, he sought a way of describing natural processes through pure quantification. His major term, the *ecosystem,* was derived from the newly emerging science generally known as systems theory. All units within any society exist together by exchanging energy; and in this process, there will inevitably be a tendency toward entropy, or irreplaceable loss of energy. An ecological system operating at peak efficiency integrates all its parts so that entropy is minimized. Although economics was by no means irrelevant to this way of thinking—that science has its own fascination with automatically functioning mechanisms for ensuring efficiency—the intellectual model for the new ecology became cybernetics. By viewing nature as a complex system driven by self-regulating laws, ecologists could avoid the conservatism of social Darwinism in favor of a doctrine stressing harmony of interests and beneficial outcomes.

With the development of computers and artificial intelligence, a cybernetic way of understanding the automatic functioning of the natural world was reinforced. "In this age of computer-run organizations and the carefully arbitrated resolution of all discords," Donald Worster has written, "it was probably inevitable that ecology too would come to emphasize the flow of goods and services—or of energy—in a kind of automated, robotized, pacified nature."[23] The computer—a machine that seemed capable of exchanging vast bits of information with little (or almost immeasurable) loss of energy—represented the ultimate in cybernetic theory. From an ecological perspective, both nature and artifice seemed to be linked together by the dynamics of systems theory.

The application of systems theory to an understanding of nature represented a gigantic step in the scientific development of ecology. It also had important ethical and moral implications. Ecology, after all, is not simply a descriptive science but also contains elements of an ethical system; the general normative belief associated with ecological understandings of nature is that the system as a whole, rather than the individual parts that compose the system, ought to be respected. As long as biology was the dominant science associated with ecology, a holistic ethics could be reconciled with individual parts: we ought to preserve living species because life itself, understood as the life of any individual organism, is valuable. When the information sciences became the model of an ecological system, by contrast, either life could no longer be the ultimate justification for a holistic ethic or the meaning of life would have to be redefined to include all self-regulating systems— even systems such as oceans, mountain ranges, and computers, which were once thought of as lifeless.

Under the influence of Erwin Schrödinger, life was, in fact, redefined. A living being increasingly came to be understood as any organism that avoids decay by "attracting, as it were, a stream of negative entropy upon itself, to compensate the entropy increase it produces by living and thus to maintain itself on a stationary and fairly low entropy level."[24] Schrödinger's definition was important because, by shifting the scientific basis of life from biology to quantum physics, he made possible a broad and all-encompassing conception of what it means to live. Later on, when information science and artificial intelligence developed, it became possible to argue that all self-reproducing things are living things. This was something of a radical notion for the information sciences. We know that computers are self-reproducing. Are they therefore alive?

At least some thinkers, even if in a playful spirit, wanted to entertain the notion. Computer hackers, for example, are familiar with a game called Life, invented by John Horton Conway in 1970. This game enables the player to use a few basic algorithms to generate systems so complex and unpredictable from the first moves that they resemble living things; "among finite Life patterns there is a very small proportion behaving like self-replicating animals. . . . It's probable, given a large enough Life space, initially in a random state, that after a long time, intelligent, self-reproducing animals will emerge and populate some parts of the space." This, of course, was not likely to happen soon, since " 'sufficiently large' means very large indeed, and we can't prove that 'living' animals of any kind are likely to emerge in any Life space we can construct in practice."[25] But as an indication of how the information sciences change the meaning of what it means to live, the idea suffices.

From a biological perspective, a holistic emphasis on the species could be justified out of respect for the life of individual organisms. Such an emphasis is no longer justified when an information science perspective becomes the basis for an ecological understanding of the world. Animal rights thinkers undervalue human interpretative capacities by defining life in sensate terms. But their conception of why life is important—however thin it may appear in comparison to human life—is thick in comparison to ecological models based on the information sciences. Since many cybernetic systems, including computers, have no sensations at all, even the sensate features of living species are devalued in favor of the capacity to engage in self-reproduction. From such a perspective, human interpretative capacities are at a double remove from any position of privilege: we are equated first with all other creatures that can feel pain, and then with all other creatures whose affairs can be governed algorithmically.

Algorithmic systems operate the way they do because they are concerned with the autonomy of the system itself and not the autonomy of the parts that compose the system. For a system to be smart, the parts, as we saw in the previous chapter, have to be as dumb as possible. If, following the tenets of what is now called the "new" ecology, we base our understanding of the natural world on systems theory, and if we then include humans as part of the system that is self-functioning, it follows that the lives of particular and specific human individuals are of no particular import.

What this new holism would mean for human beings became clear when a new political movement called "deep ecology" appeared in the 1970s and 1980s. According to the distinction first advanced by the Norwegian philosopher Arne Naess in 1973, "shallow" ecology, associated with traditional environmentalism, is an effort to protect nature for man's use. "Deep"

ecology, by contrast, represents a vigorous effort to ensure
that nature will be understood and appreciated in its own right,
irrespective of whatever uses man might have in mind for it.[26]
Naess himself is somewhat moderate in his application of deep
ecological principles; he recognizes that the question of
whether hunting whales is justified depends upon the economic circumstances of those who hunt whales.[27]

No such concession to real people and their activities and
practices can be found in the writings of George Sessions, Bill
Devall, J. Baird Callicott, and other American theorists of the
deep ecology movement.[28] Like John Muir, who felt little obligation to do anything about slavery but was moved to anguish
by the plight of bears, these writers share the perspective of
John Howard Moore, Clarence Darrow's brother-in-law, who
thought of humans as "the most unchaste, the most drunken,
the most selfish and conceited, the most miserly, the most
hypocritical, and the most bloodthirsty of terrestrial creatures."[29] Just as the novelist Edward Abbey would rather kill
a man than a snake, deep ecologists turn their backs on the
human race.[30] The extent of one's misanthropy, as Callicott
put it, became a good measure of the extent of one's commitment to ecological principles.[31] Eighteenth-century humanism, from such a perspective, is simply a form of arrogance,
the sooner done away with, the better.[32] There is no special
moral advantage to any practice that improves and extends
human life. Indeed, some activists associated with the deep
ecological organization Earth First! have suggested that the
famine in Ethiopia or the AIDS epidemic serves the function
of reducing the human population and thereby protecting the
natural world.[33] In the expression of such beliefs, the full consequences of what it means to value the perpetuation of systems, rather than the people who compose those systems, become evident.

As part of the "new" ecology, deep ecology naturally privileges wholes over parts. Aldo Leopold first expressed this ethical position as follows: "A thing is right when it tends to preserve the integrity, stability, and beauty of the biotic
community. It is wrong when it tends otherwise."[34] From such
a holistic perspective, deep ecology can have little respect for

those parts we generally call human selves.[35] Deep ecologists tend to understand the self in Heideggerian terms: the everyday, inauthentic self will be overcome and transcended as we give up any false strategies of control and mastery and just let our being be.[36] Devotion to nature is one such way of overcoming the everyday self to achieve some higher form of self-realization.[37] But even mere natural appreciation will do: standing before Lake Solitude in the High Sierras, Holmes Rolston reflected that "neither lake nor self has independent being: both exist in dynamic interpenetration across a surface designed for passage and exchange, as well as for delimitation and individuation." The self therefore has little permanence: "We are participants in a shared flow, of which the self is an integral but momentary instantiation."[38] The human self has receded to the background of the landscape painting, if it even appears at all.

It is perhaps because human selves matter so little in the ethical scheme of things that deep ecological thought can be so explicitly Malthusian. Among its list of fundamental principles, as expressed by Naess and by Devall and Sessions, is "that the flourishing of human life and cultures is compatible with a substantial decrease of the human population. The flourishing of nonhuman life requires such a decrease."[39] Unfortunately, human population has been increasing over time, as a result of what William R. Catton has called the success of "death control." Human longevity "aggravated the unseen precariousness of our situation by releasing the brakes; a further acceleration of population increase followed, not linked to *any* increment of carrying capacity."[40] We might therefore have to ask government to intervene in the process, since, as Herman E. Daly puts it, "the right to reproduce must no longer be treated as a 'free good'—it should be regarded as a scarce asset, a legal right limited in total amount at a level corresponding to replacement fertility, or less, distributed in divisible units to individuals on the basis of strict equality, and subject to reallocation by voluntary exchange."[41]

But not even Malthus believed that because nature tends to kill off members of a species that grows too quickly, we ought to argue for the rights of viruses to live, even those that, if

unchecked, could kill people. Environmental ethicists such as
J. Baird Callicott reject any "psychocentric" morality that
gives human subjects the benefit of the ecological doubt.[42]
"Even Aldo Leopold, whose land ethic laid the foundation of
Callicott's thought," writes Roderick Nash, "had not drawn
such radical anti-human implications. Nor had the extreme
ecologists who defended the rights of germs admitted the necessity of sacrificing a few designated human carriers so that
the endangered smallpox virus could make its contribution to
the integrity of the ecosystem. But this was the conclusion to
which Callicott's philosophy pointed."[43] The value of any individual life, including a human self, is, from such a perspective, hardly a matter about which we ought to be sentimental.[44]

By itself, deep ecology represents an extreme position in
debates over the environment. Yet although few would agree
with the position that "in some situations, it is a *greater* wrong
to kill a wildflower than it is, in another situation, to kill a
human," the suspicion of the human self found in deep ecology
does correspond with other trends in current thought.[45] Consider the overlaps between deep ecology and literary post-
modernism, the subject of the chapter that follows.[46] Deep
ecology echoes the sense found in the world of contemporary
deconstruction that it is futile to talk of boundaries, distinctions, and subjects; for, as Devall and Sessions express it,
"there are no boundaries and everything is interrelated."[47] In
addition, both radically question the existence of any transcendental or universal standards of value; there is no special
value to human life, because, in the words of J. Baird Callicott,
who is otherwise hostile to post-modernism, "there can be no
value apart from an evaluator."[48] Moreover, just as post-modernism takes a position of neutrality toward the privileging of
texts, deep ecology is morally indifferent, believing that there
are no rights and wrongs in nature. If indeed "the skin is not
a morally relevant boundary," then all systems exist in a state
of ethical equality: any system's stability is presumably as important as any other system's stability.[49] Mountains and sea-
shores have as much right to regenerate themselves naturally
as cows and humans. Even computers, because they are self-
regulating systems, have a right to exist. As Michael Tobias

has written, "The first terrestrial matter was probably silicon, beaches. From a computer's perspective, human beings are on Earth merely to reorganize silicon into conductive chips."[50] Deep ecology is, in Paul Taylor's expression, "species impartial"; it refuses to take the position that any one species found in nature has any claims over any other.[51] Like much of the work inspired by Heidegger's interpreter Jacques Derrida, deep ecology combines radical politics with a conservative message of resignation in the face of systems that loom beyond the power of humans to alter.[52]

With deep ecology, the suspicion of individual human selves—a suspicion that always existed in ecological efforts to value the whole over the parts—extends to a recognition that human selves are, from the standpoint of nature, superfluous. "If the total, final, absolute extermination of our species (by our own hands!) should take place," Paul Taylor has written, "and if we should not carry all the others with us into oblivion, not only would the Earth's community of life continue to exist, but in all probability its well being would be enhanced. Our presence, in short, is not needed."[53] This is, even by deep ecology standards, a fairly extreme position. But Taylor's biocentrism and Callicott's environmental ethics are not without supporters. "Although few pushed environmental ethics this far," Roderick Nash writes, "support for Callicott's position appears frequently in contemporary philosophy."[54] The more extreme forms of deep ecology raise a fascinating question: What kind of world can we imagine if all human beings disappear from it? The only problem with the question is that without human beings, there is no one to do the imagining. If animal rights philosophers would sacrifice the human capacity to attribute meaning to things in order to avoid cruelty to other species, deep ecologists—in giving moral preference to the system over the units that compose the system—reduce humans not only to all other living species but to any inorganic matter that, through no choice of its own, has become part of a self-reproducing chain.

Gaia

If, indeed, our presence is not needed on the earth, the question of whether human life has any particular value is answered: it is earth, not the living species (human or animal) who inhabit it, that deserves respect; for the earth, as a planet, is also alive, and it is greater than any of its parts. Such is the conclusion reached by James Lovelock, the originator of the "Gaia" hypothesis, and his followers.

Lovelock was a space scientist visiting the Jet Propulsion Laboratory in Pasadena when he began to become aware of the beauty of the earth as a whole. Retiring to his village in Devonshire—the same village of the novelist William Golding, whose *Lord of the Flies* is one of the most antihumanistic accounts written in this century—Lovelock developed the theory that all the gasses, minerals, and life forms on earth are part of a vast, interrelated system, which adds up to more than the property of any single part. As Lewis Thomas wrote about our planet: "Although it seems at first glance to be made up of innumerable separate species of living things, on closer examination every one of its working parts, including us, is interdependently connected to all other working parts. It is, to put it one way, the only truly closed ecosystem any of us knows about."[55] Imagining the earth and its environment as "an automatic, but not purposeful, goal-seeking system," Lovelock incorporated ideas associated with thermodynamics, computer science, population biology, and autopoiesis (the self-creation of life) into his view that everything in this world is part of one complex, interdependent, global pattern.[56]

The Gaia hypothesis was articulated by Lovelock in the form of a computer program that imagined the world that would be created—he called it Daisyworld—by an ecological competition among two species of daisies, one dark, the other light. Like the models associated with theoretical ecology, or like the infinitely recurring mathematical properties associated with Mandelbrot sets, Daisyworld took off on its own course; "no foresight, planning, or purpose was invoked." If a species tries to grow uncontrollably, it will contribute to an unfavorable environment that will reduce the population of the species, leading the system always back toward stability. The point is that the model was driven purely by algorithmic rules, which, if applied firmly and consistently, would tend toward homeostasis.

From the perspective of the whole world, either this one or

all imaginable ones, the affairs of humans seem a trifle indeed. Since, according to Lovelock, "pain and death are normal and natural," it makes little sense to become exercised by unfairness or moved by sympathy. "Our humanist concerns about the poor of the inner cities or the Third World, and our near obsession with death, suffering, and pain as if these were evils in themselves—these thoughts divert the mind from our gross and excessive domination of the natural world." Humans are merely "intelligent fleas," bothering, but in no way altering the movement of, the larger system around which they buzz. With its eyes fixed upward toward the solar system, Gaia theory, as Lovelock correctly notes, "is as out of touch with the broader humanist world as it is with established science."[57]

Systems theory, as we have seen, gives ethical priority to wholes rather than parts. What makes Lovelock's version of this theory unique is that the parts that receive little sympathy are not just human selves but natural objects as well. After all, the natural world on this earth, from the perspective of the entire universe, is also not especially important. Hence, Lovelock is not bothered by nuclear power plants, no doubt understanding that even if there were a serious accident involving one, the earth would survive even if humans did not. Nor does pollution upset him, since (following Garrett Hardin) he believes that the only pollution is people. "The very concept of pollution," he writes, "is anthropocentric and it may even be irrelevant in the Gaia context."[58] The earth avoids entropy because breathing beings take free energy from the environment and excrete it back to the environment in degraded form. Our excretion—Lovelock, like Georges Bataille and Norman O. Brown, is fascinated by waste products—makes life possible; "only by pollution," he writes, "do we survive."[59] Unlike all other environmental philosophers, who respect nature but distrust society, Lovelock expresses a mood of indifference to both.

Clearly, what enables Lovelock to be so unmoved by worldly concerns is his sense that everything in the world has already been determined, or will soon be determined, by the automatic functioning of the huge system of which we are a part. Lovelock is overwhelmed by the wonders of completely rule-driven worlds. "Perhaps," he concludes, "it is a metaphor for our own experience that the family and society do better when firm, but justly applied, rules exist than they do with unrestricted freedom."[60] The belief that firm rules will always produce stable outcomes contributes to the quality of unforgiving judgment in Lovelock's outlook:

Gaia, as I see her, in no doting mother tolerant of misdemeanors, nor is she some fragile and delicate damsel in danger from brutal mankind. She is stern and tough, always keeping the world warm and comfortable for those who obey the rules, but ruthless in her destruction of those who transgress. Her unconscious goal is a planet fit for life. If humans stand in the way of this, we shall be eliminated with as little pity as would be shown by the micro-brain of an intercontinental ballistic nuclear missile in full flight to its target.[61]

Humans have broken the rules; they have not treated the earth well, and now the earth is reciprocating. "So long as we continue to change the global environment against her preferences, we encourage our replacement with a more environmentally seemly species."[62] Our disappearance from the world will never even be noticed, a sure indication of how misplaced has been our pride in ourselves.

It would not seem possible to outdo deep ecology in developing a theory more hostile to humans and their practices, but Gaia tries. At least the deep ecologists recognize a self, albeit one that blends with the natural environment in such a way that human autonomy is lost. Lovelock blends the human self not into the natural environment but into the universe: "To me Gaia is alive and part of the ineffable Universe and I am part of her."[63] Although Gaia is an earth-bound philosophy, the earth itself is part of a general system called the universe, and that larger system may be, following the hypothesis of Erich Jantsch, self-organizing.[64] One writer has suggested that the principles revealed by the computer game Life can be used to explain how the entire universe is the product of the working out of a few relatively simple algorithms over vast amounts of time.[65] From the cosmic vantage point of the entire universe, Lovelock imagines people, rocks, mountains, oxygen, and carbon dioxide as having two, and only two, states: either they function properly, so that the larger system of the universe

can avoid entropy, or they are "noise," clogging the channels
of an otherwise perfectly self-reproducing information chain.
Lovelock is too much the information scientist to believe that
the whole system is inspired by mysticism and religious spir-
itualism, but he cannot help flirting with the notion. Quoting
Gregory Bateson to the effect that "there is a larger mind of
which the individual mind is only a subsystem," Lovelock also
asks: "What if Mary is another name for Gaia?"[66]

With Gaia theory, humans and their affairs exist at a third
remove from a concern with the powers of meaning associated
with individual minds. Not only are our abilities to interpret
the world devalued in favor of our status as living things, and
not only are we equated with nonliving and inorganic matter,
but, in addition, our existence is blended into a cosmic universe
so large that even systems themselves lose their special character in favor of mystical wholeness. Far from being distinct,
we are no different from anything else found in the universe;
therefore, our behavior can be properly understood not
through social science but through a version of astrophysics
tinged with Eastern religion. Just as animal rights philosophers
question the separation between humans and nature that was
at the heart of nineteenth-century social theory, Gaia theorists
question the separation between humans and God. What were
at least three distinct realms become one, as everything, from
the cosmos to the cell, is absorbed into a single system operating by the unforgiving laws of self-reproduction.

Gaia has attracted numerous followers because of the depth
of the ecological crisis facing Western societies at the end of
the twentieth century. Anyone who appreciates nature may
well be tempted to conclude that any turn toward ecological
thinking can only be a good thing. Yet, although preserving
the natural environment ought to be one of the highest prior-
ities facing contemporary liberal democracies, we cannot do
so if we believe that the laws governing nature and the laws
that drive human affairs are the same. For if our affairs occur
algorithmically, then the very processes that led us to take so
little care of our natural environment can only continue. Humans can alter the actions that have had such a devastating
effect on the natural environment only if they are capable of

making choices, of righting wrongs, of setting off on a new course—one that is not preprogrammed. If we extend ecological reasoning from nature to society, we cannot allow for such course correction. Ultimately, as the case of James Lovelock seems to indicate, the more we allow our understanding of human affairs to be guided by a systems theoretical model that works on the basis of automatic, self-regulating rules, the more we will have to reconcile ourselves to being passive observers of nature's destruction.

The Computer in the Woods

Because human societies constitute a system, and because the units that compose that system are people, there are always temptations to turn to one or another version of systems theory to understand human societies and how they function. Early American sociology, especially the Chicago School of Robert Ezra Park and Ernest W. Burgess, was heavily influenced by the biological study of ecological systems; they argued that the rise and fall of cities could be understood as conforming to general laws by which all organisms rise and fall.[67] In the 1950s, "human ecology" became an inspiration for a good deal of social science research. As Amos Hawley expressed it, humans are unique in the complexity of their organization, but not that much: "The elements of human culture are therefore identical in principle with the appetency of the bee for honey, the nest-building activities of birds, and the hunting habits of carnivora."[68] The emphasis that ecology and other information sciences place upon system maintenance is important to some sociologists, at least one of whom believes that "all concrete control systems—both individual and collective—must overcome the same fundamental problems if they are to maintain themselves counter to entropy."[69] In addition, ecological perspectives have been used in specific fields, such as organizational sociology, where researchers have attempted to show that the dynamics by which labor unions, semiconductor firms, and newspapers are founded and go out of business can be understood algorithmically.[70]

Valuable lessons for an understanding of human society often can be learned from such applications of systems theory borrowed from the natural and information sciences. Human societies are large scale and complex, and surely there must be laws by which all complex systems, at a sufficiently general level of understanding, function. But, as the extreme versions of ecological theories discussed in this chapter suggest, social scientists cannot apply systemic models from biology and computer science too literally. For what emerges from such borrowings is a respect for both nature and technology, accompanied by little appreciation for real human beings. Theories that have a difficult time concealing their distaste for real people are not the ideal bases for building a science of how real people behave.

One of the most fascinating aspects of the journey from animal rights to deep ecology and Gaia is the way in which life becomes progressively redefined away from the individual living and breathing members of species to algorithmic systems that have no life other than their self-reproduction. The works inspired by the "new" ecology are based on the intermeshing of complex systems derived from cybernetics and the information sciences. Nature thus appears not only as a machine but as the ultimate machine, whose principles of functional dynamics establish the model by which all other machines are expected to work. "The machine in the garden" is the well-known metaphor coined by Leo Marx to describe the ambivalence between nature and technology found in much American literature.[71] The reliance on algorithmic understandings of system dynamics to understand nature, a science that in turn owes a great deal to the invention and proliferation of computers, is the current form taken by Marx's story.

Although computers represent the latest in machine technology, those who work with them are anything but apologists for the world of artifice and culture, often preferring instead ecological simplicity. "In the years after [personal computers] first appeared," Sherry Turkle writes, "people tied [them] into aspirations for ecology: decentralized technology would mean less waste because people would attend electronic meetings and conferences, do more work out of their homes, and save on transportation and energy costs. . . . Relationships with a computer became the depository of longings for a better, simpler, and more coherent life."[72] One can see the same correspondence working in the other direction as well. Bill McKibben, who argues that we have reached the "end of nature" because of our lack of appreciation for the primitive and pristine, wrote his book at his Adirondack mountain retreat on his personal computer and sent out his material to the big cities on a fax machine, relying on technology to make his withdrawal to the pastoral more possible.[73]

What seems to link natural and technological enthusiasts is their mutual distaste for one species that is neither a computing machine nor a pure product of nature: human beings. From an ecological perspective, people spoil the natural environment and are the enemies of all the other species with whom they share nature; they have a constant tendency to tamper with naturally driven ecological laws that are as beautiful in their simplicity as they are fragile in the face of our ignorance. From a technological perspective, human beings are also interfering with the machines that can do tasks much more efficiently than they can; let there be an accident at a nuclear power plant or any other complex technological system, and the first response is nearly always to point the finger at human error, thereby absolving the machines of blame.[74] The natural and the technological, their defenders claim, have no need for human beings. They are best off running themselves.

Real human beings—sloppy in their reasoning, uncertain about their choices, ambiguous in their cues, limited in their memory storage, unpredictable in their development—are a poor subject for those who appreciate the mathematical elegance and formal models that govern the evolution of computers, other animals, and nature. As the case of James Lovelock illustrates, those who appreciate the elegance of the rules that govern other species often have little taste for human peculiarities. Sherry Turkle, who has conducted ethnographic studies of people who work with computers, describes "hacker culture"—the way of life that characterizes the world of computer theorists—as a culture of mastery, individualism, nonsensuality. It values complexity and risk in relationships with things, and seeks simplicity and safety in relationships with people. It delights in ambiguities in the technological domain—where most nonscientists expect to find things straightforward. . . . Hackers try to avoid ambiguity in dealing with people, where the larger culture finds meaning in the half-defined and the merely suggested.[75]

Many of those attracted to ecological models—for instance, the sociobiologists who find our instructions hard-wired in our genes—have the same characteristics as the hackers described by Turkle. In Robert Wright's biographical study of three information scientists, for example, the sociobiologist Edward O. Wilson related a boyhood of someone "alone in the woods, free from the demands of human society" who could "enter a world oblivious to his"; and artificial intelligence theorist Edward Fredkin found the computer "preferable to every other conglomeration of matter he had encountered—more sophisticated, and more flexible, than other inorganic machines and more logical than organic machines."[76]

There are many reasons not to like real people; whether we ought to be proud or ashamed to be human is not my concern here. At issue, rather, is how we are to understand humans. For better or for worse, I have been arguing, human beings are capable of bringing to the rules that govern their affairs qualities of mind that enable them to bend and shape the rules for their own purposes. If, in frustration at the arrogance and imperial proclivities of the human species, we turn toward the more elegantly rule-governed worlds of other systems, we ought to be careful in generalizing back to ourselves. Social science, the specific study of human behavior, has long contained a dual imperative: to understand how we act and to guide our actions toward purposive ends. Neither imperative— the scientific or the moral—is possible if one holds to the assumptions of the philosophies discussed in this chapter.

A model of behavior based on self-reproducing, mindless, automatically equilibrating models is not especially appropriate for members of a species that possesses qualities of mind. That numerous theorists have used the language of society to describe nature is no reason that those who study society have to use the language of nature or any other complex system. It is difficult to imagine how a social science would achieve adequate scientific status if its assumptions about the behavior of what it studies are far removed from the actual experiences of those subjects. Human beings possess the capacity to interpret the world around them, which means they are capable of governing themselves rather than being governed by the automatic functioning of rules. What makes them poor subjects for self-reproducing systems is exactly what makes their behavior require a science capable of appreciating qualities of mind.

Much the same can be said of the moral perspective that undergirds animal rights philosophies, deep ecology, and Gaia. Humans are different from other species because they can attribute meaning to the events around them and therefore can direct their affairs to some purpose. Life itself, as important as that may be, is a means to a meaningful end, not an end in itself. The reproduction of the conditions that make life possible, as awe-inspiring as it may be, is not by itself a moral accomplishment. Ecological models achieve their attractiveness by placing themselves at three removes from real human beings: away from their cognitive capabilities toward their sensate ones, away from their sensate ones to their self-reproduction, and away from their self-reproduction to their absorption into the cosmos. Those who put nature first have much to teach about the importance of the environment shared by all species, but the scientific and moral lessons available from them for the human species—a species that not only lives but lives for meaning—are minimal.

Chapter Five

The Post-modern Void

Between the Sacred and the Profane

Out of the things that exist around them, human beings create worlds of meaning, stories that enable them to live according to a purpose. As Durkheim stressed, the study of human beings cannot proceed without an appreciation of the need for a sacred realm through which a society expresses its collective sense of itself. No other species shares the sacred with us. Other species besides the human live in a physical world of survival and even, under certain conditions, a material world of social organization. But the world of other species is entirely profane; they strive to satisfy basic needs without attributing importance to the ultimate goods those needs serve. The Durkheimian distinction between the sacred and the profane is the key distinction of an anthropocentric theory of society. Other animal species may, like humans, make war and peace, but, unlike the human species, they do not read and write *War and Peace*.

For Durkheim, the sacred is a realm above ourselves, which enables us to evaluate our mundane actions and goals against some standard of the good; if we are to be at the center of the world, there has to be something above us as well as beneath us. Durkheim wrote that the world of the sacred "must be treated in its own peculiar way: it would be a misunderstanding of its nature and a confusion of it with something that it is not, to make use of the gestures, language, and attitudes which we employ in our relations with ordinary things."[1] Yet if Durkheim recognized the need for a realm of the sacred, he also understood that the sacred does not refer to some untouchable realm of perfection that stands totally beyond our reach. One of Durkheim's great insights is that the sacred can be understood as our own creation, as the product of the way we make meaning out of the world. Society is both sacred and profane. It is sacred because it expresses our collective destiny; it is profane because we can use the cognitive powers that make us modern to understand it and chart its dynamics. As the science of this realm between the sacred and the profane, sociology, from Durkheim's perspective, would always be torn between them. A sociology that incorporates everything into its science leaves little that can serve as a source of wonder and common meaning. A sociology that cannot apply its insights everywhere preserves a world of sacred meaning, but at the cost of its scientific claim to understand everything.

As Durkheim's reflections suggest, to be modern is to live poised uneasily between the world of everyday life and a world that seeks to make meaning out of everyday life. If societies are to do more than simply reproduce themselves, if they are to direct themselves toward meaningful goals, they must establish a version of the good (or of many goods), against which their members evaluate who they are and where they are going. But if modern societies are also to be governed by those who compose them, this realm of the sacred must be understood as a product of the profane, as a realm that human beings create in the first place and then agree to elevate. The modern quest for meaning is not a search after a timeless ideal but, instead, an effort to move from the particular to truths about the human condition that are more contingent than universal. No wonder modernity is a difficult condition. There will always be the tendency either to elevate the sacred totally beyond the profane, imagining some canon of great truths existing in an ahistorical or transcendental limbo, or to ignore the sacred entirely by believing that everything we do and believe is little more than a rationalization for someone's everyday interest.

Because the quest for meaning is central to what we do together in our collective life, modern societies—unlike ant colonies, central processing units, and ecological systems—

mark off some of their everyday practices and artifacts as special: on this day, in this place, or through this text, we gain a better understanding of what we have in common and what the meaning of our common destiny may be. These practices and artifacts can take many forms: religions, holidays, philosophical systems, national rituals, norms, legal and constitutional documents, literary and artistic works, and folk cultures, to mention just a few. They provide clues about the purposes for which people come together in groups. To serve as adequate guides for meaning in the modern world, such cultural artifacts must, like social science itself, have roots in both the realm of the sacred and the world of the profane.

Most of modernity's great cultural artifacts do have such roots. As an example, consider the modern novel. Its development follows a path quite similar to the development of modern sociology. Both tend to be concerned with the particulars of time and place. The self is an essential ingredient of both, either the individual character developing through time or the individual enmeshed in social structures. Realism is the dominant mode of each form of expression, embodied in the study of real people in situations of real life, or what Ian Watt has called "the novel's closeness to the texture of daily experience."[2] Both, as we shall see in chapter 7, have a fondness for metaphors involving webs. Each has a moral dimension, an interest in exploring the impact of people on the groups and societies around them.

But perhaps the most important similarity between the modern novel and modern sociology is that each tries to take materials from the everyday world of profane activities and to transform them into more sacred and permanent objects that stand outside the rhythms of daily life. Unlike the classical tradition in literature, which understood the realm of the sacred as existing somewhere above and beyond the world of daily life, the modern novel tells stories about recognizable individuals out of whose experience lessons can be drawn about how to lead one's life. In distancing itself from neo-Platonist quests for ideal form and perfect style in favor of rough-hewn language designed to capture how real people talk and think, the modern novel has sought a middle ground be-

tween the holy world of sacred texts—great epic poems, classical tragedy, ancient philosophy—and the profane world of
folk tales never written down by real authors.

Because humans live in worlds that escape the cycles of
nature in order to build lasting monuments of meaning, their
affairs will never be properly understood without an appreciation of cultural artifacts, such as novels, that are capable of
embodying common lessons about the nature of the good. For
this reason alone—there may well be others—sociology will
always have a close relationship with literature and other quasi-
sacred cultural forms. "Literature," Alvin Kernan has written,
"belongs not to nature but to the world of culture that Vico,
who, along with Hobbes, is sometimes honored as our first
sociologist, believed we can understand fully because it was
made for human purposes."[3] In creating great works, some
human beings give to other human beings ways of making sense
out of the world around them, which may well explain why
the notion of a gift relationship is central to both literature
and sociology.[4] A human conception of literature, Kernan concludes, "leaves such cultural realities as literature and the
other arts an honorable place in the social scheme of things as
a useful partner in making a meaningful world in which to live
in the face of a nature going relentlessly and invariably on its
meaningless way."[5] No wonder that sociology, as Robert Nisbet has argued, is an art form, spinning narratives on the great
questions of modernity and how it developed.[6]

Social theory and literature are thus intimately linked because the latter gives the former a sense of meaning, while the
former reminds the latter who provides that meaning and how.
Without social theory, literature would be understood as written by gods or other animal species, neither of which would
make it a human product. Without literature, social theory
would study the complex social systems in which people live
but would fail to consider why these systems are important to
the people who live in them. Sociology cannot be an art form
when there is no art. But because there is art, and because it
is made by real people, the societies in which human beings
live have a purpose other than self-reproduction.

Beneath the Sacred and the Profane

If literary works are central to the quest for meaning, literary theory is not. There has always been a gap between literature and the study of literature, but never, seemingly, has it been as large as at the present time. The study of literature is increasingly dominated by philosophical dispositions known as post-modernism, post-structuralism, and deconstruction, which question whether there exist any fixed standards of meaning, evaluation, justice, taste, truth, or morality outside of the specific ways we make contingent rhetorical arguments about such contested terrains.[7] Although such dispositions may yet prove to be a passing fad, they now exercise significant influence over how we think about culture, philosophy, religion, history, and law in American academic life.[8] From the perspective of these approaches, nothing is eternal, all value is relative, meaning is self-referential, and the sacred is little more than an ideological construct imposed by those who hold power over those who lack it. An attitude that once attributed much to the sacred has been flipped on its side and now attributes little.

Unlike the classic thinkers of the sociological tradition, who wrote within a milieu shaped by great literary works, contemporary social theory coexists with a humanism that is no longer sure of its relationship to monuments of human creation. There is nothing necessarily wrong here; in toppling transcendental standards of the good and the true, post-modern literary criticism brings the human creative process within the reach of human beings, just as Durkheim brought religion down to earth. By debunking the idea that texts are the product of some kind of transcendental rendering of the mysterious unknown, literary iconoclasm could serve humanistic goals by reminding readers that texts were written by real human beings. But this is not what has taken place as contemporary literary theory has mounted its assault on canons of value. In its path downward from the sacred, post-modern literary theory has not been content to stop halfway at the human world but, determined to reject humanism in any form, has gone naturalistic, not humanistic; indeed, in its extreme form, literary theory has turned away from both the world of nature and the world of culture in favor of the artificial worlds of machines and self-regulating systems.[9]

The abdication of the humanities from humanism has significant consequences for society and therefore for social theory. Like animal ethology, sociobiology, and deep ecology, post-modern literary criticism establishes, for the social theorist, a fascinating thought experiment: what happens to the human quest for meaningful societies if we believe that there is no meaning? In the absence of texts that can speak to values and purposes beyond the everyday world of the profane, what will govern the quest for order that holds society together? At least two answers to these questions have been posed by thinkers influenced by post-modernism. One is that our affairs will be governed by violence, since all cultural production is force by one means or another. The other is that our affairs will be governed much like those of other species: by self-referential systems that do not need external goals because the internal goal of reproduction is sufficient.

The ubiquity of violence is a constant theme in the philosophical reflections of many post-modern literary theorists.[10] That transcendent goods merely serve the interest of the stronger was first suggested by Thrasymachus—the first post-modernist—and is repeated, in more elegant form, by Michel Foucault and those inspired by him. Everything being power, the only antidote to oppression is a transformation in the relations of power. Appeals to standards outside ourselves, from such a perspective, are naïve, self-defeating, a lingering symptom of wooly-headed humanism. Replace all humanistic talk by power talk and then we can begin to talk about who makes the rules and how. "Does might make right?" Stanley Fish asks. "In a sense the answer I must give is yes, since in the absence of a perspective independent of interpretation some interpretive perspective will always rule by having won out over its competitors." Or, more epigrammatically, "the gun is always at your head."[11]

When standards of sacred meaning reflect the power of contending forces and nothing else, the goals toward which we direct our efforts are ones that have been imposed by some

political force in the society over competing versions that did
not have sufficient power to challenge it. The world comes to
be organized not by persuasion but by coercion. Fish, who
believes that persuasion—e.g., rhetoric—is coercion, consequently holds that human agents have strikingly little freedom
in these matters: "In the end we are always self-compelled,
coerced by forces—beliefs, convictions, reasons, desires—from
which we cannot move one inch away."[12] If one adopts such
a perspective on the ubiquity of power, it is futile to discuss
the nature of the sacred: it will always be power—and not ideas,
desires, or capacities—that organizes society. In this world, our
condition resembles a popularized Darwinian struggle for existence. Animals do not fool themselves into believing that
their struggle has anything to do with transcendental purpose;
they just struggle. There is, in this vision, no essential difference between the world of nature and the world of culture;
both exist only at the most profane level: survival at all costs.

Crude forms of Darwinism are not necessarily the best
guides to the natural world; the ethologists who observe real
animal species, as recounted in chapter 2, are as impressed by
equivalents to morality and peacemaking as they are to warlike
behavior. The study of nature has in fact been heavily influenced by the study of machines, and in both cases self-reproduction, not violence, has been held to be the key process.
Much the same is true with literary theory. Self-referentiality
provides literary theorists with a second answer to the question
of how we can think about the good without elevating anything to the realm of the sacred. There being no conception
of the good outside the operation of a system, this way of
thinking concludes, our conception of the sacred must be *inside* the workings of the system. We do not, if we follow such
an approach, have to conclude that because there are no
metatruths, there are no goods. Rather, we can orient our affairs to the good, and at the same time avoid privileging any
one version of the good, by imagining that our conception of
the good is self-referential to whatever activity we are engaged
in.

Self-referentiality rules the roost in contemporary literary theory. The criteria for judging any text must lie within the text itself. There are no external judges to whom we can appeal, nothing outside of the arguments we construct. Our forms of expression, our search for a sacred realm that gives meaning to what we do, are thus no different from the eternal recurrence of an autopoietic system or the infinite Mandelbrot patterns churned out by a computer that someone forgot to turn off. The same laissez-faire approach to the environment that characterizes ecological thinking comes to characterize literary thinking: the relationship between a text and a reader is envisioned as a complicated ecological system best left to find its own equilibrium. The shift from naturalism to self-referentiality is thus like the shift from animal rights theorists, who at least respect living things, to systems theorists, for whom mere reproduction, whether sensate or not, is enough. In turning literary theory away from naturalism to the artificial world of machines, information theory, and cybernetics, post-modern writers take us down to a world beneath even the level of the profane.

Although many post-modern writers treat science as one more form of narrative that cannot appeal to any fixed truth outside its own practices and terms, there are significant areas of overlap between those who design artificial languages, those who study the evolution of other species besides our own, those who are attracted to the new ecology, and those concerned with the indeterminacy of meaning in literary and legal texts: all of them agree that those governed by the rules of a system have little autonomy in deciding for themselves how those rules will be followed. Antihumanism is as fashionable in the humanities as in the sciences, if not more so. The humanities and the sciences, which once were separated by a seemingly unbridgeable gap, may find some common ground in the notion of a self-referential system. But before celebrating this unity of knowledge, we might first pause and ask whether it constitutes progress for both the humanities and the sciences to link themselves in opposition to social theory's concern with real human beings.

Information Versus Meaning

Any conception of the sacred that can serve as a guide to actions ought to mean something to those who will be governed by its imperatives. Yet meaning is precisely what texts cannot possess, according to the philosophical inclinations under discussion here. Texts nonetheless contain words. Do those words convey anything if they do not convey meaning?

Some post-modernists believe that texts, if not capable of conveying meaning, are capable of conveying information. Information and meaning are not the same thing. Meaning, as we saw in chapter 3, is a macrophenomenon that involves making larger sense out of smaller bits, while information reduces larger complexity into smaller, and presumably more manageable, units. Information communicates through signs; meaning, through symbols. For those who seek information, context is only noise; for those concerned with meaning, context is everything. Information and meaning, in short, work at cross-purposes.

While the humanistic disciplines have traditionally been concerned with meaning, the two intellectual giants who created the framework for post-modernism and deconstruction—Friedrich Nietzsche and Ferdinand de Saussure—were both suspicious of the notion that meaning lies somewhere behind words in any fixed or certain form. Hence, both were also attracted to cybernetic notions of self-regulating systems, because the rules governing such systems made it possible for the relationships between things to keep them suspended in air without being either grounded in a reality beneath them or tied to something sacred above them. The attraction of information processing and cybernetics to those who inspired post-modernism was there even before these sciences existed.

Nietzsche's ideas are particularly instructive in this regard, given the importance that he has assumed among those who argue that whatever meaning can be found in texts lies in the perspectives that different readers bring to those texts. But another aspect of Nietzsche's thought, besides his "perspectivism," overlaps directly with theories of self-referentiality. In speaking of the metamorphosis of the lion into the child,

Zarathustra introduces the image of a "self-propelled wheel," preparing the way for his later discussion of the eternal recurrence—images and concepts similar to the ideas of Goedel, Escher, and Bach, which have been found to be compatible with the age of information machines.[13] Moreover, even if we do not accept the notion of the eternal recurrence as a cosmology (and Nehamas, in defending Nietzsche, asks us not to accept it as such), we can still accept it as "a view of the self."[14] Nietzsche's somewhat mysterious references to the notion that if we could live our lives over again, we would live them in exactly the same way can therefore be read as a kind of thought experiment designed to show that the world is still possible without selves that can be defined by essential, noncontested, features.

Given such intellectual roots, post-modernism, far from being hostile to the self-recurrence of information theory, is awed by the potential of information processing. Certainly, the inventor of the term *post-modernism*, Jean-François Lyotard, has a tendency to take extreme, and rather dubious, positions vis-à-vis the capabilities of computers. He suggests, for instance, that artificial intelligence will be capable of translating from one "natural" language to another, that computers can "aid groups discussing metaprescriptives by supplying them with the information they usually lack for making knowledgeable decisions," and that data banks will serve as "nature" for post-modern individuals.[15]

But this respect for information processing is not just a Lyotardian quirk; it can be found "eternally recurring" in every significant post-modern thinker. Paul de Man, who was fascinated by Pascal's discussion of an arithmetic machine, increasingly began to focus on language as a machine, as in this passage on Rousseau: "There can thus be no use of language which is not, within a certain perspective thus radically formal, i.e., mechanical, no matter how deeply this aspect may be concealed by aesthetic, formalistic delusions."[16] Jacques Derrida—whose picture of the world in *The Post Card* resembles the endless circuitry of a modern computer—was so attracted to mechanical imagery that, as Geoffrey Bennington has put it, "a reading machine would be needed to read all the machines in Derrida's work."[17] The writings of Deleuze and Guattari are filled with images of machines that program other machines in ever-recurring fashion, down to the notion that the structure of desire takes the form of a binary system.[18] The "mode of information" lies behind nearly all versions of post-modern theory.[19]

The extreme representative of the common ground shared by information theory and literary post-modernism is Michel Serres, who has incorporated all the reference points for information theory—entropy, Maxwell's demon, the second law of thermodynamics, Claude Shannon, and Boltzmannian quantum physics—into a theory of the origins of language. Information theory allows Serres to develop a theory of communication even though there may not be any communicators. In contrast, for example, to Habermas, who specifies two parties to a communication (and who, in so doing, inspires a heavy-handed critique from Lyotard),[20] Serres shows that language may be possible even when one knows nothing about its origins:

I know who the final observer is, the receiver at the chain's end: precisely he who utters language. But I do not know who the initial dispatcher is at the other end. I am confronted indefinitely with a black box, a box of boxes, and so forth. In this way, I may proceed as far as I wish, all the way to cells and molecules, as long, of course, as I change the object under investigation.[21]

As might be expected, Serres' theory about the origins of language has little to do with the notion of an autonomous self. "There is only one type of knowledge and it is always linked to an observer, an observer submerged in a system or in its proximity. And this observer is structured exactly like what he observes. . . . There is no more separation between the subject, on the one hand, and the object, on the other."[22]

As Serres' remarks imply, communication is possible within the terms of information theory, but interpretation is not. Information can only be processed, not read. The act of reading, by bringing an interpreting self in confrontation with a text, can only be viewed, from the perspective of information theory, as noise. Nonetheless, the computer is too fascinating a machine not to exercise a certain power over novelists and literary critics. "Perhaps the computer," one critic has written, "after first ushering in (apart from superefficiency) the games and preprogrammed oversimplifications of popular culture, will alter our minds and powers of analysis once again, and enable us to create new dimensions in the deep-down logic of characters."[23]

The same fascination can be seen as well in the writings of another critic, William Paulson, who argues that Serres' approach provides "a unique example of the possibilities opened up by bringing literary culture and scientific thinking into play with one another."[24] But even Paulson, who wants literary critics to take information theory seriously, concludes that "what literature solicits of the reader is not simply reception but the active, independent, autonomous construction of meaning."[25] Without ever explicitly saying so, Paulson seems to believe that deconstruction, despite its strong similarities to information theory in other respects, at least allows for readers, even if it does not theorize much about them. In pushing information theory to its logical conclusion, these efforts make clear why a purely self-referential approach to communication is inappropriate to the texts that human beings write and read: meaning exists when human selves attribute characteristics to the symbols around them, whereas information requires only relationships between signs.

It is not only an interest in computers that has inspired post-modernist writers to reach for self-referential conceptions of the good. The notion of rule-following contained in some forms of artificial intelligence matches the emphasis placed by sociobiologists on the role played by DNA as a transmitter of information across time. Post-modern thinkers, not surprisingly, also find biological metaphors that correspond to their understanding of the sacred. Especially relevant in this context are those who discuss the possibility that life itself is "autopoietic." "The most striking feature of an autopoietic system is that it pulls itself up by its bootstraps and becomes distinct from its environment through its own dynamics, in such a way that both things are inseparable," Maturana and Varela have written.[26] From the standpoint of autopoiesis, systems specify their own laws without the need for any external agents. Moreover, a truly Nietzschean form of eternal recurrence enables two or more units, such as cells, to interact with each other in stable ontogenies. In an autopoietic model, systems—and not individual agents—have autonomy. Systems take on a life of their own, generating the goals that they can strive to reach. In an autopoietic system, nothing exists outside the system.

Although autopoiesis may therefore seem of little relevance to human affairs, since we have powers of mind that enable us to take our development into our own hands, the notion has nonetheless been attractive to literary theorists. In particular, the work of Barbara Herrnstein Smith illustrates the quest for self-referential conceptions of the good. In her work, autopoiesis joins information processing, equilibrium theory in economics, and numerous other ways of imagining a self-reproducing system—all in an effort to demonstrate that any belief in a sacred realm of value outside our everyday activities is an illusion.

For Herrnstein Smith, the Western humanistic tradition has sought standards of "transcendence, endurance, and universality" in its evaluation of literary works, but her own personal relationship to Shakespeare's sonnets convinces her instead that "everything is always in motion with respect to everything else." If value is therefore never a fixed attribute of any particular product under evaluation, how do certain cultural products come to be seen as worthy, while others are assigned to the dustbin of culture? Herrnstein Smith begins her answer by turning to economics. Each of us has a personal economy of needs and resources: "Like any other economy, moreover, this too is a continuously fluctuating or shifting system, for our individual needs, interests, and resources are themselves functions of our continuously changing states in relation to an environment that may be relatively stable but is never absolutely fixed."[27]

Markets, then, play a role in the creation of literary standards of the good, and not only in the narrow economic sense of money. But what kind of market are we talking about: the rigged and fixed markets that, in the view of radical critics since Marx, drive capitalist societies; or the purely automatic, homeostatic markets envisioned by eighteenth-century liberals? For Herrnstein Smith, it is clearly the latter: markets are interesting to her because they work independently of the desires of the agents in the market.[28] Like contemporary rational choice theorists, Herrnstein Smith argues that self-interest drives everything we do: "We are always, so to speak, calculating how things 'figure' for us—always pricing them, so to speak, in relation to the total economy of our personal universe." But unlike rational choice theorists, Herrnstein Smith does not believe that "we" do this calculating consciously and as autonomous choosers: "Most of these 'calculations,' however, are performed intuitively and inarticulately, and many of them are so recurrent that the habitual arithmetic becomes part of our personality and comprises the very style of our being and behavior, forming what we may call our principles and tastes—and what others may call our biases and prejudices."[29]

Since Herrnstein Smith's picture of the market is far more invasive than anything found in writers like Gary Becker and Richard Posner, who see markets everywhere, it is no wonder that conceptions of self-regulating systems dominate her account of how standards of taste become established. So much is in motion at such speeds that the only possible regulation of the whole process is automatic regulation, or what Herrnstein Smith calls an "evaluative feedback loop":

Every literary work—and, more generally, artwork—is thus the product of a complex evaluative feedback loop that embraces not only the ever-shifting economy of the artist's own interests and resources as they evolve during and in reaction to the process of composition, but also the shifting economies of her assumed and imagined audiences, including those who do not yet exist but whose emergent interests, variable conditions of encounter, and rival sources of gratification she will attempt to predict—or will intuitively surmise—and to which, among other things, her own sense of the fittingness of each decision will be responsive.[30]

Thinking in terms of feedback and system reproduction, Herrnstein Smith touches on the possibility that human brains may be cognitively hard-wired in predetermined ways. She also criticizes the Habermasian notion of rational communicative standards on the ground that we speak, as we spend, only out of self-interest, so that honesty in speech, if it ever exists, is the product of a Mandevillian lack of intention. She adopts autopoiesis as the model for an epistemology in which "what is traditionally referred to as 'perception,' 'knowledge,' 'belief,' . . . would be an account of how the structures, mechanisms, and behaviors through which subjects interact with—and, accordingly, constitute—their environments are modified by those very interactions." In addition, she uses information theory to explain that evaluative classifications exist so that "energy need not . . . be expended on the process of classification and evaluation each time a similar array is produced," and she argues that often such classifications are "fixed in the DNA." Finally, she relies on Brownian motion and Nietzsche's "play of forces" to criticize those who suggest that there is an "overall, underlying, or ultimate governing outcome toward which each instance of human productive-acquisitive *or* consumptory-expenditure activity (all making, getting, and spending, we might say) is directed."[31]

The purpose of this use of self-referential imagery is to explain why certain products of culture have entered our canon. Artistic texts survive the way species do: "These interactions are, in certain respects, analogous to those by virtue of which biological species evolve and survive and also analogous to those through which artistic choices evolve and are found 'fit' or fitting by the individual artist." Evolutionary feedback loops allow Herrnstein Smith to resolve the question in aesthetic theory proposed by Hume: Why do we consider Homer great? The answer is not that Homer survived because he was great but that because he survived he is considered great. "Nothing endures like endurance." Images of eternal recurrence combine with Durkheimian functionalism to explain the secret of Homer's success:

Repeatedly cited and recited, translated, taught and imitated, and thoroughly enmeshed in the network of intertexuality that continuously *constitutes* the high culture of the orthodoxy educated population of the West (and the Western-educated population of the rest of the world), that highly variable entity we refer to as "Homer" recurrently enters our experience in relation to a large number and variety of our interests and thus can perform a large number of various functions for us.[32]

With Herrnstein Smith, the realm of the sacred has traveled full circle from a place above humans and their creations to a place below. The Greek epics no longer serve as a source of inspiration for meaningful values such as virtue, as they do in the writings of Alasdair MacIntyre.[33] That may or may not be an advantage, depending on what one thinks about MacIntyre's political and social beliefs. But in Herrnstein Smith's account, the story does not end there. For not only is Homer rejected as a meaningful text; he is also rejected as an interpreting person. There is, indeed, no longer any Homer but instead a self-reproducing artifact called "Homer." Homer could be understood as a perfect example of how a real person creates a human masterpiece that continues to inspire other humans to create masterpieces themselves and to live their lives in certain ways. When he and his work are instead understood as a feedback loop, the only accomplishment worth celebrating is that the system that produced him continues to reproduce itself without individual capacity and social meaning. To move beneath both the sacred and the profane is to enter a world in which all meaning is reduced to information, all readers to coders, and all texts to programs. An effort to equate human accomplishments, including ones as masterful as *The Odyssey*, with those of other species takes its ultimate form in the denial of any sacred realm of human value whatsoever.

Algorithmic Justice

One particular human creation has a special relevance to the way in which we govern ourselves: the law. Legal systems have been generally understood to strive after justice, one of the most important human goods. To believe that there is justice in the world is to believe that our actions are not like those of animal species. In human affairs, events that might at first glance seem random and contingent were traditionally regarded as part of some larger design, the name of which is justice. Like religious belief—to which it is often compared—the quest for justice invariably involved grand stories that took people beyond the concerns of the material world into considerations of the sacred.[34] The just act, the just person, and the just society have been viewed as possessing an otherworldly nature, as if only heroic action on the part of heroic actors could achieve, or even approximate, them. Plato's stories may be, in Geertzian language, "thick," while John Rawls's are "thin," but neither points toward standards directly observable in the everyday course of social practice—lying, as they are, either hidden in shadows or behind a veil of ignorance.

Such a transcendental vision of justice standing outside daily life in sacred confines clearly clashes with the iconoclastic and profane spirit of post-modernism. From the perspective of the post-modern, laws are texts, they are interpretable in many ways, and even the most "sacred" of such texts, such as constitutions, are the products of particular struggles over power. If literary texts can no longer offer a glimpse of the good and the true, law can no longer have much to do with transcendental conceptions of justice. It should not be surprising that post-modernism and deconstruction have brought law and literature closer together.[35]

Just as literary theorists posit evaluations of texts within the inner logic of the texts themselves, it is also possible to understand justice as a by-product of the inner workings of a system, and not as a quest for some good outside any particular system. Stanley Fish, who is both a literary and a legal theorist, is attracted to self-referential conceptions of justice. Although Fish finds truly algorithmic systems, such as Chomskyian grammars, distasteful, he emphasizes that an individual deeply situated within the habitual rules of a practice "need not look to something in order to determine where he is or where he now might go because that determination is built into, comes along with, his already-in-place sense of being a competent member of the enterprise."[36]

People, in Fish's view, are part of a preformative chain— not one, to be sure, of the automatic transmittal of information without consciousness but nonetheless one that works without requiring autonomy and self-judgment. Individuals follow rules so deeply situated that individuals probably are not aware that they are following them. For Fish, people are so deeply embedded in the practices around them that they have little autonomy and scope for choice: "the individual . . . is always constrained by the local or community standards and criteria of which his judgment is an extension."[37] Fish chose to call his collection of essays *Doing What Comes Naturally* because he wanted "to refer to the unreflective actions that come from being embedded in a context of practice. This kind of action— and in my argument there is no other—is anything but natural in the sense of proceeding independently of historical and social formations; but once those formations are in place (and they always are), what you think to do will not be calculated in relation to a higher law or an overarching theory but will issue from you as naturally as breathing."[38] Doing what comes naturally is a naturalistic act.

Although Fish understands the law as a self-referential practice, he does not call upon developments in artificial intelligence or autopoietic understandings of living creatures to provide theoretical grounding. The same cannot be said for Niklas Luhmann, who has taken systems theory as it has emerged in the natural and artificial sciences and applied it to all aspects of society, including legal aspects.

Like almost all social theorists, Luhmann is fundamentally concerned with modernity: what defines it and what consequences for human beings flow from it? The overarching theme of his work—comparable to the theme of rationalization in Weber or organic solidarity in Durkheim—is that hierarchy or stratification has given way to system differentiation. As long as the Hobbesian problem of order was resolved by strong political authority, the question of what makes society possible was easily answered. But a number of developments—primarily, the separation of society from politics in such a way that political authority no longer extends beyond a separate political subsystem—make the Hobbesian solution invalid for modern societies. A society that lacks a centering principle cannot find unity through the extension of rules from any of its parts to the system as a whole. But this inability of society to represent itself as a unity does not constitute an unsolvable legitimation problem. For the units of the system increasingly organize themselves self-referentially. It does not therefore matter that the dynamics of the legal system are inapplicable to the religious system or vice versa. As long as each system finds within itself what it needs to reproduce itself, there is the possibility of order without Order. Sociologists look in the wrong place for some centered principle or source of central authority, and they misdiagnose the problem when they fail to find such a source.

In considering how each differentiated part of a system organizes itself by its own logic in order to reduce complexity, Luhmann turns to the world of computers and other living species. Computers reduce complexity by dividing all information into bits that can be expressed as os and 1s. So, argues Luhmann, do legal systems. A legal system can exhaust the entire realm of the possible through the legal/illegal dichotomy. That distinction, in a sense, constitutes the "hardware" of a legal system. In order for the system to make a decision in a specific case, "software" programs access the system, feeding back into the "memory" and thereby creating new rules that anticipate future programs.[39]

For Luhmann, the dynamics of specific cases introduced into a legal system continuously redefine the binary codes, interacting again with new programs in ways that resemble eternal recurrence. The whole system, he argues,

is a matter of a specific technique for dealing with highly structured complexity. In practice this technique requires an endless, circular, re-editing of the law: the assumption is that something will happen, but how it will happen and what its consequences will be has to be awaited. When these consequences begin to reveal themselves they can be perceived as problems and provide an occasion for new regulations in law itself as well as in politics. Unforeseeable consequences will also occur and it will be impossible to determine if and to what extent they apply to that regulation. Again, this means an occasion for new regulation, waiting, new consequences, new problems, new regulation, and so on.[40]

Social systems achieve this circular reproduction by communication, Luhmann argues; communication is the "particular mode of autopoietic reproduction."[41] By "communication," Luhmann does not mean such human activities as talk and the use of language. When real human beings communicate, they convey what they mean not only in formal codes or grammars but also by intonation, irony, and metaphor. Sociologists from Weber to contemporary sociolinguists have therefore been interested in language as a human artifact capable of conveying meaning. But systems do not communicate through language in this sense. For Luhmann, communication is the process by which an open system obtains enough information from its environment to enable the system to reproduce itself totally from its own properties. A message is sent to the environment; the environment processes the message; this processing is transmitted back to the system so that the system can take the next step; and the entire process then repeats itself ad infinitum. Communication and language are entirely different processes.

Because sociology focuses primarily on language rather than communication, its conception of meaning, according to Luhmann, is inadequate. Sociologists from Weber to the later Durkheim understood meaning as a specific feature of the cultural or human sciences. To understand human existence, one had to take into account the capacity of humans to observe the world around them, to draw from those observations certain insights, and to use those insights to alter the conditions of their existence. For Luhmann, by contrast, meaning must be the basic concept of sociology, but it must also be divorced from the interpreting subject. Meaning is a way of bringing a Husserlian horizon closer to the immediate world of decision by organizing an infinite number of possibilities into a manageable number of choices. It is a "selection rule," a way of reducing the complexity in the world.[42] "Meaning is a representation of complexity. Meaning is not an image or a model of complexity used by conscious or social systems, but simply a new and powerful form of coping with complexity under the unavoidable condition of enforced selectivity."[43]

Without a conception of meaning capable of providing symbolic and cultural truths outside the realm of everyday communication, there can be no conception of the sacred. The ambivalence between the sacred and the profane that pervades the writings of Durkheim and Weber is missing in Luhmann, who resolves this ambivalence not by choosing between the sacred and the profane but by rejecting both. Systems cannot refer to anything outside themselves. There are no special places or traditions that convey meaning in timeless or universal ways, nor are the internal workings of a system the product of profane human considerations such as talking or doing. Communication in the world of real people—what Luhmann calls "communication of the streets"—is irrelevant to the way in which systems reproduce themselves. Human communication "is not coordinated functionally or [is] coordinated only ambiguously" and is therefore hardly worthy of scientific consideration.[44]

Since human communication and human meaning are insignificant compared to the systems that communicate and generate meaning, there is no need for a special science for that special subject the human agent. We can therefore dispense with any notion that it is possible to divide the sciences from the humanities, the former concerned with complexity and the latter with meaning. Instead, "we will have to choose system references that crosscut the unity of the human being."[45] Any theory that emphasizes the distinctive powers of mind possessed by human beings is misguided, Luhmann concludes. He shares the vigorous antihumanism found in much contemporary theorizing in the humanities. "The theory of autopoietic systems seems to bar all ways back to an anthropological conception of man," he writes.[46] This is not a "nice" theory, he points out, but it is nonetheless inevitable. "Autopoietic systems reproduce themselves; they continue their reproduction or not. This makes them individuals. And there is nothing more to say."[47]

There may, however, be at least one thing more to say. Once a shift is made to autopoiesis, the reduction of complexity becomes not a means to an end but an end in itself; autopoietic systems reduce complexity because they reduce possibility. The reduction of complexity no longer serves the happy purpose of enabling individuals to focus their choices and avoid illusory options. Instead, people and their choices stand in the way of the laws of complexity reduction. The power of Luhmann's theorizing comes from his critique of the romantic tradition in social theory, which imagines technique running wild in ever more inhumane complex systems, producing endless alienation. But in the thought of a Niklas Luhmann, it is the urge to simplify and reduce complexity that runs amok, trampling real human subjects just as thoroughly in the process. Complexity is not a state that demands reduction to algorithms; it is, rather, the raw material for making sense out of the world. It is as if the social theorist is given a choice between living with meaning and living with complexity under control; opting for the latter, as Luhmann does, may make society more possible, but the question of what kind of society it would be remains open.

A World Safe for Systems

Uncomfortable with privilege and hierarchy, open to new readings of classic texts, and responsive to those who have been excluded from the canon, the deconstructive mood in literary and legal criticism seeks to further democratic goals. Clearly, one of the reasons deconstruction and post-modernism appeal to feminists, minority scholars, and others who were once excluded from the academy is this sense that radical epistemologies open up new possibilities for inclusion and representation.

To a significant degree, the world as imagined by post-modern theorists and others attracted to self-reproducing, algorithmic imagery is a democratic one. Herrnstein Smith's theory of value, for example, has certain clearly egalitarian features. Automatic, self-regulating systems are nonhierarchical, thereby overlapping with a political commitment to egalitarianism. They are nonjudgmental in that they pose no teleological purpose to human action, and therefore are compatible with the reluctance of many post-modern thinkers to conclude that any one moral or ethical premise is superior to any other. Finally, self-regulating systems change—indeed, fluidity is their defining characteristic—and, as a result, they offer a positive alternative to the conservative rigidity found in many forms of structuralism.

Much the same is true of Luhmann's autopoietic theory of

law. Although Luhmann's intellectual orientation is anything but post-modernist—and although Lyotard rejects Luhmann's theories along with those of Habermas—his ideas about the law overlap with post-modernism because autopoietic systems are nonhierarchical. Being circular in their dynamics, they avoid privileging any one set of legal norms over any other; as Luhmann expresses it, "There can therefore be no normative hierarchies," or, somewhat more self-reflectively, "legal forms are valid because they are valid."[48] There is also a certain egalitarianism in Luhmann's vision; indeed, it would be impossible to imagine a world of more perfect equality than the world of a Luhmannian system, which resembles a state of "primitive communism," in which everything is equal because nothing is differentiated from anything else. Finally, the legal theory of Luhmann and the literary theory of Herrnstein Smith both find in autopoiesis a way of focusing on the constant change undergone by systems, not on their stasis.

The systems that lie behind many post-modern visions may be fluid and open systems, but they are not especially fit for modern human beings. Author, text, and reader must all interact if people are to live halfway between the profane world of production and a sacred realm of meaning. Authors—novelists, founding fathers, legislators—create. Their texts—novels, constitutions, laws, traditions—take on some degree of permanence but are constantly reinterpreted by those—citizens, readers, newcomers—to whom they give meaning. Post-modernists are right to claim that any system that privileges the author at the expense of texts and readers is undemocratic, for it establishes a truth independent of those governed by it. But any system that privileges the text at the expense of authors and readers is equally undemocratic, for it ignores the human beings who, alone among all species in the world, can provide meaning above and beyond self-referentiality.

People—but not all people—read the texts that other people write. Infants do not read and interpret texts, and neither do the illiterate or the brain-dead. The capacity to read and write is a potential, something that can be undertaken only by a self: a mature, socialized human individual who has grown up in a society and possesses the tools of culture given to her by that society.[49] But it is precisely people that have been factored out of post-modernism's equations.

This was not always the case. At least in some of its early versions, post-modernism was willing to consider a role for readers. Some literary theorists developed sophisticated understandings of how the responses of readers shape the interpretations given to texts; and these approaches, in assigning importance to readers, by implication assigned importance to people.[50] And if human readers supply meanings to texts, whatever their authors' intentions, it follows that the communities formed by such readers ought to be assigned a special place—as they were, for example, in the earlier work of Stanley Fish.[51] In this form, post-modern literary theory pointed toward sociological theory—as expressed, perhaps, by writers such as Mead, Schutz, Garfinkel, or Goffman—that seeks to define the self not as found in nature (for in nature there are no selves) but as the product of society and its dynamics.[52] The argument against transcendental and eternal meaning ought to be an argument for humans and their capacity to create texts that make their societies meaningful.[53]

But post-modern theory could not stop at the level of human readers and their interpretative communities without making a choice in favor of humanism, the one seemingly unpardonable sin in a perspective otherwise unwilling to make judgments. In the heady Nietzschean atmosphere of post-modern thought, talk of real people and their societies verges close to that particular combination of naïveté and arrogance alleged to be characteristic of Enlightenment thought. Leading post-modernist writers understand people not as authors of their own acts, determining for themselves what they will do in situations of choice, but as subjects ruled by structures that determine what they will do. The logic of this way of thinking, in the words of Heller and Wellbery, "negates the normative power of autonomous individuality by reducing subjective consciousness to the artifact of a self-replicating, superpersonal mechanism."[54] Novels no longer have characters who experience *bildung*; identity is historically and socially constructed; there is no longer a centered ego to discover through psychoanalysis; moral autonomy inheres in systems, not in the individuals who compose them; and the indeterminacy of the law, as Thomas Heller expresses it, "does not arise because the standpoint of the human individual is in some way privileged or central. Rather, indeterminacy is an element of the grammar of complex systems or a feature of the observation/system relationship."[55] Barbara Herrnstein Smith needs to invent a new language to dismiss the possibility of human capabilities; she coins the term *desired/able* in order to indicate

that the valued effect in question need not have been specifically desired (sought, wanted, imagined, or intended) as such by any subject. In other words, its value for certain subjects may have emerged independent of any specific human intention or agency and, indeed, may have been altogether a product of the chances of history or, as we say, a matter of luck.[56]

Post-modernism seeks to make the world safe for systems, not people. Once one walks down this road, the trinity of author, text, and reader is reduced to a unity: there is nothing outside the text, neither authors nor readers; and because there is not, meaning can reside only in the self-referential codes that constitute such texts. Reluctant to develop hierarchies, post-modernists nonetheless assign more importance to texts than to those who write them and read them.

The consequence of the post-modern turn in literary and legal theory is thus, for all the subversive talk, the same as the classical: to place texts beyond the reach of human beings. If we understand legal systems or cultural artifacts without regard to the meanings they make possible for real people, we come full circle from the features of self-referentiality that first made it attractive to post-modern theorists. Post-modernism became influential in literary and legal theory as a way of challenging the notion that the justice or value of a particular text was fixed in stone, engraved by the intentions of those who wrote it. In one sense, self-referential theories of the sacred are diametrically opposite to such conceptions, for there can be no higher realm of meaning that stands above human creative powers. But by turning to self-referential models that achieve autonomy for the whole at the expense of the parts that constitute them, theorists such as Luhmann and Herrnstein Smith overlap with those who view cultural artifacts as existing in a timeless realm beyond human intervention. In both cases, humans and their interpretative capacities are the objects of legal and literary systems, not their authors. Law and literature can be viewed as lying above real people in some heavenly realm or below them encoded into their genes, but in neither case are they understood as human and social creations.

For this reason, post-modern dispositions in literary and legal theory have more in common with the Platonic world of eternal truths than they usually recognize. If we understand the sacred as existing in a Platonic world of timeless value beyond human intervention, we elevate the sacred to such a high pedestal that it rules us rather than being ruled by us. We would then have a world of culture, but it would not be different in form from the world of nature; both systems, majestic in their transcendental timelessness, need not concern themselves with the gifts given to society by real, creative people. But little is gained by turning around and arguing that great works of human expression perpetuate themselves ad infinitum without human intervention. For then, instead of culture's replacing nature, nature—or the world of machines— would replace culture, and neither perspective would pay attention to the human beings who add capacities of mind to both.

Post-modernism, whatever its attractions and repulsions, has one advantage: it supplies an answer to the question of what a human society would look like in the absence of interpreting selves who can turn to sacred texts to help supply meaning for their lives. Such a society would have no purpose, and the individuals who compose it would eventually become codes in someone else's texts. The search for self-referential conceptions of the sacred is both futile and self-defeating. Human beings, capable of interpreting, are also free to make mistakes. We do not think as logically as computers; and, because we interfere in the ways in which our genes pass information to future generations, we do not reproduce ourselves as effortlessly as other species. It is because we are imperfect that we turn to masterpieces of human creation to find meaning for what we do; if we were as perfect as computers or DNA, we would not need the sacred. We cannot satisfy the human quest for meaning by transforming it into the processing of information that humans share with other species and machines. To live for more than self-reproduction, humans will always need the humanities; and if the study of literature does not supply social scientists with the materials for understanding this aspect of their subject, it is likely that literature itself always will.

Chapter Six

Social Science as a Way of Knowing

The Two Faces of Social Science

From biology in the late nineteenth century to information theory in the late twentieth, the social sciences have turned to the natural sciences for inspiration. Yet the expectations have never fully been satisfied. After more than one hundred years of effort, the ability of social scientists to say anything with certainty about human behavior is not impressive. We remain close to where we started, developing theories, trying to test them against data, arguing about methodology, and disputing conclusions. The social sciences have neither the public legitimacy nor the self-confidence that comes from the practice of "real" science.

There are numerous explanations for the failure of the social sciences to develop along the lines of the natural sciences, but surely among them ought to be included the special subject of the social sciences: human beings. The aim of a science is to describe and predict the behavior of the subjects it studies. Human subjects, because they can interpret the world around them, create sacred worlds of meaning out of their profane everyday affairs. A science of the human species that ignored one of the most significant aspects of what humans do would be like physics without the atom. It is anything but science to borrow the insights of those who study mindless subjects and apply them to those who possess mind. Nor does it satisfy the first criterion of science to understand those whose complex affairs are governed by the search for meaning on the basis of self-regulating systems that function without any special realm for meaning. The social sciences, unlike the natural sciences, must incorporate the study of great humanistic texts in order to be a science. Because the opposition between the sciences and the humanities is a false opposition, those who would study human affairs by using one rather than the other are doomed to discover very little.

Yet the atmosphere created by the failure of the scientific model based on the natural sciences to predict much more than the obvious has not led to a rethinking of how to do science so much as it has to a rejection of science itself. Reflecting a post-modern inability to define the world with precision, some theorists have claimed that there can be no science at all. In those accounts usually referred to as the "strong program" in the sociology of science, science is understood as little more than rhetoric. The acceptance of a truth by scientists is not the result of a clever experiment or the marshaling of convincing data; instead, it is the end product of an inexhaustible rhetorical campaign, in which the winners use every available strategy to browbeat the losers.[1] If "we must eventually come to call scientific the rhetoric able to mobilize on one spot more resources than older ones," the tables are reversed.[2] Instead of turning to the natural sciences intent on envious borrowing, sociologists now claim to have the only method capable of understanding "science in action." The imperialism of the natural sciences over the social sciences is reversed if "adequate *social* studies of the sciences turn out to be the necessary foundations upon which more comprehensive and less distorted descriptions and explanations of nature can be built."[3]

If the sciences, including the hardest of them, are in reality rhetoric, then rhetorical tools can be used to understand everything, including society. What is coming to be called "the rhetorical turn" uses the techniques of rhetoric to understand social phenomena, just as a previous generation of sociologists used the techniques of science.[4] Rhetorical tools have been applied to many disciplines, but because sociology studies social interaction, it is viewed as especially appropriate for the use of rhetorical tools. "As sociologists," Albert Hunter has written, "we cannot but see truth claims as examples of social interaction, and their refutation or acceptance is an inherently social process."[5] Once that insight has been accepted, the ways in which ideas are presented become at least as important as the ideas themselves. And the tools of literary analysis come to the fore; society is understood as a "text" to be read by sociologists sensitive to post-modernist techniques.[6]

The rhetorical turn in the social sciences adds a much-needed element of skepticism to the belief that a rigorous, almost algorithmic, understanding of human behavior is possible. But it would be a loss if the social sciences, in liberating themselves from the natural sciences, were to fall head over heels into the arms of rhetoric. If they did, those who claimed that the laws of the social sciences should be reduced to those of biology or biochemistry would be replaced by those who claim that their laws can be reduced to tropes and language games. And even more important, both the positivists and many rhetoricians, for all their differences, agree on one key issue: that human beings have no special and unique characteristics.

Positivists who would turn to the natural sciences for a model of how to do social science see no sharp break between natural and social phenomena. To argue that biology or physics provides a fruitful approach for humans is to make a case that the subjects of the one—other animal species or atoms—exist along the same continuum with the subjects of the other—people. Arguing that "the scientific analysis of social phenomena follows exactly the same general principles whether the objects of that analysis are human or nonhuman organisms," Walter Wallace believes that "sociology is, in its actual practice as well as its abstract design, one of the natural sciences—that is, much more akin to biology, chemistry, and physics than to philosophy, poetry, and religion."[7] From such a perspective, Wilhelm Dilthey's distinction between the cultural and the natural sciences would make no sense.[8] At some point, if not already now, sociology as a human science would make no sense. The study of people will become either the study of the physical parts out of which people are made or the study of all living organisms that exist together in groups, whether those organisms have human properties or not.

Approaches that deny the possibility of a firm and unshakable grounding for knowledge share with positivism an unwillingness to make a distinction between the subjects of inquiry. In much feminist and post-modern thought, any sharp break between nature and culture is suspect. It therefore follows that any effort to distinguish between a science of nature and a science of culture is also problematic. From Sandra Harding's perspective, "we must be skeptical about being able to make any clear distinctions between the physical and the nonphysical."[9] Harding, consequently, explicitly accepts the notion of a "unity of science" associated with the prime representatives of twentieth-century positivism, the Vienna Circle, even if she would reverse the hierarchy and place the moral sciences over the physical ones. Richard Rorty comes to a similar conclusion. His argument that we have no "sky hook" we can use to hitch ourselves to reality applies both to physics and the social sciences. Rorty instead urges that "we avoid using Dilthey's suggestion that we set up distinct parallel metavocabularies, one for the *Geistes-* and one for the *Naturwissenschaften.*"[10] The only difference between the social and the natural sciences, from such a perspective, lies in the way those who claim such titles do their work: "If we say that sociology or literary criticism is not a science, we shall mean merely that the amount of agreement among sociologists or literary critics on what counts as significant work, work which needs following up, is less than among, say, microbiologists."[11] In Rorty's ideal world, disciplinary designations ought to refer to communities of scholars "whose boundaries were as fluid as the interests of their members."[12] There would be no reason to divide disciplines by their claims over "chunks" of the world that interfaced with other chunks.

If reality for the positivists is seamless in its intelligibility, reality for Rorty, Harding, and many post-modernists is seamless in its opacity. They may differ sharply with positivists on epistemological grounds, but they have no essential difference with those who would model social science on the natural sciences, for in both cases the world is equally unchunkable. Just as for positivists the social world has only a transitory autonomy (it is sitting there waiting to be colonized by the tools of the natural sciences), so for the post-modernists the social world is an arbitrary convention, an illusory attempt by people to believe they can control and organize chaotic forces that are really out of control. The distaste toward the self and the society found in many post-modern writers is merely a continuation of a similar distaste once expressed by biologists and physicists, or those who would emulate them.

To be faithful to human beings and their capacity to create meaning out of the things around them, the social sciences can turn neither to the hard sciences nor to post-modern rhetorical or literary theory. Sociology has long sought a third way between the market, the subject of economics, and the state, the subject of political science. But as a social science, it joins with those disciplines in seeking a third way between science as usually understood and the humanities as currently understood. Unlike the natural sciences, it must account for the interpretative capacities of those it studies. Unlike rhetorical and post-modern understandings, it must recognize the reality of human subjects. The social sciences must combine elements of both science and literature into a synthesis that fully resembles neither.

The best social theory has, in fact, always found itself between the sciences and the humanities.[13] "While many of its roots are in the novel . . . ," Bruce Mazlish has written, "sociology still aspires, and should, to be a form of science."[14] Committed to a philosophical anthropology that understood humans as a unique species, the classic social theorists of the late nineteenth and early twentieth centuries hoped to fashion a social science that would be faithful simultaneously to science and to the human subject. Durkheim turned to biology as his guide in his earlier work, but he concluded his studies with a humanistic emphasis on meaning, before attempting to classify, like a taxonomist, everything there was to know about human beings.[15] Simmel could be both formalistic, like a scientist, and also "impressionistic," like an artist.[16] Florian Znaniecki called for a "humanistic sociology" but also argued that it should meet "the highest standard of logical exactness compatible

with the nature of social data.''[17] And Max Weber may have
been the most ambivalent of all, appreciated because of his
stress on "value-free" research, while seeming to embody a
Nietszchean heroic resistance against rationalization.[18]

In more recent years, this ambivalent position between science and the humanities has continued, even though, in postwar America, a positivistic model of the social sciences reached
its pinnacle. Under the inspiration of Talcott Parsons and especially Robert Merton, European grand theory was trans-
formed into "middle-range theorizing," which would generate
hypotheses suitable for testing by models borrowed from the
natural sciences. The idea was that knowledge would accumulate slowly but systematically, to the point at which sociologists could speak with authority about human behavior. Yet
the victory for a social science based on a normal science of
data collection and hypothesis testing was always more ap-
parent than real, for the most interesting work in the field
tended to remain ambiguous toward both science and the humanities.[19] Robert Merton himself illustrates the point. Although a consistent advocate for middle-range theorizing,
Merton was nonetheless rather ambivalent toward the natural
science model; indeed, ambivalence was one of his favorite
concepts.[20] Recognizing that sociology "oscillates" between
the humanities and the sciences, Merton noted that "only a
few sociologists adapt to these pressures by acting wholly the
scientific role . . . or the humanistic one."[21] Although he is well
known for his work in the sociology of science, Merton's sty-
listic brilliance, copious references to literary sources, and love
of irony and paradox make him a first-rate humanitarian. If we
consider the subtext (the way Merton presented himself) over
the text (his arguments for sociology as a science), the influence
of the literary model is undeniable: Merton's references are
to very old sources, such as Francis Bacon; his footnotes are
in literary, not scientific, form; and he published his books with
leading New York houses. In postwar America, the best of
scientific sociology was also humanistic at heart.

Because of its ambivalent status between the sciences and
the humanities, sociology is also ambivalent in its manner of
presenting its findings. In the sciences, as Merton has shown,

knowledge accumulates in such a way that what were mind-boggling problems to mathematicians or logicians in an earlier period become the subject matter of introductory exercises in contemporary textbooks. Hence, since only very recent work tends to be cited in scholarly production, scientific findings usually are reported in journal articles—premised upon relatively quick publication followed by relatively quick obsolescence. In the humanities, by contrast, older works are not only cited frequently but are often held to embody a wisdom beyond the reach of contemporary scholars. Given the longer expected life of the ideas involved, books—which are designed to be more permanent and more easily obtainable from shelves (as opposed to being stored on microfilm)—become the obvious mode of publication.[22] A thoroughly scientized sociology would, like the natural sciences, develop an almost exclusively article culture; yet the fact is that sociology, even to this day, has a book culture as well.[23]

Sociology's two cultures are vastly different from one another, and each claims more in common with neighborly disciplines than with others in the same discipline. They often have little to do with each other, clustering themselves in different kinds of universities and promoting careers in different ways. Yet the very fact that each culture is associated with a particular kind of university in a particular location suggests a certain arbitrariness in the way sociology is practiced. Sociology's fate, as Kai Erikson has written, is to have no permanent home:

Sociologists occupy a kind of border territory, positioned between the holdings of historians and literary critics, say, who often use language to reach out to larger audiences, and the holding of economists and statisticians who circulate material to one another written (if that is the right word) in a species of code. To the first set of neighbors we look inelegant; to the second we look inexact.[24]

Given the subject that sociology studies—human beings, who live simultaneously in the worlds of nature, culture, and mind—such bifurcated ways of doing and presenting research, however awkward, are also somewhat understandable.

It would be a mistake for the social sciences to lose their

ambivalent status. Their task is to develop a way of knowing that, on the one hand, grounds knowledge in something more than rhetorical argument and, on the other hand, recognizes that the truths so obtained are tentative and even transitory. The something on which knowledge can be grounded is the human subject, for human beings exist in the real world, have capacities that define what is special about them, and can be understood once those capacities are recognized and appreciated. But the truths obtained must be tentative because what is special and unique about human beings is their capacity to interpret, and thereby change, the rules that govern what they do. Because the subjects we investigate "talk back" to us, their behavior requires what Anthony Giddens calls a "double hermeneutic," since the subjects of study already exist in a "pre-interpreted" world.[25] The techniques, methodologies, and epistemologies of the social sciences must be as distinctive as the subjects they study.

How, then, ought we to do social science if we are to remain faithful to the interpretative capacities of the subjects we study? The question cannot be ignored, but it cannot be answered too literally, as if there were one way, and one way only, to do social science. Recognizing the particular capacities of human subjects leads to at least three general injunctions: (1) we ought to develop multiple methodologies because the people we study have multiple characteristics; (2) we ought to be committed to a form of sociological realism, because once one dismisses other animal species or machines as analogous to humans, real humans are all one has left; and (3) we ought to understand and take seriously our calling as social scientists, because we, like the people we study, are ultimately responsible for what we do.

Methodological Pluralism

In the ever present struggle to represent reality, academic disciplines traditionally begin by putting methodology first and the real world second. Those who would use the tools of the natural sciences to describe human social behavior already know, even before looking at the behavior they plan to observe, how it should best be studied. There are certain tools that have been perfected by the natural sciences. These tools—the experimental method, the verification of hypotheses, the accumulation of data, the interlinking of confirmed propositions into a theory about the world—are what define science, rather than the world that the scientist seeks to understand. The facts of the social world are there waiting to be discovered, but it is more the search than the discovery that stimulates the intellectual juices. Indeed, once found, the facts often turn out to be trivial or boring. To practice social science on the basis of assumptions gleaned from the study of nature is to spend far more time learning method than learning content.

The application of rhetorical technique to the social sciences also puts method in the foreground and examines real-world behavior as an afterthought. Rhetorical analysis is concerned primarily with the techniques used to persuade an audience and only secondarily—if at all—with actual discoveries of fact. From a rhetorical perspective, real-world facts are not so much trivial as they are slippery. In some accounts, they have no real existence at all but are instead the construction of the investigator, who, knowingly or unknowingly, is engaged in a struggle for power with his or her audience. To practice social science from a rhetorical perspective is to spend far more time examining how the world is presented than how it actually is.

There is a long-standing debate in the social sciences—one that parallels the division between science and the humanities—regarding the predictability of human behavior. Some social scientists claim that human behavior is constant and therefore can be predicted; others argue that humans are so unpredictable that their affairs can never achieve the regularity needed by science. Both positions miss the point. Humans live in both nature and culture. They possess qualities of mind but do not always use those qualities. The first task of any social science investigation is to gain a sense of the degree to which the individuals one is studying have accepted their world as given by nature or culture or have made the world around them through mind. The social sciences need a methodology for determining which methodology is appropriate.[26] There can be no fixed methodology for the social sciences, because there can be no fixed assumptions about human nature.

Nonetheless, a certain methodological imperialism runs rampant in the social sciences, and from all sides. Those who argue from positivistic premises usually share a commitment to a certain kind of methodology, even if they are pluralistic with respect to theory. Walter Wallace, for example, has attempted to provide an eclectic theoretical overview of all contemporary schools of sociology, in the belief that a latent consensus exists among them. Wallace's reach is broad: he finds common ground not only among Marxists, Parsonians, symbolic interactionists, and neofunctionalists but also between sociobiologists and ethologists. But if his theoretical range is inclusive, his methodological focus is exclusive. When he turns to methodological questions, consequently, Wallace looks only at techniques borrowed from the natural sciences. None of the objections to the appropriateness of such techniques for the study of human behavior strikes him as convincing.[27]

Those who dissent from the positivistic consensus also—ultimately—adhere to a monistic methodology. Herbert Blumer, whose conception of sociology as embodying "symbolic interactionism" is probably closest to the emphasis I have been making on human beings as interpreting creatures, has little positive to say about methods borrowed from positivistic conceptions of science. According to Blumer, the use of concepts and methods from the natural sciences imposes a kind of "captivity" on the researcher, from which he ought to be "released." Only a close "inspection" of the real situations in which people find themselves, Blumer argues, constitutes an empirical science. Scientific approaches are a "travesty on methodology," generating techniques that "are grossly inadequate on the simple ground that they deal with only a limited aspect of the full act of scientific inquiry." Techniques borrowed from the natural sciences might supplement Blumer's emphasis on symbolic interactionism, but he never specifies how. What begins as an effort toward methodological pluralism winds up polarizing "rather sharply the opposition between naturalistic inquiry, in the form of exploration and inspection, and the formalized type of inquiry so vigorously espoused in current methodology.''[28]

All forms of methodological monism reduce human beings to one of their capacities or another. Either they are organisms essentially similar to all other living organisms, as they are in Wallace's view, or what characterizes them is always and everywhere their irreducible need to make sense out of the situations they are in, as in Blumer's account. Yet whether human beings act as predictably as honeybees or are so idiosyncratic that no science can chart their affairs is not an a priori but an empirical question. Even sociobiology does not argue that all living organisms act in similar ways; some species can symbolize and others cannot, and among those fifteen or so species believed to be capable of imitation and learning, relative abilities vary.[29] Nor does it follow that the capacity to use mind to shape both culture and nature is a given, as if the development of modernity automatically produces autonomous individuals capable of mindful action. There is clearly a historical relationship between the kind of subject one studies and the way one studies it; modern people, in general, are more likely to use their minds than people living in traditional society (and perhaps more than the post-modern selves who come after them). Still, on some occasions very modern people will act instinctively and unthinkingly. To argue that mind is always and invariably present is to negate what is important about mind.

Human behavior is never the product only of nature, of culture, or of mind. In the interactions among them, three general parameters of human action can be discovered. To the degree that human beings struggle for mere existence, their behavior, like that of other animal species, will be more or less amenable to a natural science such as biology. (Or, to consider the world of machines, to the degree that people adapt their behaviors to the computers around them, they would be appropriate subjects for the sciences that explain those computers.) To the degree that human beings exist closer to the cultural world, by contrast, their behavior will be best charted by a combination of physical and cultural science—in the fashion, for example, of Durkheimian sociology or *fin de siècle* anthropology. And to the degree that human beings liberate themselves from the constraints of both nature and culture, in the process using their minds to alter the rules that govern what they do, an understanding of their behavior requires more of an interpretative science.

Some combination of methodologies will in most cases be necessary to understand human behavior in all its forms. There is no reason to denounce methodologies borrowed from the natural sciences on the grounds that people are never predictable. Sometimes their behavior is very predictable. They do tend to vote in ways that one can anticipate. Reduce their income, and they will most likely be less generous toward strangers. Put them in crowded jail cells with little hope for release, and they may act like rats in a cage. Remove socialization, and biology may well become more important. Understood as one methodology among many—appropriate for particular circumstances if not for others—the traditional techniques of science have an important role to play in the social sciences. Unfortunately for those who would model social science on the natural sciences, that role is not only limited but also becomes more irrelevant as society becomes more and more modern, if modernity is understood as the ability of people to understand the world around them. The flaw in positivist conceptions of social science is the belief that the more societies rely on natural science, the more its tools can be borrowed by the human sciences. The relationship is actually the other way around.

In a similar way, there is little or no reason for adherents to a positivistic conception of social science to rule out hermeneutical approaches. Even if most people's behavior is in general predictable, science still should seek to understand those who deviate from the statistical norm. Surely, any insight that one might gain by applying the methodological tools of the natural sciences to a social phenomenon could be deepened and improved by an accompanying "thick description" of particular cases.[30] What kind of science can possibly result when the assumptions that govern its view of its subject are simplistic, the tools used to gather evidence are partial, and the theoretical perspective into which the findings are to be incorporated ignores the special features of the subject under investigation? Self-referential sciences are only partially appropriate to subjects that possess culture. Cultural sciences—especially those committed to strong versions of structuralism, which attribute little importance to human agency—are only partially appropriate to subjects that possess mind. When both nature and culture loosen their grip, hermeneutical methods provide the straightest road to a human science.[31]

A commitment to methodological pluralism makes the demand that social science not be formulaic. It makes little sense to study phenomena in the real world by developing a tight research design that, to achieve presumed scientific validity, takes all the imagination out of doing social research. The predictability of much "scientific" social science is generally matched, however, by the formulaic quality of much "rhetorical" social science, which also applies its own pre-experiential methods to the study of social reality. If the social sciences are to be neither science nor rhetoric, their methodology has to be open-ended and multiple. There is nothing wrong, and a good deal right, about studying the same thing from many methodological standpoints. To the scientists, the results will be untrustworthy because they cannot be replicated. To the rhetoricians, some of the methodology will smack of positivism. But because neither alone can grasp the complexity of real human beings in all their biological, cultural, and mindful complexity, both together will have to suffice.

Avoiding furious battles for the soul of the social sciences, methodological pluralism picks and chooses from all contending parties, depending on circumstance and situation. Driven by subject rather than method, such choices will tell us something about the world we want to understand. Methods borrowed from the natural sciences will dominate when people are not using the powers of mind that modernity makes available. Hermeneutic methods will dominate when people's interpretative capacities are at their fullest. In this way, the social sciences as disciplines will be intimately linked with society as a subject, the one telling us what the other requires, and vice versa.

Sociological Realism

Methodological pluralism is rooted in the idea that the social scientist must begin with real-world facts and then develop the appropriate methodology for understanding them. But are there real-world facts? Anyone who argues from a "realist" position tends to be on the defensive in a post-modern epistemological atmosphere marked by skepticism toward such grandiose claims.[32] But my argument for realism is a minimalist one, based on the distinction between the human and other species, both natural and artificial. In the real world, I have been arguing, there are some chunks of reality that possess interpretative capabilities and others that do not. It then follows that one should try to determine which kind of subject one wants to study, and how that subject is acting and thinking, before deciding which methodology is appropriate to understanding it. Rather than methodology first and reality second, this way of proceeding would put a slice of reality first and tailor its methodology afterward.

The term *realism* not only has a philosophical meaning but is also used in a political sense—as the opposite of idealism. A "realist" is one who, in deciding between strategic alternatives, takes the world as given. Statesmen are realists to the degree that they accept human nature as they believe it is. They ask what is in their own and their opponents' interest, not what is right or ethical according to some impartial standard of justice. Although there need not be any relationship between these two meanings of the term, some thinkers embody them both. Max Weber was one, Raymond Aron another.

To be an appropriate science for the humans it would study, the social sciences have to be realistic in both senses of the term. But if the belief in philosophical realism can be weak, premised only on the assumption that some chunks of reality possess mind while others do not, the belief in a political form of realism ought to be strong. Once one drops the assumption that human behavior can be modeled on the study of rats, pigeons, or computers, there are no appropriate subjects left for a human science except humans. Social scientists have to understand people as they really are, because people as they really are are the only things social scientists can study.

The best social science, therefore, is inevitably marked by a commitment to realism that is similar to the *realpolitik* of a great statesman. Such realism has usually been associated with the ethnographic tradition in the social sciences—a tradition especially under attack from post-modernism's suspicion of authorial omnipotence. Ethnography prides itself on understanding people as they really are, not as we would like them to be. Such realism is closely aligned with a "debunking" tendency in modern sociology, a tendency to look at the "realities" hidden behind official rationales, platitudes, and spaces. For this reason, the sociology of the professions has long had a realistic dimension, since professionals are usually defined by their formal commitments to codes that are often violated in practice.[33] Also influenced by realism is what used to be called "deviant behavior," for merely by calling attention to problems that society generally prefers to ignore, the social scientist plays a realistic role. Studies of crime, for example, are grist for the realist's mill, rarely better exemplified than in Jack Katz's indictment of criminologists for not understanding why crime is pleasurable to the criminal.[34] Even the perception of crime so drastically changes the way in which people live that only an observer sensitive to the silent codes of dress, deportment, and language can obtain a realistic picture of urban life at the present time.[35]

Few sociological careers have better illustrated this commitment to realism than that of Herbert Gans.[36] At a time when white ethnic cultures were barely understood, Gans painted a vivid picture of Italian life in Boston.[37] A few years later, when it was common among intellectuals to denounce as tacky and inhuman the newly built suburbs that sprouted in the years after World War II, it took Gans to discover that inside those little houses were not conforming dupes spawned by an abstraction called "mass society" but real people struggling with the dilemmas of real life.[38] Finally, in his recent account of "middle American individualism," Gans continues to bring real people face to face with the prejudices that intellectuals and academics often have against them.[39] Reflecting on the methodology that he used in *The Urban Villagers*, Gans concluded that he did not carry out a "scientific study" in Merton's sense of the term. His goal, rather, was "to get close to the realities of social life."[40] The juxtaposition is what is most interesting here—assuming, as it does, that what is realistic is not necessarily scientific and vice versa, as if a science of human behavior could be based on something other than the real world.

Given this juxtaposition, it is perhaps not surprising that realism actually has a number of opponents in contemporary social science. The reasons advanced are generally of two kinds: theoretical and political.

C. Wright Mills made his reputation through his criticisms of theory and method that were divorced from reality.[41] Much of what he says about abstracted empiricism and grand theory is still relevant, even if the matters to which it need be applied have changed. Rational choice theory, which has its origins in biology as well as in economics, is one theory-driven approach to the social sciences that is primarily concerned with modeling behavior according to certain assumptions and only occasionally with testing those assumptions against real-world behavior. In James Coleman's view, for example, there are two significant kinds of actors: natural actors, or persons, and corporate actors, or organizations. The assumption that both will act to maximize utility ignores many "deviations from rationality," such as, in Coleman's terms, "weakness of will, precommitment, preference reversals with changes in proximity, failure to meet the criterion of independence from irrelevant alternatives, and others." This failure to account for the reality of the self in the empirical world represents a "central weakness of a theory based on rational action."[42] But Coleman is convinced that the problem is not as important as critics have made it out to be. On the one hand, "the theoretical predictions made here will be substantially the same whether the actors act precisely according to rationality as commonly conceived or deviate in the ways that have been observed."[43] On the other hand, we can imagine the internal structure of actors by generalizing back from corporate actors to natural persons in ways that will enable us to develop a more complete view of the self. Coleman's understanding of the self actually resembles a self-recurring computer rather than a flesh-and-blood person: "The receptor, linkage, and actuator constitute a kind of control system, and the perfect purposive actor could also be described as an optimal control system."[44] Determined to solve the problem of deviations from the model of rationality as a thought experiment, Coleman never considers providing an ethnographic account of real people living in conditions of real life.

If theoretical interests were not enough of an obstacle to understanding real-world people in all their complexity, there are also political ones. While social theory and politics always overlap, there are differences between them, and the most important of those differences involves the question of realism. To be true to social science, one must suspend judgment about how people ought to be and first consider how they are. But to be a political activist, one necessarily wants to overcome people as they really are and make them into people as one wants them to be. Just as methodologists put an approach first and consider reality secondarily, political activists have a theory of human nature to which reality has to be adjusted. Conservatives think of people as inherently limited, whereas radicals tend to view them as essentially good. But both believe what they want to believe about people and fail to consider people as they actually are. That is why social scientists can be political but can never let their politics substitute for their commitment to social science.

A commitment to realism cuts across the existing right-left dimension that characterizes political attitudes. Conservatism, for example, was once almost synonymous with realism, but no longer. Contemporary conservatives yearn for a world that no longer exists, lamenting, in the process, the fact that real-world people have not only made their compromises with modernity but sometimes find it appealing. Women are unlikely to leave the workplace, even if families could afford it, stop having abortions, and devote full-time to their families, no matter how vigorously conservatives urge them to do so. To be a realist is to accept the fact that gender relations have changed precisely because people have minds as well as bodies and that, once changed, they are never again likely to be the same. Conservatives who demand legislation requiring parental approval for abortions, in appealing to an imagined family structure, are much the same as post-modernists calling for androgynous social arrangements; the one demand is as unreal as the other. If liberals often have a hard time believing that people can be racist or inegalitarian, conservatives refuse to believe that homosexuals will not go away, secularism is here to stay, most people have minds of their own, and modernity survives because most people find it beneficial. It is precisely because conservatives have lost touch with realism that their proposals often seem so radical.

But radicals and leftists also have difficulty accepting realism. At first glance, this seems surprising, since being able to accept the real world, even in all its unpleasantness, is a prelude for changing it, which is perhaps why Marx and Engels understood themselves as realists (and why they liked novelists such as Balzac). Yet many on the left seem unwilling even to acknowledge unwanted realities for fear that to admit their existence is to accept their inevitability. This is a particular problem for many sociologists, who generally lean toward the left in their personal politics. To the degree that sociologists understand themselves as critics and dissenters from society as it is, realism seems just another term for reaction. A book like Jonathan Rieder's *Canarsie*, which allows its subjects to express a point of view that most sociologists would find racist and repugnant, exemplifies sociological realism at its best; but it remains, for many sociologists, an uncomfortable book. Critics of the book confuse the messenger with the message, objecting because Rieder did not confront his subjects with their politically incorrect attitudes—as if the task of sociology were to create a world other than the one that exists, rather than understanding the world we have. Even as sophisticated a realist as Herbert Gans was disturbed by Rieder's book, wishing the author to be "less the dutiful ethnographer" and more the "systematic" analyst of the causes of what he found.[45]

For those who see sociology as a way of taking the side of the underdog, realism is treacherous, a dangerous, lurking presence that will, if we are not careful, seduce us into a false complacency. In developing what she calls "a feminist sociology," Dorothy Smith argues that the everyday world is "problematic": "we cannot understand how it is organized or comes about by remaining within it." Instead, we have to shift our attention from the world of everyday practices to the world of discourse. Ethnography can never stop with the real world but only can begin there. "The ethnographic process of inquiry is one of exploring further into those social, political, and economic processes that organize and determine the actual bases of experience of those whose side we have taken." And if realism is dangerous, so is sociology, for it too is, in Smith's phrase, "part of the ruling apparatus."[46] Realism in general and sociological realism in particular are epiphenomenal. What really counts are structures of power, and we need to work through the real world to find them. In imagining how her subjects ought to be, the sociologist deprives them of their own imaginative capacities—failing to understand, for instance, a subject who chooses to imagine herself in roles—such as loving mother, wife, or homemaker—that the sociologist believes inauthentic because inscribed in power. By contrast, realistic feminist ethnographers should, as one of them put it, "learn to respect and understand some of the social appeals of widespread nostalgia for eroding family forms" characteristic of the political movements they otherwise oppose.[47]

The denial of reality is strongest among those influenced by post-modernism. If reality is little more than the arguments one makes about reality, one can always look elsewhere, beyond the text of everyday life, endlessly deconstructing what appears to be until finally one is satisfied that the imperfections have been removed. Pauline Rosenau has shown why post-modernist assumptions, so attractive in the humanities, are of more limited appeal to social scientists.[48] The reason surely is that, taken to its logical conclusion, post-modernism leaves no real social facts to be discovered or analyzed. Any particular social fact could illustrate the point, but the one that is most salient is the fact of difference. For the sociologist, borders, boundaries, and divisions are the heart of the matter; people are organized, or organize themselves, by time, space, ethnicity, race, age, gender, taste, status, and any one of a number of relevant sociological categories.[49] For the post-modernist, difference is suspect. Distinctions and boundaries are artificial.

Socially constructed, they can be deconstructed. A product of power, they can be abolished by power. The task becomes one of imagining worlds, or at least trying to develop public policies, where difference is no longer invidious.[50] Sociology tends toward exclusion, since groups usually develop their identity by keeping others out. Post-modern thought tends toward inclusion, the incorporation of the other as no longer foreign and strange. An imagined world without distinctions may be more fair and more just, but, from a sociological standpoint, it is also likely to be less interesting and less richly textured. With post-modernism, we reach the pole that is diametrically opposite sociology's long fascination with the real world.[51]

Despite pressures that derive from theoretical or political premises, sociology must be a realistic science. When we prejudge people's actions and beliefs—by approaching them with a predetermined methodology or a predetermined set of political attitudes—we fail to give them the benefit of what makes them human: the capacity to interpret the world in their own ways. The only check we have on the tendency for either our theories or our politics to run wild is an obligation to turn to the real world from time to time to see where we are. The people we find in the real world are unlikely to give full support for any theoretical or political position advanced in their name. Their motives are likely to be mixed, conforming neither to the dictates of rational self-interest nor to an automatic recognition of the claims of other people. And their politics will rarely be as decisive as the politics of those studying them; therefore, any effort to substitute our politics for theirs becomes not only bad social science but also, in the long run, bad politics. To be a sociological realist is to recognize that people are neither perfect nor imperfect, neither biologically determined nor socially created, neither embedded in structures nor free of constraint, neither predictable nor idiosyncratic. What makes them real is precisely that they resist monistic assumptions—whether methodological, theoretical, or political—of who and what they are.

Social Science as a Vocation

Neither the scientific nor the rhetorical approach to social science has an adequate understanding of the obligations of those doing social research. Just as the subjects one studies are not very interesting if one knows in advance which methodologies or political attitudes are appropriate to them, the person who studies them is not very interesting if that person follows formulaic conventions without much regard for his or her own interpretative qualities. Being true to the human subject requires taking seriously not only the people one studies but also one's method of studying them.

The scientific model that became so attractive for sociologists in the years after World War II never did generate the patient accumulation of facts upon which complex theories could be built. Surely, part of the reason, as I have argued throughout this book, is that, in borrowing models from the study of other than human species, much of scientific social science failed to understand its own subject. But whatever the reason for its failure, the scientific model did possess one significant advantage, which may explain why it continued to live. Under the scientific model, the rules suggesting how social scientists were expected to comport themselves in their professional work were fairly clear. Unlike earlier thinkers (in America, sociology developed as an explicitly moralistic substitute for Protestant theology), scientific sociologists would be circumspect about injecting their own values into their scholarship.[52] Instead of writing books for general audiences, which any good journalist could do as well, they would subject themselves to the hard discipline of peer review, submitting articles for publication in journals that would be read—anonymously— by impersonal judges concerned only with fidelity to agreed-upon standards.[53] Decisions about hiring, promotion, and tenure would be based not on what Parsons dismissed as affective and subjective criteria associated with premodern *Gemeinschaft* communities but, instead, on the universalistic judgments of the "invisible college" and its standards. (The Parsonian scheme—stressing affective neutrality over affectivity, universalism over particularism, achievement over ascription, specificity over diffuseness, and collectivity orientation over self-orientation—may not have been an adequate description of how sociologists understood the world, but it was undoubtedly an accurate description of how professional sociologists wanted the world to understand them.)

The scientific model may not, finally, have taught all that much about social reality, but it did deal extremely well with the reality of who social scientists were and what they aspired to be. Its set of rules for professional behavior enabled its practitioners to resolve some exceptionally awkward questions about what social scientists, as opposed to social science, ought to do. Social scientists could attempt to be objective, even if social science could not. Social scientists could follow well-known rules, even if reality did not. Methodological debates involved the behavior of practitioners, not the nature of the social world. A model of science as a profession was far more appealing to American social scientists than a model of science as an epistemology.

Nonetheless, the inability of the scientific model to generate significant new increments in social knowledge created a void in which at least some have been tempted toward a post-modern response—asserting that no one reality exists outside of the efforts of observers to describe it. But if epistemological assumptions structure not only how we try to comprehend reality but also how we establish standards of professional comportment, what would be the consequences of a post-modern understanding of professional obligations? Can one retain one's belief in the neutrality of knowledge—and continue to respect the relatively dispassionate, value-free professional code based on this belief—if knowledge itself is understood to be so slippery as to be almost beyond grasp? If we can no longer be sure which practices are "deviant" and which "straight," if norms are contingent and contextual rather than universal, if the self is little else than a series of presentations, then an entire structure of professional obligations based on the assumption that what validates academic inquiry is an adequate description of social reality becomes difficult to maintain.

There may well be dangers in practicing the post-modernism one might be tempted to preach.[54] If there is no real social world whose laws can be understood, there is no way to judge whether any social scientist has a better understanding of the world than any other. The academic enterprise is essentially concerned with making distinctions; yet distinctions themselves are suspect from post-modern assumptions. Unable to make judgments and distinctions based on merit, since merit would likely be dismissed as a construction through which some try to obtain domination over others, universities would have to resort to other criteria for making judgments about appointments, publication, and tenure. Such criteria would include politics, on the grounds that all knowledge is tainted by politics in any case. It might include the background of the scholar, if one believes that those who have been excluded from dominant ways of knowing "can provide the grounds for a less distorted understanding of the world around us."[55] A vocation organized by post-modern assumptions would not recognize social science as an autonomous way of knowing. Sociology would be another form of politics, just as for the positivists sociology was another form of science.

Both those who would model sociology on the natural sciences and those who would turn toward post-modern epistemologies have an insufficient understanding of what the vocation of a scholar demands. When sociology modeled its professional standards on the practices of physical scientists, its practitioners believed, even if incorrectly, that they could count on reality to help them out: ideas would be proven by hypothesis testing or they would not. Because it was reality that was believed to hold the secrets, the observer of reality played an essentially passive role. The multiple authorship and jargon-laden language of scientific sociology—represented in the side of sociology that sought publication in journal articles—symbolized the impersonal and antibiographical nature of the quest for truth. Good writing was unimportant, since nature wrote and the scientist merely transcribed what nature had in mind. No strong theory of vocational conduct was necessary because it finally did not matter what the sociologist did or did not do; reality itself would determine what happened in the world.

Although practitioners of the new post-modern epistemologies disdain positivistic science, their understanding of the scholar's vocation is essentially the same. Since reality can never help us out, since the whole quest to discover laws of the real world can only uncover the rhetorical strategies by which its investigators frame their arguments, attention shifts from the world to the observer of the world. But such a point of view attaches no particular importance to the observer, since texts take on their own dynamics, irrespective of the intentions or desires of their authors. The death of the author means the death of the sociologist as author. There need not be any conception of the right way to carry out one's vocational duties if one has no autonomy, no selfhood, no authorship. Not surprisingly, therefore, although post-modernists tend to publish books rather than articles, their books contain the same jargon-filled prose and "authorless" quality found in scientific journal articles. In both cases, research writes itself, making irrelevant any notion that observers of the world have any particular responsibility when carrying out their observations.

Sociological realists and methodological pluralists, who cannot find satisfactory rules of conduct in either scientific or rhetorical approaches, have to resurrect the notion of an authorial responsibility that is missing in both. Because the sociologist cannot allow the nature of the world to solve problems of conduct for her, she, as author, has to solve them herself. Skepticism toward epistemological assumptions demands faith in professional standards. An understanding that social reality is colored by politics must be accompanied by a search to understand reality that is divorced from politics. The more one appreciates interpretation, the less one can rely on algorithmic models that focus on information, not meaning. Post-modernism, for those who like it, comes with a price: if we allow the content of what we do to be influenced by post-modernism, we must resist allowing the form by which we do it to be similarly influenced. Indeed, the case can be put even more strongly. Precisely because we can no longer be convinced that there is a relatively uncomplicated social reality out there to be measured and described, we need even more to have deeply entrenched professional standards by which we go about conducting our business.

Because social scientists, in trying to understand the world, are also trying to understand themselves as part of the world, the subject and object of social investigation are difficult to distinguish. If humans have no special capacities of interpretation, then social scientists—who are also human—lack them as well. Thinkers like Niklas Luhmann, who imagine the world in completely self-referential terms, allow little room for autonomous social scientists because there is little room for autonomous selves of any sort. But if the concern of the social sciences is with chunks of reality that possess mind, then included within that chunk of reality are social scientists themselves. An adequate theory of the human subject can never be developed if it stops short of including those who study and write about other humans.

Is Sociology Necessary?

Although they once regarded their profession as the queen of the sciences, sociologists are no longer certain that they have anything to offer the world. Surely, the tendency to borrow from elsewhere—to turn to the sciences and then to the humanities, to economics and then political science—reflects an intellectual insecurity quite at odds with the assertive, often imperial, tone of Comte and Durkheim. The longer sociology has been in existence, the less it seems to know what it wants to do—a state of affairs that seems to vindicate those who believe that sociology is little more than jargon in the first place.

In the 1960s, sociology was a booming business; today there are some who question whether sociology is any longer necessary. It was, after all, a field that established itself not only late but also with some difficulty, since conservative elites in both Germany and France viewed sociology as little different from socialism.[56] With the dramatic turn against socialism that started in the 1980s, a turn against sociology would also become inevitable.[57] And to the degree that any anthropocentric assumptions have been challenged by the emerging worldviews described in this book, the case for a distinct science for the human species seems even more problematic. An intellectual milieu that distrusts utopianism and is simultaneously attracted to antihumanism is not one in which sociology is going to flourish.

One response to this state of affairs would be to proclaim the death of sociology, to view its classic objectives as overtaken by developments in neighboring fields. This is essentially what both the scientific and the rhetorical turns imply, the one absorbing sociology into biology and physics, the other into argumentation and textual analysis. But it is also possible to view sociology's ambivalence as a sign of strength—an indication of the need for a mature science to stand on its own feet, accept its own subject matter, and develop its own methodology, irrespective of whether what it does conforms to the epistemological and ontological views of others. In that sense, the challenge to sociology that emerges from events in the real world, as well as from developments in the realm of thought, forces sociology back to its origins.

Both science and rhetoric tend not to lead back to origins such as classic texts, founding documents, or significant statements. It is a hallmark of science to ignore works written long ago, no matter how important for their time, on the grounds that new knowledge is always the most relevant knowledge. It is a hallmark of contemporary literary criticism to treat classic texts iconoclastically, as if their appearance were a matter of contingency and luck. Because sociology is concerned— some would say obsessed—with its founding classics, it is, once more, different from both science and rhetoric.[58] In their location between the sciences and the humanities, in their attempt to discover a science of the human between the world of god and the world of nature, in their effort to find a place between the sacred and the profane, the classic thinkers in the sociological tradition broke new ground. Whatever has changed since, the ground is firm enough to provide the footing necessary for a distinct science for a distinct subject to walk forward.

But it has to be a walk, not a run. To practice a social science that recognizes its subjects as interpretative creatures in the real world means learning to live with ambiguity. The social scientist, as Thomas Scheff has argued, will practice "being a jack-of-all-trades, as well as an expert in a particular field."[59] Such a social science will present itself in many ways. It will publish its findings in both book and article form. Its methodology will be inherently pluralistic, borrowing from the biological and cultural sciences while stressing social science as a distinct way of knowing. It will accept the existence of a real world, but not in a strong sense and never in the sense that what is found in the real world settles all epistemological and moral issues. Its conception of a calling will be rooted in its belief that the social scientist lives in the same world as those he or she studies. This is not a formula for certainty; it does not imply that social science can unlock the secrets of human beings. But it is a formula for a more realistic social science— one that, in rejecting both science and rhetoric as its proper model, meets the human beings it presumes to understand more than halfway.

Chapter Seven

Society on Its Own Terms

Competing Metaphors

It is impossible to capture the complexity and interconnectedness of human society without metaphors. One in particular—the image of the web—has dominated not only social theory but also the literary and scientific texts with which it has been linked. The web, as Steven Marcus has written, "is to be found almost everywhere. It is prominently there in the later Dickens, it is all over the place in George Eliot, particularly in *Middlemarch*, and it figures centrally for Darwin in *The Origin of Species*. It forms as it were the underlying structural conception of sociology, which regards society as a web of relations."[1] Its popularity has continued in this century: Robert MacIver spoke of the "web" of government, Georg Simmel of the "web" of group affiliations, and Clifford Geertz of man living in webs of significant symbols.[2]

Existing somewhere between science and literature and the sacred and profane, social science has looked both to nature and to culture to develop metaphors for human action. Webs are thus appropriate; spiders spin them, and humans make them. But if the metaphor of the web remains ubiquitous, it has been supplemented, and in many cases superseded, by terms that have far more explicitly cultural connotations. The most famous metaphor of all—Max Weber's iron cage—conveys the very opposite of the natural: a technological artifact designed by humans to keep wild nature contained. Even those who find the iron cage too tragic and pessimistic an image for modernity nonetheless rely on cultural rather than natural terms. The weave is not the same as the web, whatever linguistic origins the two terms may share, for the one refers to an explicit human artifact while the other is ambiguous. To speak, therefore, as Louis Wirth does, of cities as having "woven diverse areas, peoples, and activities into a cosmos," suggests the importance of culture.[3] So do numerous references to other artifacts, such as a "fabric," "tapestry," or "mosaic" made by the efforts of the people who constitute it.[4] This shift in metaphor from nature to culture has implications for how social scientists think about modern society. From a biological perspective, the world creates us; from a cultural perspective, we create the world. The change from one to the other thereby suggests a greater willingness to understand social institutions as the products of people's own intentional actions.

Rugs, mosaics, and fabrics hold a particular metaphorical significance for social scientists, not only because they are made but also because they are made out of patterns. The task of the social scientist is to find the order in the pattern, as Talcott Parsons did with his discovery of "pattern variables" believed to be present in all forms of social organization. To be sure, Parsons would be criticized because of his emphasis on well-ordered, always harmonious, and somewhat unoriginal patterns; C. Wright Mills wrote that "what social science is properly about is the human variety, which consists of all the social worlds in which men have lived, are living, and might live." But Mills had as little doubt as Parsons that society could be understood in an orderly way, just as a rug is woven in an orderly way; for, he concluded, variety "is not as 'disorderly' as the mere listing of a small part of it makes it seem."[5]

Social scientists reach almost automatically for fabric metaphors to describe society for yet an additional reason: threads can unravel. Cloth objects are not as strong and seemingly permanent as those made out of steel or carborundum. As opposed to industrial products, which have hard-metal properties, social properties can disintegrate if not handled properly. In contrast to the legal system, bureaucratic authority, or the state, social practices—embodied in families, local community networks, and churches—have usually been described in more "feminine" terms associated with bonding and weaving.[6] The informal institutions of society create a "healing web" or a "human bond."[7] This structure is a fragile one, constantly endangered by the universalistic and legalistic institutions of a more formal welfare state; as if to indicate how natural it has become to talk this way about the social, Nathan Glazer, who makes an argument along these lines, speaks of "strengthening the natural social network."[8] Networks are yet one more metaphor for understanding human ties. Such networks may not be "natural" in the sense of found in nature, but when they work properly, they appear "natural" in the sense that we do not pay explicit attention to them.[9]

Whatever the differences between all these metaphors, it is likely that a newer one will increasingly come to be used in the analysis of modern society. We are now more aware than ever of the fragility—indeed, the possible extinction—of the natural world. When this sense of natural fragility is linked to the notion that the threads that make society possible are also in danger of unraveling, it is inevitable that we will rely more on ecological understandings of social institutions and how they function. Yet a term like *social ecology*, by referring to both the world of nature and the world of culture, begs the question of which kind of ecology it is: discovered or invented, spontaneous or planned, running down or building up. Too literal an application of naturalistic metaphors for understanding modern society may not be especially helpful when the most important dimensions of modernity are cultural and mindful. As attractive an idea as ecology may be, we should not adopt the term if in so doing we were to shift our understanding of social dynamics back to nature. There are at least three reasons why.

First, none of the currently available models for understanding biological and ecological systems is appropriate for the complexities of social dynamics. The notion that the natural ecology will always find its own self-regulating solutions has, in the theories of Herbert Spencer, already been tried as a model for human and social affairs, and without much success. Given the popularity of conservative political ideas toward the end of the twentieth century, social Darwinist ideas, this time helped by often simplistic understandings of sociobiology, have been invoked to argue for inherent inequality in gender relations.[10] Not only are such ideas often unattractive, especially to those whose affairs are now to be understood on the basis of instincts and drives, but the scientific evidence for them is controversial and disputed. Conservatism has more intellectual tools in its repertoire than borrowings from biology; we are unlikely to have to confront Spencer once again.[11]

Not all forms of social Darwinism were associated with laissez-faire; thinkers as diverse as Engels and the founders of the eugenics movement were also inspired by naturalistic metaphors. These theorists, especially those in the eugenics movement, advocated hands-on intervention into nature to ensure the survival of the fit and to limit the damage of the unfit. Eugenic metaphors, when applied to the human and social world, rationalized strong state intervention, often in the form of population control; the provision of social services; and, when necessary, the application of strong discipline. (As L. T. Hobhouse, who was both a liberal and a sociologist, put it, "Now we fully agree with the evolutionists in their main position. It is desirable that the fit should succeed and the unfit fail; we are ready to exclude the utterly unfit from society altogether by enclosing them in prison walls.")[12] But this picture, which uses nature to justify the state just as laissez-faire used nature to justify the market, is also not especially attractive. Humans are not roses in a rose garden in need of pruning. The regulation of their affairs ought to be carried out in other ways than with shears and poisons.

A second reason to be cautious about applying ecological understandings directly to the social world is that, as poorly as we understand the dynamics of the former, we probably understand them better than we do the dynamics of the latter. Ecology and biology are both recent sciences, and each has made false starts. The theories that guide research into the affairs of other species, including sociobiology and ecology, are best viewed as theories in the making. Revised frequently to take account of new insights and new research, such theories are more like theories in the social sciences than they are like theories in physics. Indeed, it has been suggested that there can be no biological theory valid across all animal species, only theories for specific species.[13] Compared to physics, biology is far from a theoretically sophisticated science.

But as young as the biological sciences may be, they are far better grounded than any theories we have about culture, mind, agency, structure, and the other aspects of human behavior that bedevil sociologists. If biologists and ecologists had made as many mistakes in predicting the effect of various changes on the environment as social policy analysts made in predicting the effects of new programs on the ecology of families or communities, we might not have a natural environment. We are in the very beginning stages of developing a distinct science for a distinct species; what we do not know about the social worlds around us is staggering. We ought to be acquiring knowledge about human institutions and practices before jumping to the conclusion that we can understand ourselves by adopting laws borrowed from the world of nature.

Third, and most important, the rigid distinction made by nineteenth- and earlier-twentieth-century theorists between nature and culture needs revision. As we have already seen, some animal ethologists and sociobiologists believe that other animal species possess the rudiments of culture. Similarly, human culture has some resemblance to the natural order. The very word *culture* comes from the verb "to cultivate," and, as Hannah Arendt has suggested, we often use the term *culture* to mean "taking care of," rather than "dominating," the world around us.[14] As Mark Sagoff notes, the natural habitats of some animal species cannot be conserved without human intervention, while the costs and benefits of human activities cannot be calculated without including effects on the natural world.[15] He argues that both preservationists, who want to protect nature against man, and conservationists, who want to protect man against nature, are increasingly irrelevant as the gap between nature and culture diminishes.

To suggest that the opposition between culture and nature is not as sharp as it once was is not, however, to suggest that the worlds of humans and other animal species are converging toward similar patterns of behavior. Neither the world of nature nor the world of culture can supply the metaphors we need to understand society, at least in its modern forms. What we learn by comparing ourselves to other species is that we have added mind to culture, just as earlier sociologists argued that we added culture to nature. If we are not roses in a rose garden, neither are we threads in a piece of cloth. The patterns that make rugs, the threads that can be spun into webs, the ties that bind, the links in a network—none of these parts of the whole possesses capacities of mind. As I have argued throughout this book, the social sciences, in trying to develop a philosophical anthropology that seeks to understand the human difference, should not look to culture per se but, instead, to the interpreting capacities of humans, which enable them to imagine alternative worlds.

In the face of serious threats to both the natural and the social worlds, we may well choose to speak of a social ecology that needs care, just as we speak of a natural one. But we will not discover the ways in which social institutions work, and therefore the kinds of care they need, by looking at how other species govern their own affairs. We cannot leave social institutions alone to grow on their own accord, nor can we cultivate them by regulating their growth in predetermined ways. Neither tame nor wild, the institutions that together constitute the social world flourish best when treated as what they are: structures that people have developed to regulate their affairs and that people themselves can change. We will never understand society properly unless we are prepared to understand it on its own terms.

What Social Institutions Are For

Toward the end of the twentieth century, social scientists began to rediscover social institutions. This rediscovery seems best understood as a response to a paradox too striking to be tolerated: just as society was increasingly being organized by large-scale companies that manufactured goods and provided services, social scientists seemed increasingly attracted to models of human behavior emphasizing the solitary character of individual decision-making. The resulting gap between the real world and theories purporting to analyze the real world became, finally, a source of some embarrassment to social scientists.

Neo-institutionalism, consequently, has become the watch-word of developments in all the social sciences. Political scientists are less content to look at individual votes, whether of citizens at the polls or legislators in legislatures, and have increasingly concerned themselves with how institutional cultures shape individual options.[16] Economists, who in general are sympathetic to models of individual decision-making, have also begun to pay more attention to the role of large-scale institutions that inhibit individual choices.[17] And sociologists, whose discipline from the start has been more receptive to the role of large-scale organizations than the other social sciences, have increasingly, in this sense, returned to their origins.[18] The rediscovery of institutions is a development to be welcomed by those interested in the human dimensions of social science, for one of the things that human beings do is to form the institutions that give their lives meaning.

Institutions themselves come in many forms; it has been argued, for example, that "a No Smoking sign is an institution."[19] Some institutions, such as a business corporation or a governmental bureau, appear relatively sturdy and permanent. Others, especially the more intimate institutions of society, such as families and communities, are usually understood as more fragile. When social scientists are tempted to think in ecological terms, they have in mind these more intimate institutions. As with the natural ecology, an important debate is taking place about the future of these fragile institutions. Many social scientists find that the microworlds of civil society are in decline, replaced by large, efficient, but also alienating structures that operate on the basis of impersonal universalism.[20] Yet at least one sociologist who has studied local neighborhoods extensively has discovered no such thing. In the worlds he investigated, people are still in contact with each other, kinship remains important, and individuals do not report high levels of loneliness and alienation.[21] The same kind of debate takes place over just about every other face-to-face social institution. Either these institutions are no longer reinforcing the moral fabric that makes society possible or they are adapting to new environments and new challenges, strengthening themselves in the process. If there is a threat to the social ecology, it surely lies here.

For this very reason, the institutions of civil society provide an especially appropriate arena for looking at why mindful metaphors are more appropriate than natural ones in trying to understand the social groupings into which human beings organize themselves. And of those microworlds of civil society, no other institution has received as much attention as the family. The family, we have been told, is in crisis, as evidenced by low birthrates, working wives, high divorce rates, latch-key children, child abandonment, and an increasing tendency to rely on governmental and legal mechanisms to carry out what were once family functions.[22] Others dispute nearly every point in this indictment, pointing out that the nuclear family of the 1950s was itself a recent invention and attributing any crisis over the family to the failure of public policy to keep up with essentially positive family developments.[23] For yet others, the family is the central question of feminism, and from a feminist perspective, one ought to examine the relations of power involved in all family forms.[24] From these latter points of view, the family as an institution is not necessarily weaker just because both parents work, or because there is only one parent, or because same-sex couples want to get married; it has simply changed its form, as all institutions always do.[25]

As different as each of these positions on the viability of the family may be, all of them have a tendency to reach, directly or indirectly, for naturalistic—and sometimes ecological—imagery. According to one set of metaphors, adhered to by the left in the nineteenth century and by the right in the late twentieth century, nature is essentially wild and consequently requires strict cultivation and regulation. Because humans are driven by instincts and desires, what they say they want must give way to what is best for them. Strong, patriarchal, traditional families are needed, from this point of view, to ensure the survival of the social order. If the individual members of the family unit are allowed to decide for themselves what they want to do—if women, for example, want to pursue a career or limit the number of children they will have—the institution will no longer serve its function.

Those who would defend social institutions against change find naturalism along these lines appealing. From their point of view, some practices, such as the nuclear family, are "natural," while others—homosexuality, for example—are not. The reason they resort to natural metaphors, it seems clear enough, is to further a political objective; for if something is natural, then efforts to change it will be futile. But natural metaphors can backfire on those who use them. If we understand families as part of a social ecology that resembles the natural ecology, then they will certainly change. The change may be slow, the consequences delayed, but there will be evolution; therefore, any particular form existing at any particular time and place will be temporary. Defenders of social institutions as they are think of themselves as traditionalists, yet tradition is a very unnatural phenomenon; there are in fact few phenomena more sociological in nature than traditions.[26] Conservative defenders of social institutions ought to be arguing from sociological premises; when they shift to biology and nature, they undermine their own position.

Those who argue that families are not in decline, and may be in the process of a certain strengthening, tend to rely on sociological premises. All particular family forms, they argue, are socially constructed, the product of particular arrangements of power and discourse. Created this way, the family can be re-created that way. Humans are malleable and adaptable, so much so that their institutions are epiphenomenal and contingent. But as important as such sociological language is in understanding rapidly changing family forms, a naturalistic set of images also comes into play among those sympathetic to family change. Sometimes these images are explicit; early radical feminism, in particular, absorbed, in Alison M. Jagger's account, " 'naturalistic' assumptions about human biology," hoping to turn them in different directions from those inherent in conservative biological accounts.[27] More commonly, such metaphors are implicit and more directly ecological. Family forms are assumed to "evolve" from one historical stage to another, and this evolution, like the natural ecology, occurs so automatically as to take on an inevitable character. Because family forms evolve progressively, to go backward, to reimpose the nuclear family and the subordinate position of women, would be as futile as trying to bring an extinct species back to life. "American families have repeatedly had to change in order to adapt to novel circumstances," two historians have written. It is therefore "futile" to worry about whether the family will survive, "nor do we need to worry obsessively about the increasing diversity of family arrangements, since ethnic, religious and economic diversity has always been a defining characteristic of American family life."[28] The ecological optimism of such passages, reminiscent of the language of nineteenth-century Spencerian laissez-faire, raises the question of whether the assumption that nature is essentially tame and will find its own harmonious resolutions if let alone to follow its own evolutionary dynamics has simply shifted from the right (and economics) in the nineteenth century to the left (and social institutions) now.

The use of naturalistic or ecological metaphors to analyze human institutions such as families is limited because human beings live not merely for reproduction but also for meaning. We cannot understand social institutions such as the family without raising the question of what they are for—what larger purpose, besides the reproduction of the species, they are to serve. Naturalistic and ecological metaphors turn us away from such concerns. Except in a functional sense, we rarely ask what the practices of other animal species are for. Darwinian theory encourages a perspective in which the answer to the question of what something is for is contained already in the terms of the theory: animals develop particular behavioral patterns or physical features in order to help their species survive efficiently. When social science models itself on natural sciences like biology, it usually adopts one or another form of such a functionalism; human practices are adopted or not adopted because of their socially reproductive consequences. From a functionalist perspective, nuclear families were explained by their success in contributing to successful social integration or by the way they seemed to "fit" the need for mobile wage labor in an industrial economy.[29] In either case, nuclear families were simply assumed to function best, with little attention paid to what values and capacities were being furthered by the family's reproduction. One of the limiting conditions of a social science borrowed from biology was its inability to evaluate institutions with respect to the specific human qualities of those who compose them. Because it could not take account of real people and their needs, especially women, functionalism predicted the continuation of one particular family form that was soon to lose its inevitable character. Understanding human families on terms borrowed from functionalist biology did not make for a good predictive science.

Functionalists are not the only ones, however, who fail to ask what families are for. The argument that families are social constructions has been enormously helpful to feminists, for it calls into question any "natural" division of labor within the family. But the argument for social construction can, in post-modern theory, take some fairly extreme forms, which also ignore the question of what a family ought to do. Not only are institutions understood as socially constructed; so are all conventions, all moralities, and all systems of ethical conduct, including, more than a few feminists have noticed, feminist values themselves.[30] When normative standards have no independent justification but represent the story told by the victor in a political struggle that has used discourse as the primary weapon, any discussion of purpose or meaning is irrelevant. Post-modern literary theories, such as those discussed in chapter 5, turn to naturalistic and mechanical understandings of the world precisely to avoid concluding that human affairs are directed toward some end. To study an institution like the family from such a post-modern perspective is finally to come to the same conclusion that one would from a functionalist perspective; in both cases, families are what families do.

In contrast to such naturalistic metaphors, a social science faithful to the meaning-producing qualities of human beings should examine social institutions as sources for the cultivation of meaning. Families are for telling stories, teaching moral lessons, ensuring that qualities of mind are developed, and imagining possible futures. They are places where members of society who have not yet developed the capacity to understand the world around them—children—develop that capacity in a trial-and-error fashion under the influence of people who feel a special and unique responsibility for them. Because familial relationships are intimate and personal, they cannot proceed on the basis of abstract and universal rules. They either take account of the specific features of each individual or they fail to work. None of this is meant to idealize families; it is well demonstrated that families are the location for a considerable amount of violence and injustice. My argument is simply that modern humans, faced with a bewildering variety of cues coming to them from biology, tradition, and their own inclinations, cannot be expected to leap into the world fully formed and ready to make decisions. Their capacities to participate as interpretative beings have to be shaped and developed, and families are among the most important institutions for so doing.

Stories about nature come in two versions, neither of which is especially appropriate to regulate a human social institution such as a family. Evolutionary ideas that stress how "natural" it is for family forms to evolve in new and unexpected ways are remarkably sanguine in the face of how difficult it is for modern families to do what our capacities as interpreting beings require that they do. Parents can, and do, ignore their responsibilities for the next generation when pressures on them are too severe. We ought to be concerned with whether people have children at all, how much time they have to spend with them, and what they do with that time. These things cannot be left to some optimistic sense that all change is necessarily for the best. One reason why leftists, who are statist in the economic sphere, are nonetheless laissez-faire in society and culture is their belief that humans are so plastic a species that there is no use cultivating their moral growth at all. But a family unconcerned with morality is not a human family.

The argument that individuals can discharge their responsibilities to the next generation by following unchanging rules determined by nature also fails to take account of what modern families ought to do. Families can be overregulated and unthinkingly strict, teaching imitation rather than imagination. When the discussion of the family is so restrictive, premised on the belief that there is only one proper family form, consequences similar to the eugenics movement will likely follow: an effort to reward "fit" families and an effort to discourage those that are "unfit." One reason that conservatives, who tend to be believers in laissez-faire in economics, are nonetheless firm statists in the cultural sphere is their belief that humans, because they are wild, are in need of trainers who understand the importance of strong discipline.

There may well be reason to find that families in modern society are fragile and worth tending. Because they are, the temptation to rely on metaphors for understanding them that are similar to the possible extinction of species or other threats to the natural ecology is strong. But if we are to pay attention to the social ecology of families—and the other institutions of civil society as well—it ought to be on the basis of metaphors that appreciate the mindful capacities of family members and the mindful tasks of family life. Only a species capable of exercising powers of interpretation can balance the two somewhat contradictory tasks modern families are called upon to perform: to carry values and moral beliefs from one generation to the next, but to do so in a way that allows moral beliefs and values to change from one generation to another. Because sex roles are not determined by biology, they can change as people themselves change. But because human beings live in social worlds that are distinct from those of all other species found in nature, their social ecology requires attention paid to the social values and moral obligations that surround them. Finding this balance—between versions of the good as either completely fixed or completely flexible—is difficult. Because it is difficult, the institutions that comprise the social ecology are under constant pressure. What makes them fragile, however, is not so much threats from the environment around them as the contradictory demands within them.

Philosophical Anthropology Revisited

The social sciences have never been able to make up their minds whether they are scientific or moral enterprises. Yet there is something problematic in either category. The notion that the social scientist can be objective and value-free, treating crime or poverty with the same detachment as a biologist treats caterpillars, seems especially naïve when knowledge has been so often used as power. Social science's pursuit of pure knowledge along the lines of the physical sciences may go down as one of the great false steps in modern intellectual history. Knowledge can be gained, data analyzed, and findings confirmed, but these activities are part of social science, not the whole. Because the social sciences study human behavior, their use of scientific procedures must reflect the characteristics of human subjects.

Yet it is equally unsatisfactory to argue that social inquiry cannot be grounded in anything at all. All too often, critics of the scientific turn in social science seem to believe that the mere assertion of an idea is sufficient to establish its validity. With the decline of the scientific model, social science becomes advocacy for this position or that, as if volume or vehemence could be a substitute for knowledge. Under conditions such as these, social science not only loses whatever legitimacy it may have won, but its practice becomes indistinguishable from rhetoric. To the degree that they replace their belief in science with a belief in the impossibility of science, social scientists have no special claims to make or particular insights to offer. Once again, the possibility of understanding something about humans and how they act is lost.

In all likelihood, a satisfactory solution to the conflict inherent in social science will never be found. Because they concern themselves with human beings, social scientists will always have to deal with such contentious topics as meaning, morality, and purpose. But because they must aspire to something more than rhetoric, the social sciences will have to find ways to ground their conclusions in something real. The discussion of an institution as debated as the family indicates why social science is both scientific and evaluative: as social scientists, we need to understand and predict what will happen to families; but as human beings, we need to be concerned with what they do and how they do it. Moreover, the scientific and evaluative tasks are linked: those who do not understand what families are for, and who therefore fail to appreciate that families have moral and meaningful tasks, are less prepared to understand and predict their future; those who insist that they know what families must be for, but refuse to look at real families in the real world, become hectoring moralists without understanding the institution whose moral behavior they would regulate.

The scientific and evaluative aspects of social science are linked because human beings are both the subjects and the objects of social research. The laws that govern their behavior must include the possibility that they can change the laws that govern their behavior, even as those who try to formulate such laws are themselves part of the whole process. In the face of all these difficulties, the concerns of the classic thinkers in social theory with the unique characteristics of the human species—concerns that many contemporary observers consider old-fashioned and quaint, best left in the Victorian attic where they have been stored for a century—are not so peculiar after all. Philosophical anthropology was important to the founders of modern social theory because it enabled them to be scientists and moralists simultaneously.

Late-nineteenth-century social theorists understood the distinctions between humans and other species as scientific fact. Biology could provide some grounding for the social sciences because it could establish the features of human life that were not shared by others. The reliance on evolutionary models, the use of biological categories such as organic and mechanical solidarity, and the development of ecological models of cities were all efforts to establish uncontested truths about the human condition. That hope, of course, was unfounded. All too often, the moral values came first, and the search to find support in natural science followed, as the intellectual history of social Darwinism shows. Moreover, we now know that science, which itself has become an essentially contested notion, does not constitute the grounding it once did. Nonetheless, classical social theorists were struggling to find a way to be faithful both to science and to the moral features of human beings.

At the same time, reminding oneself of the distinct qualities of the human species was a way of refusing to go all the way in modeling the social sciences on the natural sciences; philosophical anthropology was a last refuge of the humanist lingering within the social scientist, expressing the realization "Wait a minute; this subject is different." If they could show that certain values are particularly associated with humans—that as a species we are rational or inherently equal or productive—then, these earlier social theorists hoped, maximizing those values would bring about social improvement. These theorists, then, were concerned not with society per se but, instead, with a vision of the good society.[31] Marx, Weber, and Durkheim, because they speculated freely about the unique qualities of humans, were moral theorists as much as they were social scientists.

Of course, a better understanding of what makes humans different from other animal species or machines will not enable us to resolve once and for all the inherent conflict in social science between understanding the world and making it better. At the same time, we have to understand the special nature of human beings if we are to develop a social science appropriate to its human subject. The more we know about the human species—especially its capacity to interpret the environment and bring meaning to the world—the more likely we will be to avoid the pitfalls of both excessive scientism and excessive moralism. What we need, and what a modified philosophical anthropology can provide, are provisional answers to the question of how we act and what we act for.

The post-modern challenge to scientific epistemology makes it difficult ever again to believe that reality, including social reality, is completely uncontested terrain. The quest for scientific certainty has surely been affected by considerations of gender and power. The rhetorical tools used to present scientific findings cannot be divorced from the findings themselves. Science is a human enterprise, influenced by all the peculiarities of the way humans carry out their affairs. But none of these things should lead us to conclude that there can never be any grounding for our observations of the social world. There are differences between humans and other animal species, and these differences can be understood by scientific observation. When we make claims for human capacities, evidence can be examined, experiments can be interpreted, and conclusions can be drawn. The study of other animal species and the possibilities and limitations of artificial intelligence are real, and they tell us things about human uniqueness that we need to know. In spite of the pretensions of earlier sociology, the grounding we achieve by comparing ourselves to other species is minimal: such a comparison does not provide universal knowledge about behavior applicable to anything that behaves; it only provides insights about modern humans, and these insights, because they apply to humans, are understood to be transient, contingent, socially constructed, and capable of change. We can have a certain security in what we are talking about, even while recognizing that what is secure can also change.

At the same time, to call attention to the meaning-producing abilities of human beings is to make an evaluative decision about what is important in the world. Good societies are those that enhance the capacity of human beings to attribute meaning to the things around them; bad societies are those that do not. Modern societies, if the United States is any indication, are not especially confident with respect to meaning. The lack of an appropriate language for discussing meaning is felt in a wide variety of contemporary institutions: schools, which are unsure what to teach; legal systems, which look more at procedure than substance; politics, which increasingly focuses on winning office rather than governing; and families, which flourish in diverse forms but are uncertain about their purpose. Social scientists need not feel helpless in the face of institutions that seem to have lost their way. To be sure, there is always the danger—warned about so eloquently by Max Weber—of seeking ultimate values along the avenues of politics.[32] But the quest for meaning need not be a quest for ultimate meaning. Just as an appreciation of the meaning-producing capacities of humans contributed to a minimal, but real, epistemology, it also contributes to a minimal, but real, morality. Social science can play a role in enhancing the capacity of social institutions to enrich what is human about human beings, without necessarily deciding what particular set of values any institution, such as the family, ought to maximize. Since human beings are meaning-producing creatures, they can figure out for themselves what their most important values ought to be. The social scientist's task is to help them by protecting and appreciating what makes it possible for them to be more fully human.

Theory and society habitually mirror each other. Throughout most of the post–World War II period, stability in both were assumed. An ever-progressing, gradualist, and increasingly better society found its match in a similarly gradualist understanding of social science, in which the patient accumulation of facts would contribute to knowledge, just as the patient accumulation of knowledge contributed to social stability. Neither understanding remains. A sense that society is in chaos is matched by a feeling that all efforts to describe and categorize social reality are problematic, that knowledge itself is little more than a tool in the hands of groups struggling to achieve mastery over other groups. It would be a shame if the excessive optimism of earlier versions of social science were to result in the excessive pessimism and nihilism of those who question any groundings for knowledge. Rather, we should appreciate that there is room both for those who once argued that social science can solve society's problems and for those who now argue that social science cannot exist. Social science is made possible not when science is divorced from values but when the links between the two are found.

Whatever the future of social science, it is unlikely to be pursued with the optimistic spirit and imperialistic pretensions of the nineteenth-century theorists. Animal ethology, artificial intelligence, ecology, post-modernism, and other trends in contemporary thought teach a certain humility toward the human species and a respect for subjects once considered so inferior to ourselves that little attention was paid to them. But the various components of the antihumanistic cosmology that seem popular in many disciplines finally add up to a greater, if more circumspect, appreciation of human capacities, rather than to a rejection of humanism. Because we can interpret the world around us, we can build societies that enable us to search after the good. The existence of these interpretative capacities is not a universal constant: at one time in our history, they were undeveloped; and at some future time in our history, perhaps they will be again. Precisely because human subjects and human societies are modern, important, fragile, and contested, we owe it to ourselves to keep humanism alive; and the social sciences, properly understood as a distinctive way of knowing for a distinct subject, remain one of our most important ways of doing so.

Notes

Chapter 1

1. Wolf Lepenies, *Between Literature and Science: The Rise of Sociology,* trans. R. J. Hollingdale (Cambridge: Cambridge University Press, 1988).

2. For an excellent treatment of these issues, see Roger Sullivan, *Immanuel Kant's Moral Theory* (Cambridge: Cambridge University Press, 1989).

3. Stephen Horigan, *Nature and Culture in Western Discourses* (London: Routledge, 1988), 84.

4. Stephen Jay Gould, *Wonderful Life: The Burgess Shale and the Nature of History* (New York: Norton, 1989), 233–34.

5. Emile Durkheim, "The Dualism of Human Nature and Its Social Conditions," in Durkheim, *On Mortality and Society,* ed. Robert N. Bellah (Chicago: University of Chicago Press, 1973), 149.

6. Barry Commoner, *The Closing Circle: Nature, Man, and Technology* (New York: Knopf, 1971), 41.

7. Carolyn Merchant, *The Death of Nature: Women, Ecology, and the Scientific Revolution* (New York: Harper and Row, 1980).

8. Evelyn Fox Keller, *Reflections on Gender and Science* (New Haven, Conn.: Yale University Press, 1985), 61.

9. A great many writers make this point. See, for example, Ruth Hubbard, *The Politics of Woman's Biology* (New Brunswick, N.J.: Rutgers University Press, 1990); Sandra Harding, *The Science Question in Feminism* (Ithaca, N.Y.: Cornell University Press, 1986); and *Whose Science? Whose Knowledge? Thinking from Women's Lives* (Ithaca, N.Y.: Cornell University Press, 1991).

10. Donna Haraway, *Primate Visions: Gender, Race, and Nature in the World of Modern Science* (New York: Routledge, 1989), 8.

11. See Susan Griffin, *Woman and Nature* (New York: Harper and Row, 1978); and Ariel Kay Sallah, "Deeper Than Deep Ecology? The Eco-Feminist Connection," *Environmental Ethics* 6 (Winter 1984): 323–38.

12. This opposition between sociobiology and feminism need not be inherent. For an effort to reconcile them, see Alice Rossi, "A Biosocial Perspective on Parenting," *Daedalus* 106 (Spring 1977): 1–31, and "Gender and Parenthood," *American Sociological Review* 49 (February 1984): 1–19.

13. Carl Degler, *In Search of Human Nature: The Decline and Revival of Darwinism in American Social Thought* (New York: Oxford University Press, 1991), 215–327.

14. Merchant, *Death of Nature*, 188. See also Susan Bardo, "The Cartesian Masculinization of Thought," *Signs* 11 (Spring 1986): 439–56.

15. Michel Foucault, *The Order of Things: An Archeology of the Human Sciences* (New York: Vintage, 1970), 387.

16. For Heidegger's influence on deep ecology, see Bill Devall and George Sessions, *Deep Ecology: Living as If Nature Mattered* (Salt Lake City: Peregrine Smith Books, 1985), 98–100; and the literature cited in chapter 5 of this volume. For an entertaining account of Heidegger's influence on artificial intelligence (and many other areas of thought), see Anthony Gottlieb, "Heidegger for Fun and Profit," *New York Times Book Review*, 7 January 1990, 1, 22, 23.

17. Luc Ferry and Alain Renaut, *French Philosophy of the Sixties: An Essay on Antihumanism*, trans. Mary Schnackenberg Cattani (Amherst: University of Massachusetts Press, 1990), 130.

18. Barbara Herrnstein Smith, *Contingencies of Value: Alternative Perspectives for Critical Theory* (Cambridge, Mass.: Harvard University Press, 1988), 78.

19. Quoted in Kerry W. Buckley, *Mechanical Man: John Broadus Watson and the Beginnings of Behaviorism* (New York: Guilford Press, 1989), 75.

20. Emile Durkheim, *The Division of Labor in Society*, trans. George Simpson (New York: Free Press, 1963), 407 (originally published in 1893).

21. Niklas Luhmann, *Political Theory in the Welfare State*, trans. John Bednarz, Jr. (Berlin and New York: de Gruyter, 1990), 30.

22. Niklas Luhmann, *Essays on Self-Reference* (New York: Columbia University Press, 1990), 6.

23. Gary Becker, "Altruism, Egoism, and Genetic Fitness," *Journal of Economic Literature* 14 (September 1976): 817–26.

24. Jon Elster, *Nuts and Bolts for the Social Sciences* (Cambridge: Cambridge University Press, 1989), 79.

25. Robert Frank, *Passions Within Reason: The Strategic Role of the Emotions* (New York: Norton, 1988).

26. Roderick Frazier Nash, *The Rights of Nature: A History of Environmental Ethics* (Madison: University of Wisconsin Press, 1989), 5–7.

27. Christopher Stone, *Earth and Other Ethics: The Case for Moral Pluralism* (New York: Harper and Row, 1987).

28. The classic defense of animal rights is Peter Singer, *Animal Liberation: A New Ethics for Our Treatment of Animals* (New York: Avon Books, 1975). On the legal standing of trees, see Christopher Stone, "Should Trees Have Standing? Toward Legal Rights for Natural Objects," *Southern California Law Review* 45 (Spring 1972): 450–501.

29. The suggestion comes from Gary Drescher, at the time a graduate student at MIT, cited in Sherry Turkle, *The Second Self: Computers and the Human Spirit* (New York: Touchstone Books, 1984), 261.

30. For a recent statement of such a point of view, see Philip N. Johnson-Laird, *The Computer and the Mind: An Introduction to Cognitive Science* (Cambridge, Mass.: Harvard University Press, 1988).

31. For one set of claims to this effect, see Hans Moravec, *Mind Children: The Future of Robot and Human Intelligence* (Cambridge, Mass.: Harvard University Press, 1988).

32. The argument for many kinds of intelligence is contained in Howard Gardner, *Frames of Mind: The Theory of Multiple Intelligence* (New York: Basic Books, 1983).

33. For an overview of the differences (and similarities) between human and computer intelligence, see Morton Wagman, *Artificial Intelligence and Human Cognition: A Theoretical Comparison of Two Realms of Intellect* (New York: Praeger, 1991).

34. Karl Marx and Frederick Engels, *The German Ideology*, ed. C. J. Arthur (New York: International Publishers, 1970), 42.

35. Max Weber, "Religious Rejections of the World and Their Directions," in *From Max Weber: Essays in Sociology*, ed. Hans Gerth and C. Wright Mills (New York: Oxford University Press, 1958), 356.

36. George Herbert Mead, *Mind, Self, and Society from the Standpoint of a Social Behaviorist* (Chicago: University of Chicago Press, 1962), 73 (originally published in 1934).

37. For an excellent overview, see Axel Honneth and Hans Joas, *Social Action and Human Nature* (Cambridge: Cambridge University Press, 1988).

38. All cited in Horigan, *Nature and Culture*, 22–29.

39. Jürgen Habermas, *The Theory of Communicative Action*, vol. 1: *Reason and the Realization of Society*, trans. Thomas McCarthy (Boston: Beacon Press, 1984), 8; Peter Berger and Thomas Luckmann, *The Social Construction of Reality: A Treatise in the Sociology of Knowledge* (Garden City, N.Y.: Doubleday, 1967), 47; Anthony Giddens, *The Constitution of Society: Outline of the Theory of Structuration* (Berkeley: University of California Press, 1984), 237.

40. See Bernard Barber, "Introduction," in *L. J. Henderson on the Social System: Selected Writings*, ed. Bernard Barber (Chicago: University of Chicago Press, 1970), 1–53.

41. Talcott Parsons, *The Social System* (Glencoe, Ill.: Free Press, 1951), 32–33.

42. Benjamin DeMott, "Rediscovering Complexity," *The Atlantic* 262 (1988): 67–74.

43. See notes 21 and 22 and Niklas Luhmann, *Ecological Communication*, trans. John Bednarz, Jr. (Chicago: University of Chicago Press, 1989).

44. Niklas Luhmann, *The Differentiation of Society*, trans. Stephen Holmes and Charles Larmore (New York: Columbia University Press, 1982), 72. In his later work, Luhmann pays less attention to human languages than to the communicative properties that all self-regulating systems have in common.

45. There is one conspicuous exception: Erving Goffman. See, for example, *Relations in Public: Microstudies of the Public Order* (New York: Harper Torchbooks, 1971), 238–56.

46. Cited in Hannah Arendt, *The Human Condition* (Chicago: University of Chicago Press, 1958), 99.

47. Ibid.

48. Charles Taylor, *Sources of the Self: The Making of Modern Identity* (Cambridge, Mass.: Harvard University Press, 1989).

49. Charles Taylor, *Philosophical Papers*, vol. 1: *Human Agency and Language* (Cambridge: Cambridge University Press, 1985), 45–76.

50. Edward O. Wilson, *The Insect Societies* (Cambridge, Mass.: Belknap Press of Harvard University Press, 1971).

51. On this point see Derek L. Phillips, *Toward a Just Society* (Princeton, N.J.: Princeton University Press, 1986).

52. Clifford Geertz, *The Interpretation of Cultures: Selected Essays* (New York: Basic Books, 1973), 5.

53. Isaiah Berlin, *The Crooked Timber of Humanity: Chapters in the History of Ideas* (New York: Knopf, 1991), 62.

54. Degler, *In Search of Human Nature.*

55. Cited in Degler, *In Search of Human Nature,* 103.

Chapter 2

1. For a recent example, see Jane Goodall, *Through a Window: My Thirty Years with the Chimpanzees of Gombe* (Boston: Houghton Mifflin, 1990).

2. For an account of some of those linkages, see Howard L. Kaye, *The Social Meaning of Modern Biology: From Social Darwinism to Sociobiology* (New Haven, Conn.: Yale University Press, 1986).

3. On this point, see Peter Wagner, "Science of Society Lost: On the Failure to Establish Sociology in Europe During the Classical Period," in *Discourses on Society,* vol. 15, ed. Peter Wagner, Bjorn Wittrock, and R. Whitley (Amsterdam: Kluwer, 1990), 219–45.

4. For an example, see Marshall Sahlins, *The Use and Abuse of Biology* (Ann Arbor: University of Michigan Press, 1976). For a somewhat different approach, see Walter R. Gove, "Sociobiology Misses the Mark: An Essay on Why Biology but Not Sociobiology Is Very Relevant to Sociology," *American Sociologist* 18 (Fall 1987): 258–77.

5. For a political critique of sociobiology, see Richard C. Lewontin, Steven Rose, and Leon J. Kamin, *Not in Our Genes: Biology, Ideology, and Human Nature* (New York: Pantheon Books, 1984). A philosophical critique is Philip Kitcher's *Vaulting Ambition: Sociobiology and the Quest for Human Nature* (Cambridge, Mass.: MIT Press, 1985). For a critique of some of the critiques, see Mary Midgley, "Rival Fatalisms: The Hollowness of the Sociobiology Debate," in *Sociobiology Examined,* ed. Ashley Montague (New York: Oxford University Press, 1980), 15–38.

6. Thomas A. Sebeok, ed., *How Animals Communicate* (Bloomington: Indiana University Press, 1977).

7. Donald E. Koodsma, "Aspects of Learning in the Ontogeny of Bird Song: Where, from Whom, When, How Many, Which, and How Accurately," in *The Development of Behavior: Comparative and Evolutionary Aspects,* ed. Gordon M. Burghardt and Marc Beckoff (New York: Garland STPM Press, 1978) 215–30. The reference to Mead is from George Herbert Mead, *Mind, Self, and Society from the Standpoint of a Social Behaviorist* (Chicago: University of Chicago Press, 1962; originally published in 1934).

8. W. John Smith, "Communication in Birds," in Sebeok, *How Animals Communicate,* 545–74.

9. B. T. Gardner and R. A. Gardner, "Teaching Sign Language

to a Chimpanzee," *Science* 165 (15 August 1960): 664–72; David Premack and Guy Woodruff, "Does the Chimpanzee Have a Theory of Mind?" *Behavioral and Brain Sciences* 1 (December 1978): 515–26; Duane M. Rumbaugh and Timothy V. Gill, "Lana's Acquisition of Language Skills," in *Language Learning by Chimpanzee: The LANA Project*, ed. Duane M. Rumbaugh (New York: Academic Press, 1977), 165–92.

10. Philip Lieberman, "The Phylogeny of Language," in Sebeok, *How Animals Communicate*, 3–25.

11. A review of the features that make human speech and syntax different from those of other species is contained in Philip Lieberman, *Uniquely Human: The Evolution of Speech, Thought, and Selfless Behavior* (Cambridge, Mass.: Harvard University Press, 1991).

12. The term *metacommunication* comes from Gregory Bateson, "A Theory of Play and Fantasy," *Psychiatric Research Reports* 2 (1955): 39–51.

13. Stuart A. Altmann, "The Structure of Primate Social Communication," in *Social Communication Among Primates*, ed. Stuart A. Altmann (Chicago: University of Chicago Press, 1967), 356.

14. Edward O. Wilson, *Sociobiology: The New Synthesis* (Cambridge, Mass.: Harvard University Press, 1975), 191.

15. Dorothy L. Cheney and Robert M. Seyfarth, *How Monkeys See the World: Inside the Mind of Another Species* (Chicago: University of Chicago Press, 1990), quoted at 304.

16. Ibid., 7.

17. Frans de Waal, *Chimpanzee Politics: Power and Sex Among Apes* (New York: Harper and Row, 1982).

18. Cheney and Seyfarth, *How Monkeys See the World*, 307.

19. For the idea that thought has its own language, see Jerry Fodor, *The Language of Thought* (New York: Crowell, 1975).

20. Stephen Walker, *Animal Thought* (London: Routledge and Kegan Paul, 1983); Donald R. Griffin, *The Question of Animal Awareness: Evolutionary Continuity of Mental Experience*, rev. ed. (Los Altos, Calif.: William Kaufmann, 1981), and *Animal Thinking* (Cambridge, Mass.: Harvard University Press, 1984); Joseph Mortensen, *Whale Songs and Wasp Maps: The Mystery of Animal Thinking* (New York: Dutton, 1987).

21. Griffin, *The Question of Animal Awareness* and *Animal Thinking*, passim.

22. Griffin, *Animal Thinking*, 37.

23. Ibid., 111.

24. Duane M. Rumbaugh, "Current and Future Research on

Chimpanzee Intellect," in *Understanding Chimpanzees*, ed. Paul G. Heltne and Linda A. Marquardt (Cambridge, Mass.: Harvard University Press, 1989), 296.

25. Claude Lévi-Strauss, *The Elementary Structures of Kinship*, trans. James Harle Bell, John Richard von Sturmer, and Rodney Needham (Boston: Beacon Press, 1969), 6 (originally published in 1949).

26. Martin Lindauer, *Communication Among Social Bees*, rev. ed. (Cambridge, Mass.: Harvard University Press, 1971), and "The Functional Significance of the Honey Bee Waggle Dance," *American Naturalist* 105 (March–April 1971): 89–96.

27. Charles Peirce, "How to Make Our Ideas Clear," in *Philosophical Writings of Peirce*, ed. Julius Buchler (New York: Dover, 1955), 23–41 (originally published in 1878). See also Charles W. Morris, "Introduction: George H. Mead as Social Psychologist and Social Philosopher," in Mead, *Mind, Self, and Society*, ix–xxxv.

28. Peirce, "How to Make Our Ideas Clear," 29.

29. Griffin, *The Question of Animal Awareness*, 48. The reference to Morris is from Charles W. Morris, *Signs, Language, and Behavior* (Englewood Cliffs, N.J.: Prentice-Hall, 1946), 25. Altmann, "The Structure of Primate Social Communication," also relies on Morris in his discussion of social communication among primates.

30. Heinz Pagels, *The Dreams of Reason* (New York: Simon and Schuster, 1988), 192–94.

31. Jane Goodall, *In the Shadow of Man* (Boston: Houghton Mifflin, 1971), 117–20.

32. Benjamin B. Beck, *Animal Tool Behavior* (New York: Garland STPM Press, 1980).

33. Benjamin B. Beck, "Primate Tool Behavior," in *Socioecology and Psychology of Primates*, ed. Russell H. Tuttle (The Hague: Mouton, 1977), 414–15.

34. Griffin, *Animal Thinking*, 126.

35. John Tyler Bonner, *The Evolution of Culture in Animals* (Princeton, N.J.: Princeton University Press, 1980), 153.

36. For Cooley's conception of the looking-glass self, see Charles Horton Cooley, *Human Nature and the Social Order* (New York: Schocken Books, 1964).

37. Gordon Gallup, "Self Recognition in Primates: A Comparative Approach to the Bidirectional Properties of Consciousness," *American Psychologist* 32 (May 1977): 329–38.

38. Gordon Gallup, "Towards an Operational Definition of Self-Awareness," in Tuttle, *Socioecology*, 335.

39. Mead, *Mind, Self, and Society,* passim.

40. Edward O. Wilson, *The Insect Societies* (Cambridge, Mass.: Belknap Press of Harvard University Press, 1971).

41. On reciprocal altruism, see R. L. Trivers, "The Evolution of Reciprocal Altruism," *Quarterly Review of Biology* 46 (March 1971): 35–57; Richard Dawkins's reformulation is contained in *The Selfish Gene* (New York: Oxford University Press, 1976).

42. Maynard J. Smith, "The Concepts of Sociobiology," in *Morality as a Biological Phenomenon: The Presuppositions of Sociobiological Research,* ed. Gunther S. Stent (Berkeley: University of California Press, 1980), 21–30; Frans de Waal, *Peacemaking Among Primates* (Cambridge, Mass.: Harvard University Press, 1989), 7.

43. William D. Hamilton, "The Genetical Evolution of Social Behavior, I and II," *Journal of Theoretical Biology* 7 (July 1964): 1–52; Robert Axelrod, *The Evolution of Cooperation* (New York: Basic Books, 1984).

44. Gunther S. Stent, "Introduction," in *Morality as a Biological Phenomenon,* 14.

45. Tom Regan, *The Case for Animal Rights* (Berkeley: University of California Press, 1983).

46. Donna Haraway, "A Manifesto for Cyborgs: Science, Technology, and Socialist Feminism in the 1980s," in *Feminism/Postmodernism,* ed. Linda J. Nicholson (New York: Routledge, 1990), 190–233, quoted at 193.

47. Charles J. Lumsden and Edward O. Wilson, *Genes, Mind, and Culture: The Coevolutionary Process* (Cambridge, Mass.: Harvard University Press, 1981), 58.

48. Dawkins, *The Selfish Gene,* passim.

49. Richard Dawkins, *The Blind Watchmaker* (New York: Norton, 1986).

50. Lumsden and Wilson, *Genes, Mind, and Culture,* 332.

51. Wilson, *The Insect Societies,* 226.

52. Lumsden and Wilson, *Genes, Mind, and Culture,* 5.

53. Ibid., 332.

54. Ibid., 96.

55. Charles J. Lumsden and Edward O. Wilson, *Promethean Fire: Reflections on the Origin of the Mind* (Cambridge, Mass.: Harvard University Press, 1983), 117.

56. Lumsden and Wilson, *Genes, Mind, and Culture,* 21.

57. Dawkins, *The Selfish Gene,* 205–8.

58. Edward O. Wilson, *On Human Nature* (Cambridge, Mass.: Harvard University Press, 1978), 78.

59. David P. Barash, *The Hare and the Tortoise* (New York: Viking, 1986).

60. Norbert Elias, *The Civilizing Process* (New York: Urizen Books, 1978).

61. See C. G. N. Lasker and G. W. Lasker, eds., *Biological Aspects of Human Migration* (Cambridge: Cambridge University Press, 1988); and Robert Boyd and Peter J. Richardson, *Culture and the Evolutionary Process* (Chicago: University of Chicago Press, 1985).

62. Albert J. Ammerman and L. L. Cavalli-Sforza, *The Neolithic Transformation and the Genetics of Population in Europe* (Princeton, N.J.: Princeton University Press, 1984), 60.

63. Lumsden and Wilson, *Promethean Fire*, 152.

64. Kaye, *Social Meaning of Modern Biology*, 120.

65. François Jacob, *The Logic of Life: A History of Heredity*, trans. Betty E. Spillman (New York: Pantheon Books, 1973), 3.

66. Dawkins, *The Selfish Gene*, 203.

67. Ibid., 206.

68. Gabriel de Tarde, *The Laws of Imitation*, trans. Elsie Clews Parsons (New York: Holt, 1903).

69. Lumsden and Wilson, *Promethean Fire*, 154 (emphasis added).

70. Lumsden and Wilson, *Genes, Mind, and Culture*, 5.

71. Lumsden and Wilson, *Promethean Fire*, 173.

72. See, for example, Joseph Lopreato, *Human Nature and Biocultural Evolution* (Boston: Allen and Unwin, 1984); Paul R. Wozniak, "Making Sociobiological Sense out of Sociology," *Sociological Quarterly* 25 (Spring 1984): 191–204; and David Rindos, "The Evolution of the Capacity for Culture: Sociobiology, Structuralism, and Cultural Selectiveness," *Current Anthropology* 27 (August–October 1986): 315–32.

73. See, for example, the essays in Albert Somit, ed., *Biology and Politics: Recent Explorations* (The Hague: Mouton, 1976); Thomas Landon Thorson, *Biopolitics* (New York: Holt, Rinehart and Winston, 1970); and Fred H. Willhoite, Jr., "Primates and Political Authority: A Biobehavioral Perspective," *American Political Science Review* 70 (December 1976): 1110–26.

74. John H. Beckstrom, *Sociobiology and the Law: The Biology of Altruism in the Courtroom of the Future* (Urbana: University of Illinois Press, 1985), and *Evolutionary Jurisprudence: Prospects and Limitations in the Use of Modern Darwinism Throughout the Legal Process* (Urbana: University of Illinois Press, 1989).

75. See, for example, Charles Dyke, *The Evolutionary Dynamics of Complex Systems: A Study in Biological Complexity* (New York:

Oxford University Press, 1988); and Robert A. Hinde, *Individuals, Relationships, and Culture: Links Between Ethology and the Social Sciences* (Cambridge: Cambridge University Press, 1987).

76. Carl Degler, *In Search of Human Nature: The Decline and Revival of Darwinism in American Social Thought* (New York: Oxford University Press, 1991).

77. Cynthia Fuchs Epstein, *Deceptive Distinctions: Sex, Gender, and the Social Order* (New Haven, Conn.: Yale University Press, 1988); David Greenberg, *The Construction of Homosexuality* (Chicago: University of Chicago Press, 1988).

78. Joan Wallach Scott, *Gender and the Politics of History* (New York: Columbia University Press, 1988), 2. Scott's approach differs from Epstein's, but both would agree on this point.

79. Epstein, *Deceptive Distinctions*, 71.

80. See Jeff Coulter, *The Social Construction of Mind* (London: Macmillan, 1979), although Coulter bases his argument on different theoretical grounds than those proposed here.

Chapter 3

1. Edward A. Feigenbaum and Pamela McCorduck, *The Fifth Generation: Artificial Intelligence and Japan's Computer Challenge to the World* (Reading, Mass.: Addison-Wesley, 1983), 41.

2. Hans Moravec, *Mind Children: The Future of Robot and Human Intelligence* (Cambridge, Mass.: Harvard University Press, 1988), 5.

3. The quote is from Pamela McCorduck, *Machines Who Think* (San Francisco: Freeman, 1981), 210. Fredkin's comment is cited in Feigenbaum and McCorduck, *The Fifth Generation*, 57. For the term *machina sapiens*, see Jeremy Campbell, *The Improbable Machine: What the Upheavals in Artificial Intelligence Reveal About How the Mind Really Works* (New York: Simon and Schuster, 1989), 38.

4. Richard Dawkins, *The Selfish Gene* (New York: Oxford University Press, 1976), 157.

5. For various expressions of this idea, see M. Mitchell Waldrop, "Toward a Unified Theory of Cognition," *Science* 241 (1 July 1988): 27–29, and "Soar: A Unified Theory of Cognition?" *Science* 241 (15 July 1988): 296–98; and Patricia S. Churchland and Terrence J. Sejnowski, "Perspectives on Cognitive Neuroscience," *Science* 242 (4 November 1988): 741–45. For a different point of view, see Gerald M. Edelman, *Topobiology* (New York: Basic Books, 1988).

6. Herbert A. Simon, *Sciences of the Artificial* (Cambridge, Mass.: MIT Press, 1969), 83.

7. Sherry Turkle, *The Second Self: Computers and the Human Spirit* (New York: Touchstone Books, 1984), 13.

8. For the original statement, see Alan Turing, "Computing Machines and Intelligence," *Mind* 49 (1950): 433–60. On the way the test has been used or misused, see Charles Karelis, "Reflections on the Turing Test," *Journal for the Theory of Social Behaviour* 16 (July 1986): 161–72; and Benny Shannon, "A Simple Comment Regarding the Turing Test," *Journal for the Theory of Social Behaviour* 19 (July 1989): 249–56.

9. For more recent work in this area, which uses a different terminology than Mead's, see Gerald M. Edelman, *Neural Darwinism* (New York: Basic Books, 1987).

10. George Herbert Mead, *Mind, Self, and Society from the Viewpoint of a Social Behaviorist* (Chicago: University of Chicago Press, 1962), 133 (originally published in 1934).

11. The ELIZA program is fully described in Joseph Weizenbaum, *Computer Power and Human Reason* (San Francisco: Freeman, 1976).

12. Ibid., 188–93.

13. Derek Sleeman, "Inferring Student Models for Intelligent Computer-Aided Instruction," in *Machine Learning: An Artificial Intelligence Approach*, ed. Ryszard S. Michaelski, Jaime G. Carbonell, and Tom M. Mitchell (Palo Alto, Calif.: Tioga, 1983), 483–509; Derek Sleeman and John Seely Brown, "Intelligent Tutoring Systems: An Overview," in Sleeman and Brown, *Intelligent Tutoring Systems* (New York: Academic Press, 1982), 1–11.

14. William J. Clancey, "Use of MYCIN's Rules for Tutoring," in *Rule-Based Systems: The MYCIN Experiments of the Stanford Heuristic Programming Project*, ed. Bruce G. Buchanan and Edward H. Shortliffe (Reading, Mass.: Addison-Wesley, 1984), 464–89.

15. For a review, see Etienne Wenger, *Artificial Intelligence and Tutoring Systems* (Los Altos, Calif.: William Kaufmann, 1987).

16. Mead, *Mind, Self, and Society*, 46, 164.

17. Michael S. Gazzaniga, *The Social Brain* (New York: Basic Books, 1985).

18. Jerry Fodor, *The Language of Thought* (New York: Crowell, 1975), and *Representations: Philosophical Essays on the Foundations of Cognitive Science* (Cambridge, Mass.: MIT Press, 1981). For a sociological critique, see Jeff Coulter, *Rethinking Cognitive Theory* (New York: St. Martin's Press, 1983), and "On Comprehension and 'Mental Representation,' " in *Social Action and Artificial Intelligence: Surrey Conferences on Sociological Theory and Method* 3, ed. C. Nigel Gilbert and Christian Heath (Aldershot: Gower, 1985), 8–23.

19. Patricia Smith Churchland, *Neurophilosophy: Toward a Unified Science of the Mind-Brain* (Cambridge, Mass.: MIT Press, 1986).

20. On perceptrons, see Frank Rosenblatt, *Principles of Neurodynamics* (New York: Spartan, 1962). For a critique, see Marvin Minsky and Seymour Papert, *Perceptrons* (Cambridge, Mass.: MIT Press, 1969).

21. Marvin Minsky, "A Framework for Representing Knowledge," in *Mind Design*, ed. John Haugland (Montgomery, Vt.: Bradford, 1981), 95–128.

22. Cited in Howard Gardner, *The Mind's New Science: A History of the Cognitive Revolution* (New York: Basic Books, 1985), 18.

23. Jerry R. Hobbs and Robert C. Moore, *Formal Theories of the Commonsense World* (Norwood, N.J.: Ablex, 1985).

24. Allan Newall and Herbert A. Simon, *Human Problem Solving* (Englewood Cliffs, N.J.: Prentice-Hall, 1972); Edward A. Feigenbaum and Julian Feldman, eds., *Computers and Thought* (New York: McGraw-Hill, 1963).

25. Minsky, "A Framework for Representing Knowledge"; Roger C. Schank and Robert P. Abelson, *Scripts, Plans, Goals, and Understanding* (Hillsdale, N.J.: Erlbaum, 1977).

26. John R. Searle, "Minds, Brains, and Programs," in Haugland, *Mind Design*, 282–306.

27. Israel Rosenfield, *The Invention of Memory: A New View of the Brain* (New York: Basic Books, 1988), 113.

28. Hubert L. Dreyfus, *What Computers Can't Do: The Limits of Artificial Intelligence*, rev. ed. (New York: Harper Colophon Books, 1979); Weizenbaum, *Computer Power and Human Reason*.

29. Edelman, *Neural Darwinism*; Rosenfield, *The Invention of Memory*; George N. Reeke, Jr., and Gerald M. Edelman, "Real Brains and Artificial Intelligence," *Daedalus* 117 (1988): 143–73.

30. Edelman, *Neural Darwinism*, 44.

31. Gerald M. Edelman and Vernon B. Mountcastle, *The Mindful Brain: Cortical Organization and the Group-Selective Theory of Higher Brain Function* (Cambridge, Mass.: MIT Press, 1978).

32. Rosenfield, *The Invention of Memory*, 158.

33. Harold Garfinkel, *Studies in Ethnomethodology* (Englewood Cliffs, N.J.: Prentice-Hall, 1967), 38.

34. David Good, "Sociology and AI: The Lessons from Social Psychology," in Gilbert and Heath, *Social Action and Artificial Intelligence*, 82–103.

35. Emmanuel Schegloff and Harvey Sacks, "Opening Up Closings," in *Ethnomethodology: Selected Readings*, ed. Ray Turner (Baltimore: Penguin Books, 1979), 262.

36. Thomas J. Scheff, *Microsociology: Discourse, Emotion, and Social Structure* (Chicago: University of Chicago Press, 1990), 57, 97.

37. John Bateman, "The Role of Language in the Maintenance of Intersubjectivity: A Computational Investigation," in Gilbert and Heath, *Social Action and Artificial Intelligence*, 40–81.

38. Dreyfus, *What Computers Can't Do*, 56–57.

39. Donald N. Levine, *The Flight from Ambiguity: Essays in Social and Cultural Theory* (Chicago: University of Chicago Press, 1985), ix.

40. Cited in John Heritage, *Garfinkel and Ethnomethodology* (Cambridge, England: Polity Press, 1984), 61.

41. Erving Goffman, *Encounters: Two Studies in the Sociology of Interaction* (Indianapolis: Bobbs-Merrill, 1961), 67.

42. Arnold Gehlen, *Man in the Age of Technology*, trans. Patricia Lipscomb (New York: Columbia University Press, 1980), 3. See also Arnold Gehlen, *Man: His Nature and Place in the World*, trans. Clare McMillan and Karl Pillemer (New York: Columbia University Press, 1988), 79–92.

43. Rosenblatt, *Principles of Neurodynamics*, passim.

44. Geoffrey E. Hinton and James A. Anderson, eds., *Parallel Models of Associative Memory* (Hillsdale, N.J.: Erlbaum, 1982); D. E. Rumelhart, P. Smolensky, J. L. McClelland, and G. E. Hinton, "Schematic and Sequential Thought Processes in PDP Models," in David E. Rumelhart, James L. McClelland, and the PDP Research Group, *Parallel Distributed Processing: Explorations in the Microstructure of Cognition*, vol. 2: *Psychological and Biological Models* (Cambridge, Mass.: MIT Press, 1986), 7–57; Stephen Grossberg, *Neural Networks and Natural Intelligence* (Cambridge, Mass.: MIT Press, 1988); Carver Mead, *Analog VLSI and Neural Systems* (Reading, Mass.: Addison-Wesley, 1988).

45. For clear accounts of the connectionist revolution in AI by journalists, see Campbell, *The Improbable Machine*; and William F. Allman, *Apprentices of Wonder: Inside the Neural Network Revolution* (New York: Bantam Books, 1989).

46. Rumelhart et al., "Schematic and Sequential Thought Processes," 21.

47. J. L. McClelland, D. E. Rumelhart, and G. E. Hinton, "A General Framework for Parallel Distributive Processing, " in Rumelhart et al., *Parallel Distributed Processing*, vol. 1: *Foundations* (Cambridge, Mass.: MIT Press, 1986), 32.

48. Ibid., 39–40.

49. D. A. Norman, "Reflections on Cognition and Parallel Distributive Processing," in Rumelhart et al., *Psychological and Biological Models*, 531–52.

50. On the homunculi problem, see Daniel C. Dennett, *Brainstorms: Philosophical Essays on Mind and Psychology* (Montgomery, Vt.: Bradford, 1978), 123; and Zenon W. Pylyshyn, "Complexity and the Study of Artificial and Human Intelligence," in Haugland, *Mind Design*, 68. Gerald Edelman also believes that his research into human brains solves the homunculi problem; see *Neural Darwinism*, 45.

51. Dennett, *Brainstorms*, 123–24. For a more recent statement, and one that relies on Richard Dawkins's conception of memes, discussed in chapter 2, see Daniel C. Dennett, *Consciousness Explained* (Boston: Little, Brown, 1991).

52. Douglas R. Hofstader, *Gödel, Escher, and Bach: An Eternal Golden Braid* (New York: Basic Books, 1979), 26.

53. Marvin Minsky, *The Society of Mind* (New York: Simon and Schuster, 1986), 17. For Papert's reflections on the new approach to AI, see Seymour Papert, "One AI or Many?" *Daedalus* 117 (1988): 1–14.

54. Reeke and Edelman, "Real Brains and Artificial Intelligence," 152.

55. Rosenfield, *The Invention of Memory*, 8, 145.

56. Norman, "Reflections on Cognition and Parallel Distributive Processing," 544, 546.

57. C. Nigel Gilbert and Christian Heath, "Introduction," in Gilbert and Heath, *Social Action and Artificial Intelligence*, 1.

58. For examples, see Marie Jahoda, "Artificial Intelligence: An Outsider's Perspective," *Science and Public Policy* 13 (December 1986): 333–40; David Oldman and Charles Drucker, "The Nonreducibility of Ethno-Methods: Can People and Computers Form a Society?" in Gilbert and Heath, *Social Action and Artificial Intelligence*, 144–59; and Steve Woolger, "Why Not a Sociology of Machines? The Case of Sociology and Artificial Intelligence," *Sociology* 19 (November 1985): 557–72.

59. Edward E. Brent, "Knowledge-Based Systems: A Qualitative Formalism," *Qualitative Sociology* 9 (Fall 1986): 256–82; Robert R. Weaver, "Some Implications of the Emergence and Diffusion of Medical Expert Systems," *Qualitative Sociology* 9 (Fall 1986): 237–57; and the collected articles in Gilbert and Heath, *Social Action and Artificial Intelligence*.

60. See especially Niklas Luhmann, *Ecological Communication*, trans. John Bednarz, Jr. (Chicago: University of Chicago Press, 1989).

61. Charles Horton Cooley, *Human Nature and the Social Order* (New York: Schocken Books, 1964), 81–97.

62. Turkle, *The Second Self*, 81, 83.

63. Cited in Allman, *Apprentices of Wonder*, 186.

64. Heinz Pagels, *The Dreams of Reason* (New York: Simon and Schuster, 1988), 192–94.

65. Ibid., 193.

66. Jerry Fodor, "Methodological Solipsism," in Haugland, *Mind Design*, 315.

67. Dennett, *Brainstorms*, 3–22.

68. Niklas Luhmann, *Essays on Self-Reference* (New York: Columbia University Press, 1990), 21–79.

69. For representative examples, see Richard A. Shweder, *Thinking Through Cultures: Explorations in Cultural Psychology* (Cambridge, Mass.: Harvard University Press, 1991); James V. Wertsch, *Voices of the Mind: A Sociocultural Approach to Mediated Action* (Cambridge, Mass.: Harvard University Press, 1991); and Alan Page Fiske, *Structures of Social Life: The Four Elementary Forms of Human Relations* (New York: Free Press, 1991).

70. Jerome Bruner, *Acts of Meaning* (Cambridge, Mass.: Harvard University Press, 1990), 4.

Chapter 4

1. The philosophical differences between animal rights and environmental ethics are explored by Mark Sagoff, "Animal Liberation and Environmental Ethics: Bad Marriage, Quick Divorce," *Osgoode Hall Law Journal* 22 (Summer 1984): 297–321.

2. Tom Regan, *The Case for Animal Rights* (Berkeley: University of California Press, 1983), 353.

3. Peter Singer, *Animal Liberation: A New Ethics for Our Treatment of Animals* (New York: Avon Books, 1975), 218.

4. Ibid., xi, 34, 168, 175, 186–88, 226, 228. According to Richard Ryder, who coined the term *speciesm*, to claim that the British treat animals better than people in other countries do is "rather like arguing that the concentration camp at Belsen was more humane than the one at Dachau" (quoted in Singer, *Animal Liberation*, 73).

5. Even Singer says that "no doubt there are some people of whom this is true" (ibid., 234). For data on the personal background of animal rights activists, see Susan Sperling, *Animal Liberators: Research and Morality* (Berkeley: University of California Press, 1988); and James M. Jasper and Dorothy Nelkin, *Animal Rights: Dynamics of a Moral Crusade* (New York: Free Press, 1992).

6. See, for example, Michael Allen Fox, *The Case for Animal Experimentation: An Evolutionary and Ethical Perspective* (Berkeley:

University of California Press, 1986); for a critique of experimentation on animals, see Bernard E. Rollins, *The Unheeded Cry: Animal Consciousness, Animal Pain, and Society* (New York: Oxford University Press, 1990).

7. Regan, *The Case for Animal Rights*, 356.

8. Hannah Arendt, *The Human Condition* (Chicago: University of Chicago Press, 1958), 95–97.

9. Keith Thomas, *Man and the Natural World: Changing Attitudes in England, 1500–1800* (New York: Penguin Books, 1984); John Berger, *Pig Earth* (New York: Pantheon Books, 1979); Mary Douglas, *Natural Symbols: Explorations in Cosmology* (New York: Pantheon Books, 1982).

10. Singer, *Animal Liberation*, 156.

11. Although there may be a conflict between animal rights and the practices of some religions, an effort to reconcile environmental concerns generally with religious ethics is contained in Eugene C. Hargrove, ed., *Religion and Environmental Crisis* (Athens: University of Georgia Press, 1986).

12. Dale Jamieson, "Against Zoos," in *In Defense of Animals*, ed. Peter Singer (New York: Harper and Row, 1985), 108–17.

13. Regan, *The Case for Animal Rights*, 353–54.

14. Clifford Geertz, "Deep Play: Notes on the Balinese Cockfight," in *The Interpretation of Culture: Selected Essays* (New York: Basic Books, 1973), 434.

15. Singer, *Animal Liberation*, 206.

16. See Andrea Dworkin, *Pornography: Men Possessing Women* (New York: Putnam, 1981).

17. For an argument to the effect that we have obligations to hypothetical creatures in outer space, see J. Baird Callicott, "Moral Considerability and Extraterrestrial Life," in *Beyond Spaceship Earth: Environmental Ethics and the Solar System*, ed. Eugene C. Hargrove (San Francisco: Sierra Club Books, 1986), 227–59.

18. Judith Shklar, *Ordinary Vices* (Cambridge, Mass.: Harvard University Press, 1984); Richard Rorty, *Contingency, Irony, and Solidarity* (New York: Cambridge University Press, 1989).

19. Singer, *Animal Liberation*, 179.

20. This all-too-brief survey of the development of ecology is indebted to Donald Worster, *Nature's Economy: The Roots of Ecology* (San Francisco: Sierra Club Books, 1977).

21. Ibid., 294–301; J. Baird Callicott, *In Defense of the Land Ethic: Essays in Environmental Philosophy* (Albany: State University of New York Press, 1989), 82.

22. Richard Hofstader, *Social Darwinism in American Thought, 1860–1915* (Philadelphia: University of Pennsylvania Press, 1945).

23. Worster, *Nature's Economy*, 313.

24. Erwin Schrödinger, *"What Is Life? The Physical Aspect of the Living Cell" and "Mind and Matter"* (Cambridge: Cambridge University Press, 1967), 78.

25. Elwyn R. Berklekamp, John H. Conway, and Richard K. Guy, *Winning Ways (for Your Mathematical Plays)* (New York: Academic Press, 1982), 2: 848–49. A program developed by Thomas S. Ray charts evolutionary patterns and in its own way, according to its advocates, creates a form of computer life. See Malcolm W. Browne, "Lively Computer Creation Blurs Definition of Life," *New York Times*, 27 August 1991, C1.

26. Arne Naess, "The Shallow and the Deep, Long-Range Ecology Movement: A Summary," *Inquiry* 16 (Spring 1973): 95–100.

27. Arne Naess, *Ecology, Community, and Lifestyle: Outline of an Ecosophy*, rev. ed., trans. David Rothenberg (Cambridge: Cambridge University Press, 1989), 30.

28. Callicott, *In Defense of the Land Ethic*; Michael Tobias, ed., *Deep Ecology* (San Marcos, Calif.: Avant Books, 1988); Bill Devall and George Sessions, *Deep Ecology: Living as If Nature Mattered* (Salt Lake City: Peregrine Smith Books, 1985); Bill Devall, *Simple in Means, Rich in Ends: Practicing Deep Ecology* (Salt Lake City: Peregrine Smith Books, 1988).

29. Cited in Roderick Frazier Nash, *The Rights of Nature: A History of Environmental Ethics* (Madison: University of Wisconsin Press, 1989), 39, 53.

30. Ibid., 153.

31. Callicott, *In Defense of the Land Ethic*, 27.

32. David Ehrenfeld, *The Arrogance of Humanism* (New York: Oxford University Press, 1978).

33. As discussed in Kirkpatrick Sale, "Deep Ecology and Its Critics," *The Nation*, 14 May 1988, 670–75.

34. Cited in Callicott, *In Defense of the Land Ethic*, 84.

35. The holistic perspective of environmental ethics would ultimately come under some criticism from an environmentalist perspective. See Harley Cahan, "Against the Moral Considerability of Ecosystems," *Environmental Ethics* 10 (Fall 1988): 195–216; and Frederick Ferre, "Obstacles in the Path to Organismic Ethics: Some Second Thoughts," *Environmental Ethics* 11 (Fall 1989): 231–41.

36. Michael F. Zimmerman, *Eclipse of the Self: The Development of Heidegger's Concept of Authenticity* (Athens: Ohio University

Press, 1981); Laura Westra, "Let It Be: Heidegger and Future Generations," *Environmental Ethics* 7 (Winter 1985): 341–50; Michael F. Zimmerman, "Toward a Heideggerian *Ethos* for Radical Environmentalism," *Environmental Ethics* 5 (Summer 1983): 99–132; and Joanna Macy, "The Ecological Self: Postmodern Ground for Right Action," in *Sacred Interconnections: Postmodern Spirituality, Political Economy, and Art*, ed. David R. Griffin (Albany: State University of New York Press, 1990), 35–48.

37. Freya Matthews, "Conservation and Self-Realization: A Deep Ecology Perspective," *Environmental Ethics* 10 (Winter 1988): 347–55.

38. Holmes Rolston III, *Philosopohy Gone Wild: Essays in Environmental Ethics* (Buffalo, N.Y.: Prometheus Books, 1986), 65, 224.

39. Devall and Sessions, *Deep Ecology*, 70.

40. William R. Catton, Jr., "On the Dire Destiny of Human Lemmings," in Tobias, *Deep Ecology*, 83. See also William R. Catton, Jr., *Overshoot: The Ecological Basis of Revolutionary Change* (Urbana: University of Illinois Press, 1980).

41. Herman E. Daly, "Economics and Sustainability: In Defense of a Steady-State Economy," in Tobias, *Deep Ecology*, 98.

42. Callicott, *In Defense of the Land Ethic*, 85.

43. Nash, *The Rights of Nature*, 154.

44. In a response to an earlier publication of some of these ideas, Callicott rejects both Nash's and my own interpretation of his ideas. For his counterclaims, see his letter in *The American Prospect* 5 (Spring 1991): 18–20.

45. Paul W. Taylor, "In Defense of Biocentrism," *Environmental Ethics* 5 (Fall 1983): 337–43, quoted at 342.

46. Some of those overlaps are explored in Griffin, *Sacred Interconnections*.

47. Devall and Sessions, *Deep Ecology*, 68.

48. Callicott, *In Defense of the Land Ethic*, 26.

49. Holmes Rolston III, *Environmental Ethics: Duties to and Values in the Natural World* (Philadelphia: Temple University Press, 1988), 190.

50. Michael Tobias, "Introduction," in *Deep Ecology*, vii.

51. Paul W. Taylor, *Respect for Nature: A Theory of Environmental Ethics* (Princeton, N.J.: Princeton University Press, 1986), 45–46.

52. On the conservative bias in radical ecology, see Tim Luke, "The Dreams of Deep Ecology," *Telos* 76 (1988): 65–92.

53. Cited in William Aiken, "Ethical Issues in Agriculture," in *Earthbound: New Introductory Essays in Environmental Ethics*, ed. Tom Regan (Philadelphia: Temple University Press, 1984), 269.

54. Nash, *Rights of Nature*, 154.

55. Quoted in Norman Myers, "Epilogue," in *Gaia: An Atlas of Planet Management* (Garden City, N.Y.: Doubleday, 1984), 258.

56. James E. Lovelock, *The Ages of Gaia: A Biography of Our Living Earth* (New York: Norton, 1988), 39.

57. Ibid., 14, 155, 211.

58. James E. Lovelock, *Gaia: A New Look at Life on Earth* (New York: Oxford University Press, 1979), 110.

59. Lovelock, *Ages of Gaia*, 26. See also Georges Bataille, *Visions of Excess: Selected Writings, 1927–1939*, ed. and trans. Allan Stoekl (Minneapolis: University of Minnesota Press, 1985); and Norman O. Brown, *Life Against Death: The Psychoanalytic Meaning of History* (Middletown, Conn.: Wesleyan University Press, 1959).

60. Lovelock, *Ages of Gaia*, 52.

61. Ibid., 212.

62. Ibid., 236.

63. Ibid., 218.

64. Erich Jantsch, *The Self-Organizing Universe* (Oxford: Pergamon Press, 1980).

65. William Poundstone, *The Recursive Universe: Cosmic Complexity and the Limits of Scientific Knowledge* (New York: Morrow, 1985), 24–32.

66. Lovelock, *Ages of Gaia*, 206.

67. Robert Ezra Park, *Human Communities: The City and Human Ecology* (Glencoe, Ill.: Free Press, 1952). Morris Janowitz, however, found this emphasis on natural ecology "progressively less persuasive" as time went by. See "The Social Ecology of Citizenship," in *Morris Janowitz on Social Organization and Social Control*, ed. James Burk (Chicago: University of Chicago Press, 1991), 262.

68. Amos H. Hawley, *Human Ecology: A Theory of Community Structure* (New York: Ronald Press, 1950), 69.

69. James R. Beniger, *The Control Revolution* (Cambridge, Mass.: Harvard University Press, 1986), 68. See also Kenneth D. Bailey, *Social Entropy Theory* (Albany: State University of New York Press, 1990).

70. Michael T. Hannan and John Freeman, *Organizational Ecology* (Cambridge, Mass.: Harvard University Press, 1989).

71. Leo Marx, *The Machine in the Garden: Technology and the Pastoral Ideal in America* (New York: Oxford University Press, 1964).

72. Sherry Turkle, *The Second Self: Computers and the Human Spirit* (New York: Touchstone Books, 1984), 172–74.

73. Bill McKibben, *The End of Nature* (New York: Random House, 1989), 65, 190.

74. Charles Perrow, *Normal Accidents* (New York: Basic Books, 1984).

75. Turkle, *The Second Self,* 223.

76. Robert Wright, *Three Scientists and Their Gods: Looking for Meaning in an Age of Information* (New York: Times Books, 1988), 32, 120.

Chapter 5

1. Emile Durkheim, *The Elementary Forms of Religious Life,* trans. Joseph Ward Swain (New York: Free Press, 1965), 357 (originally published in 1912).

2. Ian Watt, *The Rise of the Novel: Studies in Defoe, Richardson, and Fielding* (Berkeley: University of California Press, 1957), 22. The ideas in this paragraph are based on Watt's book.

3. Alvin Kernan, *The Death of Literature* (New Haven, Conn.: Yale University Press, 1990), 194. My own view is that Hobbes is more a naturalistic thinker than a sociological one.

4. Marcel Mauss, *The Gift* (New York: Norton, 1967); Lewis Hyde, *The Gift: Imagination and the Erotic Life of Poetry* (New York: Vintage, 1983).

5. Kernan, *The Death of Literature,* 194.

6. Robert Nisbet, *Sociology as an Art Form* (New York: Oxford University Press, 1976).

7. There are obvious differences between these terms, as the polemics between Derrida and Foucault indicate. Nonetheless, for purposes of the argument presented here, all these approaches are suspicious of transcendental standards of the good and therefore can be linked in this chapter.

8. The impact of post-modernism on the social sciences has been less pronounced, but it is growing. For an overview, see Pauline Marie Rosenau, *Post-modernism and the Social Sciences: Insights, Inroads, and Intrusions* (Princeton, N.J.: Princeton University Press, 1991).

9. For examples of the overlap between literary theory and contemporary information science, see William R. Paulson, *The Noise of Culture: Literary Texts in a World of Information* (Ithaca, N.Y.: Cornell University Press, 1988); N. Katherine Hayles, *Chaos Bound: Orderly Disorder in Contemporary Literature and Science* (Ithaca, N.Y.: Cornell University Press, 1990); and N. Katherine Hayles, ed., *Chaos and Order: Complex Dynamics in Literature and Science* (Chicago: University of Chicago Press, 1991). For ways in which post-modern

literary theory appreciates both high technology and the world of other animal species, see Constance Penley and Andrew Ross, eds., *Technoculture* (Minneapolis: University of Minnesota Press, 1991).

10. For one example of this fascination with violence, see Jacques Derrida, "Force of Law: The 'Mystical Foundation of Authority,'" *Cardozo Law Review* 11 (July/August 1990): 921–1045.

11. Stanley Fish, *Doing What Comes Naturally: Change, Rhetoric, and the Practice of Theory in Literary and Legal Studies* (Durham, N.C.: Duke University Press, 1989), 10, 520.

12. Ibid., 520.

13. Friedrich Nietzsche, *Thus Spoke Zarathustra*, trans. Walter Kaufmann, in *The Portable Nietzsche*, ed. Walter Kaufmann (New York: Viking, 1954), 139; Douglas R. Hofstader, *Gödel, Escher, and Bach: An Eternal Golden Braid* (New York: Basic Books, 1979).

14. Alexander Nehamas, *Nietzsche: Life as Literature* (Cambridge, Mass.: Harvard University Press, 1985), 150.

15. Jean-François Lyotard, *The Postmodern Condition: A Report on Knowledge*, trans. Geoff Bennington and Brian Massumi (Minneapolis: University of Minnesota Press, 1984), 4, 51, 67, quoted at 67.

16. Paul de Man, *Allegories of Reading: Figural Language in Rousseau, Nietzsche, Rilke, and Proust* (New Haven, Conn.: Yale University Press, 1979), 294, 298, 299. Cited in Geoffrey Bennington, "Aberrations: de Man (and) the Machine," in *Reading de Man Reading*, ed. Lindsay Waters and Wlad Godzich (Minneapolis: University of Minnesota Press, 1989), 215.

17. Jacques Derrida, *The Post Card: From Socrates to Freud and Beyond*, trans. Alan Bass (Chicago: University of Chicago Press, 1987); Bennington, "Aberrations," 221.

18. See, for example, Gilles Deleuze and Félix Guattari, *Anti-Oedipus: Capitalism and Schizophrenia*, trans. Robert Hurley, Mark Seem, and Helen R. Lane (Minneapolis: University of Minnesota Press, 1983), 14.

19. Mark Poster, *The Mode of Information: Poststructuralism and the Social Context* (Chicago: University of Chicago Press, 1990).

20. Lyotard, *The Postmodern Condition*, 60–67. Lyotard also has strongly critical views toward Luhmann; yet, at least with respect to their joint fascination with cybernetics, they share more than he is prepared to admit.

21. Michel Serres, "The Origin of Language: Biology, Information Theory, and Thermodynamics," in *Hermes: Literature, Science, Philosophy*, ed. Josue V. Harari and David F. Bell (Baltimore: Johns Hopkins University Press, 1982), 82.

22. Ibid., 83.

23. Christine Brooke-Rose, "The Dissolution of Character in the Novel," in *Reconstructing Individualism: Autonomy, Individuality, and the Self in Western Thought,* ed. Thomas C. Heller, Morton Sosna, and David E. Wellbery (Stanford, Calif.: Stanford University Press, 1986), 195.

24. Paulson, *The Noise of Culture,* 31.

25. Ibid., 139.

26. Humberto R. Maturana and Francisco J. Varela, *The Tree of Knowledge: The Biological Roots of Human Understanding* (Boston: New Science Library, 1987), 46–47. For another treatment of autopoiesis, see Milan Zeleny, *Autopoiesis: A Theory of Living Organisms* (New York: North-Holland, 1981).

27. Barbara Herrnstein Smith, *Contingencies of Value: Alternative Perspectives for Critical Theory* (Cambridge, Mass.: Harvard University Press, 1988), 15, 28, 31.

28. There are occasions in her text, however, where Herrnstein Smith takes the opposite tack and argues that markets are rigged: "The linguistic market can no more be a 'free' one than any other market, for verbal agents do not characteristically enter it from positions of equal advantage or conduct their transactions on an equal footing" (ibid., 111).

29. Ibid., 42–43.

30. Ibid., 45.

31. Ibid., 95, 191, 108–9, 122, 144.

32. Ibid., 50, 53.

33. Alasdair MacIntyre, *After Virtue* (South Bend, Ind.: Notre Dame University Press, 1981).

34. The analogy between religion and justice is elaborated in Sanford Levinson, *Constitutional Faith* (Princeton, N.J.: Princeton University Press, 1988), 9–53.

35. For one example among many, see Sanford Levinson, "Law as Literature," in *Interpreting Law and Literature: A Hermeneutic Reader,* ed. Sanford Levinson and Steven Mailloux (Evanston, Ill.: Northwestern University Press, 1988), 155–73.

36. Fish, *Doing What Comes Naturally,* 388.

37. Ibid., 323.

38. Ibid., ix.

39. Niklas Luhmann, *Ecological Communication,* trans. John Bednarz, Jr. (Chicago: University of Chicago Press, 1989), 64–66.

40. Ibid., 66.

41. Niklas Luhmann, *Essays on Self-Reference* (New York: Columbia University Press, 1990), 3.

42. Ibid., 30.

43. Ibid., 84.

44. Luhmann, *Ecological Communication*, 36.

45. Luhmann, *Essays on Self-Reference*, 85.

46. Ibid., 117.

47. Ibid., 119.

48. Niklas Luhmann, "The Unity of the Legal System," in *Autopoietic Law: A New Approach to Law and Society*, ed. Gunther Teubner (Berlin and New York: de Gruyter, 1988), 21, 23.

49. For a study of the impact that the ability to write (and, by implication, the ability to read) has on the structure of society, see Jack Goody, *The Logic of Writing and the Organization of Society* (Cambridge: Cambridge University Press, 1986).

50. Jane Tompkins, ed., *Reader-Response Criticism from Formalism to Post-structuralism* (Baltimore: Johns Hopkins University Press, 1980).

51. Stanley Fish, *Is There a Text in This Class? The Authority of Interpretative Communities* (Cambridge, Mass.: Harvard University Press, 1980).

52. For a conception of the self close to the one I am discussing here, see Charles Taylor, *Sources of the Self: The Making of Modern Identity* (Cambridge, Mass.: Harvard University Press, 1989).

53. One literary critic who works in this humanistic fashion, and with an appreciation for sociological accounts of real people, is Wayne Booth. See *The Company We Keep: An Ethics of Fiction* (Berkeley: University of California Press, 1988).

54. Thomas C. Heller and David E. Wellbery, "Introduction," in Heller et al., *Reconstructing Individualism*, 7.

55. Thomas C. Heller, "Accounting for Law," in Teubner, *Autopoietic Law*, 307.

56. Herrnstein Smith, *Contingencies of Value*, 193.

Chapter 6

1. Barry Barnes and David Bloor, "Relativism, Rationalism and the Sociology of Knowledge," in *Rationality and Relativism*, ed. Martin Hollis and Steven Lukes (Cambridge, Mass.: MIT Press, 1982), 21–47.

2. Bruno Latour, *Science in Action: How to Follow Scientists and Engineers Through Society* (Cambridge, Mass.: Harvard University Press, 1987), 61.

3. Sandra Harding, *Whose Science? Whose Knowledge? Thinking*

from Women's Lives (Ithaca, N.Y.: Cornell University Press, 1991), 15.

4. Herbert W. Simons, ed., *The Rhetorical Turn: Invention and Persuasion in the Conduct of Inquiry* (Chicago: University of Chicago Press, 1990); Donald McCloskey, *The Rhetoric of Economics* (Madison: University of Wisconsin Press, 1985); John S. Nelson, Allan Megill, and Donald McCloskey, eds., *The Rhetoric of the Human Sciences: Language and Argument in Scholarship and Public Affairs* (Madison: University of Wisconsin Press, 1987).

5. Albert Hunter, "Introduction: Rhetoric in Research, Networks of Knowledge," in *The Rhetoric of Social Research, Understood and Believed*, ed. Albert Hunter (New Brunswick, N.J.: Rutgers University Press, 1990), 3.

6. Richard Harvey Brown, *Society as Text: Essays on Rhetoric, Reason, and Reality* (Chicago: University of Chicago Press, 1987).

7. Walter L. Wallace, *Principles of Scientific Sociology* (New York: Aldine, 1983), 4, 5.

8. Wilhelm Dilthey, *Selected Works*, vol. 1: *Introduction to the Human Sciences*, ed. Rudolf A. Makkreel and Frithjof Rodi (Princeton,N.J.: Princeton University Press, 1989), 55–72.

9. Sandra Harding, *The Science Question in Feminism* (Ithaca, N.Y.: Cornell University Press, 1986), 23, 246.

10. Richard Rorty, *Philosophical Papers*, vol. 1: *Objectivity, Relativism, and Truth* (New York: Cambridge University Press, 1991), 79.

11. Ibid., 40.

12. Ibid., 45.

13. Wolf Lepenies, *Between Literature and Science: The Rise of Sociology*, trans. R. J. Hollingdale (Cambridge: Cambridge University Press, 1988).

14. Bruce Mazlish, *A New Science: The Breakdown of Connections and the Birth of Sociology* (New York: Oxford University Press, 1989), 24.

15. Besides the writings of Durkheim cited throughout this book, see Emile Durkheim and Marcel Mauss, *Primitive Classification*, trans. Rodney Needham (Chicago: University of Chicago Press, 1963; originally published in 1903).

16. David Frisby, *Sociological Impressionism* (London: Heinemann, 1981). See also Donald N. Levine, "Simmel as a Resource for Sociological Metatheory," *Sociological Theory* 2 (Fall 1989): 161–73.

17. Robert Bierstedt, "Introduction," in Florian Znaniecki, *On Humanistic Sociology: Selected Papers* (Chicago: University of Chicago Press, 1969), 1–34, quoted at 16.

18. The first effort to insist that the "value-free" Weber was the incorrect one is Wolfgang J. Mommsen, *Max Weber and German Politics, 1890–1920*, trans. Michael Steinberg (Chicago: University of Chicago Press, 1984). Many recent books bring out Weber's relationship to literary themes, especially Harvey Goldman, *Max Weber and Thomas Mann: Calling and the Shaping of the Self* (Berkeley: University of California Press, 1988); Lawrence A. Scaff, *Fleeing the Iron Cage: Culture, Politics, and Modernity in the Thought of Max Weber* (Berkeley: University of California Press, 1989); and Alan Sica, *Weber, Irrationality, and Social Order* (Berkeley: University of California Press, 1988).

19. This point is made forcefully by Donald N. Levine, *The Flight from Ambiguity: Essays in Social and Cultural Theory* (Chicago: University of Chicago Press, 1985).

20. Robert K. Merton, *Sociological Ambivalence* (New York: Free Press, 1976).

21. Robert K. Merton, *On Theoretical Sociology: Five Essays, Old and New* (New York: Free Press, 1967), 28.

22. Ibid., 1–37.

23. I have explored these differences at much greater length in "Books Versus Articles: Two Ways of Publishing Sociology," *Sociological Forum* 5 (September 1990): 477–89.

24. Kai Erikson, "On Sociological Prose," in Hunter, *The Rhetoric of Social Research*, 26.

25. Anthony Giddens, *New Rules of Sociological Method* (New York: Basic Books, 1976), 158. Rorty disagrees; see *Objectivity, Relativism, and Truth*, 97.

26. On this point, see Donald W. Fiske and Richard Shweder, eds., *Metatheory in Social Science: Pluralisms and Subjectivities* (Chicago: University of Chicago Press, 1986).

27. Wallace, *Principles of Scientific Sociology*, 477–93.

28. Herbert Blumer, *Symbolic Interactionism: Perspective and Method* (Berkeley: University of California Press, 1969), 24, 26, 47.

29. The argument that fifteen or so species have an advanced form of protoculture comes from Charles J. Lumsden and Edward O. Wilson, *Genes, Mind, and Culture: The Coevolutionary Process* (Cambridge, Mass.: Harvard University Press, 1981), 2–5.

30. The reference, as every social scientist knows, is to Clifford Geertz, "Thick Description: Toward an Interpretative Theory of Culture," in *The Interpretation of Cultures: Selected Essays* (New York: Basic Books, 1973), 3–30.

31. On the role of interpretation in social science, see Paul Ra-

binow and William M. Sullivan, eds., *Interpretive Social Science: A Second Look* (Berkeley: University of California Press, 1987).

32. One exception is the school generally labeled "new social realist," whose assumptions are close to, but not the same as, my own. See Roy Bashkar, *A Realist Theory of Science* (Sussex: Harvester Press, 1978); Rom Harré and Paul Secord, *The Explanation of Human Behavior* (Totowa, N.J.: Rowman and Littlefield, 1972); and Giddens, *New Rules of Sociological Method.*

33. Howard S. Becker et al., *Boys in White: Student Culture in Medical School* (Chicago: University of Chicago Press, 1961).

34. Jack Katz, *Seductions of Crime: Moral and Sensual Attractions of Doing Evil* (New York: Basic Books, 1988).

35. Elijah Anderson, *Streetwise: Race, Class, and Change in an Urban Community* (Chicago: University of Chicago Press, 1990).

36. For Gans's description of his own career, see Herbert J. Gans, "Relativism, Equality, and Popular Culture," in *Authors of Their Own Lives: Intellectual Autobiographies by Twenty American Sociologists,* ed. Bennett M. Berger (Berkeley: University of California Press, 1990), 432–51.

37. Herbert Gans, *The Urban Villagers: Group and Class in the Life of Italian-Americans* (New York: Free Press, 1962).

38. Herbert Gans, *The Levittowners: Ways of Life and Politics in a New Suburban Community* (New York: Pantheon Books, 1967).

39. Herbert J. Gans, *Middle American Individualism: Political Participation and Liberal Democracy* (New York: Oxford University Press, 1988).

40. Gans, *The Urban Villagers,* 349–50.

41. C. Wright Mills, *The Sociological Imagination* (New York: Grove Press, 1959).

42. James S. Coleman, *Foundations of Social Theory* (Cambridge, Mass.: Belknap Press of Harvard University Press, 1990), 932–46.

43. Ibid., 506.

44. Ibid., 504.

45. Herbert J. Gans, "They Drew the Line," *New York Times Book Review,* 31 March 1985, 26.

46. Dorothy E. Smith, *The Everyday World as Problematic: A Feminist Sociology* (Boston: Northeastern University Press, 1987), 109, 119, 177.

47. Judith Stacey, *Brave New Families: Stories of Domestic Upheaval in Late Twentieth Century America* (New York: Basic Books, 1990), 5.

48. Pauline Marie Rosenau, *Post-modernism and the Social Sci-*

ences: Insights, Inroads, and Intrusions (Princeton, N.J.: Princeton University Press, 1991), 42.

49. For some recent treatments, which themselves demonstrate the tension between sociology and post-modernism, see Eviatar Zerubavel, *The Fine Line: Boundaries and Distinctions in Everyday Life* (New York: Free Press, 1991); Judith Gerson and Kathy Peiss, "Boundaries, Negotiations and Consciousness: Reconceptualizing Gender Relations," *Social Problems* 32 (April 1985): 317–31; and Michele Lamont and Marcel Fournier, eds., *Cultivating Differences: Symbolic Boundaries and the Making of Inequality* (Chicago: University of Chicago Press, 1992).

50. An interesting effort along these lines is Martha Minow, *Making All the Difference: Inclusion, Exclusion, and American Law* (Ithaca, N.Y.: Cornell University Press, 1990).

51. I have elaborated the themes of this paragraph at greater length in "Democracy Versus Sociology: Boundaries and Their Political Consequences," in Lamont and Fournier, *Cultivating Differences*, 309–25.

52. Arthur Vidich and Stanford Lyman, *American Sociology: Worldly Rejections of Religion and Their Directions* (New Haven, Conn.: Yale University Press, 1985).

53. For an argument to the effect that such methods of publication constitute "quality control" standards for the profession, and that such standards are breaking down, see Hubert M. Blalock, "The Real and Unrealized Contributions of Quantitative Sociology," *American Sociological Review* 54 (June 1989): 447–60.

54. I have written about these dangers at greater length in "Sociology as a Vocation," *American Sociologist* 21 (Summer 1990): 136–48.

55. Harding, *The Science Question in Feminism*, 191.

56. For interesting accounts of the hostile reception of sociology on the part of German and French officials, see Karl-Siegbert Rehberg, " 'Anti-Sociology': A Conservative View on Social Sciences," *The History of Sociology* 5 (Spring 1985): 45–60; and Steven Lukes, *Emile Durkheim: His Life and Work: A Critical Study* (London: Penguin Books, 1973), 100–108.

57. On the relationship between sociology and socialism, see Tom Bottomore, *Sociology and Socialism* (New York: St. Martin's Press, 1984).

58. An effort to reexamine the founding texts of sociology for future purposes is Buford Rhea, ed., *The Future of the Sociological Classics* (Boston: Allen and Unwin, 1981).

59. Thomas J. Scheff, *Microsociology: Discourse, Emotion, and Social Structure* (Chicago: University of Chicago Press, 1990), 151.

Chapter 7

1. Steven Marcus, *Engels, Manchester, and the Working Class* (New York: Random House, 1974), 57–58, cited in Daniel Bell, *The Cultural Contradictions of Capitalism* (New York: Basic Books, 1978), 9.

2. Robert MacIver, *The Web of Government* (New York: Free Press, 1965); Georg Simmel, *Conflict and the Web of Group Affiliations* (New York: Free Press, 1955); Clifford Geertz, *The Interpretation of Cultures: Selected Essays* (New York: Basic Books, 1973), 5.

3. Louis Wirth, *On Cities and Social Life: Selected Essays*, ed. Albert J. Riess, Jr. (Chicago: University of Chicago Press, 1964), 61.

4. James F. Short, Jr., ed., *The Social Fabric of the Metropolis: Contributions of the Chicago School of Urban Sociology* (Chicago: University of Chicago Press, 1971); James F. Short, Jr., *The Social Fabric* (Beverly Hills, Calif.: Sage, 1985); Bettina Aptheker, *Tapestries of Life: Women's Work, Women's Consciousness and the Meaning of Daily Life* (Amherst: University of Massachusetts Press, 1989); Phillip E. Hammond, *American Mosaic: Social Patterns of Religion in the United States* (New York: Random House, 1970); Alvin Boskoff, *The Mosaic of Sociological Theory* (New York: Crowell, 1972).

5. C. Wright Mills, *The Sociological Imagination* (New York: Grove Press, 1959), 132–33.

6. Pam McAllister, ed., *Reweaving the Web of Life: Feminism and Non-violence* (Philadelphia: New Society, 1982); Judith Plaskow and Carol P. Christ, eds., *Weaving the Visions: New Patterns of Feminist Spirituality* (San Francisco: HarperCollins, 1989).

7. Marc Pilisuk and Susan Hillier Parks, *The Healing Web* (Hanover, N.H.: University Press of New England, 1986); Harry Wasserman and Holly E. Danforth, *The Human Bond: Support Groups and Mutual Aid* (New York: Springer, 1988).

8. Nathan Glazer, *The Limits of Social Policy* (Cambridge, Mass.: Harvard University Press, 1988), 112.

9. Elizabeth Bott, *Family and Social Network: Roles, Norms, and External Relations in Ordinary Urban Families* (London: Tavistock, 1971).

10. George Gilder, *Men and Marriage* (London: Pelican, 1986); Stephen Goldberg, *The Inevitability of Patriarchy* (New York: Norton, 1973).

11. For an analysis of some of these tools, see Albert O. Hirschman, *The Rhetoric of Reaction: Perversity, Futility, Jeopardy* (Cambridge, Mass.: Belknap Press of Harvard University Press, 1991).

12. Quoted in Greta Jones, *Social Darwinism and English Thought: The Interaction Between Biological and Social Theory* (Sussex: Harvester Press, 1980), 62.

13. N. Blurton Jones and Melvin J. Konner, "!Kung Knowledge of Animal Behavior," in *Kalahari Hunter Gatherers*, ed. R. B. Lee and I. DeVore (Cambridge, Mass.: Harvard University Press, 1976), 347, cited in Richard A. Shweder, *Thinking Through Cultures: Expeditions in Cultural Psychology* (Cambridge, Mass.: Harvard University Press, 1991), 311.

14. Hannah Arendt, *Between Past and Future: Eight Exercises in Political Thought*, 2d ed. (New York: Viking, 1968), 211.

15. Mark Sagoff, "What Is Environmentalism?" in *Three Essays on Ethics and the Environment* (unpublished manuscript, 1990).

16. For a theoretical overview, see James G. March and Johan P. Olson, *Rediscovering Institutions: The Organizational Bases of Politics* (New York: Free Press, 1989); and Kenneth Shepsle, "Studying Institutions: Some Lessons from the Rational Choice Approach," *Journal of Theoretical Politics* 1 (April 1989): 131–47.

17. Oliver E. Williamson, *Markets and Hierarchies* (New York: Free Press, 1975); Andrew Schotter, *The Economic Theory of Social Institutions* (New York: Cambridge University Press, 1981).

18. A collection of both "classic" texts and newer revisions of neo-institutionalism in sociology is contained in Walter W. Powell and Paul J. DiMaggio, eds., *The New Institutionalism in Organizational Analysis* (Chicago: University of Chicago Press, 1991).

19. John W. Meyer and Brian Rowan, "Institutionalized Organizations: Formal Structure as Myth and Ceremony," in Powell and DiMaggio, *The New Institutionalism*, 42.

20. Two recent, and quite different, statements of this position are Robert N. Bellah et al., *Habits of the Heart: Individualism and Commitment in American Life* (Berkeley: University of California Press, 1985); and Jürgen Habermas, *The Theory of Communicative Action*, vol. 2: *Lifeworld and System: A Critique of Functionalist Reason*, trans. Thomas McCarthy (Boston: Beacon Press, 1987).

21. Claude Fischer, *To Dwell Among Friends* (Chicago: University of Chicago Press, 1982).

22. David Popenoe, *Disturbing the Nest: Family Change and Decline in Modern Societies* (New York: Aldine de Gruyter, 1988); Sylvia Ann Hewlitt, *When the Bough Breaks: The Cost of Neglecting Our Children* (New York: Basic Books, 1991).

23. For a recent statement of this position, see Arlene Skolnick, *Embattled Paradise: The American Family in an Age of Uncertainty* (New York: Basic Books, 1991), 199–225. An effort to accumulate the relevant data on the subject is Frances K. Goldscheider and Linda J. Waite, *New Families, No Families? The Transformation of the American Home* (Berkeley: University of California Press, 1991).

24. For various statements of these positions, see Rayna Rapp, "Family and Class in Contemporary America: Notes Toward an Understanding of Ideology," in *Rethinking the Family: Some Feminist Questions*, ed. Barrie Thorne and Marilyn Yalom (New York: Longmans, 1982), 168–87; Evelyn Nakano Glenn, "Gender and the Family," in *Analyzing Gender: A Handbook of Social Science Research*, ed. Beth Hess and Myra Marx Ferree (Newbury Park, Calif.: Sage, 1987), 348–80; and Judith Stacey, "Are Feminists Afraid to Leave Home? The Challenge of Profamily Feminism," in *What Is Feminism?* ed. Juliet Mitchell and Ann Oakley (New York: Pantheon Books, 1986), 208–37.

25. For accounts along these lines, see Stephen Mintz and Susan Kellogg, *Domestic Revolutions: A Social History of American Family Life* (New York: Free Press, 1988); Stephanie Coontz, *The Social Origins of Private Life: A History of the American Family, 1699–1900* (London: Verso, 1988).

26. Edward Shils, *Tradition* (Chicago: University of Chicago Press, 1981).

27. Alison M. Jagger, *Feminist Politics and Human Nature* (Totowa, N.J.: Rowman and Allanheld, 1983), 106.

28. Mintz and Kellogg, *Domestic Revolutions*, 243.

29. Talcott Parsons, "The American Family: Its Relation to Personality and to the Social Structure," in Talcott Parsons and Robert F. Bales, *Family, Socialization and Interaction* (New York: Free Press, 1955), 3–33; William J. Goode, *World Revolution and Family Patterns* (New York: Free Press, 1963).

30. The overlaps and differences between feminism and postmodernism are explored in Linda Nicholson, ed., *Feminism/Postmodernism* (New York: Routledge, 1990).

31. A return to this focus is evident in Robert N. Bellah et al., *The Good Society* (New York: Knopf, 1991).

32. Max Weber, "Politics as a Vocation," in *From Max Weber: Essays in Sociology*, ed. Hans Gerth and C. Wright Mills (New York: Oxford University Press, 1958), 126.

Bibliography

Aiken, William. "Ethical Issues in Agriculture." In *Earthbound: New Introductory Essays in Environmental Ethics*, ed. Tom Regan, 247–88. Philadelphia: Temple University Press, 1984.

Allman, William F. *Apprentices of Wonder: Inside the Neural Network Revolution*. New York: Bantam Books, 1989.

Altmann, Stuart A. "The Structure of Primate Social Communication." In *Social Communication Among Primates*, ed. Stuart A. Altmann, 325–62. Chicago: University of Chicago Press, 1967.

Ammerman, Albert J., and L. L. Cavalli-Sforza. *The Neolithic Transformation and the Genetics of Population in Europe*. Princeton, N.J.: Princeton University Press, 1984.

Anderson, Elijah. *Streetwise: Race, Class, and Change in an Urban Community*. Chicago: University of Chicago Press, 1990.

Aptheker, Bettina. *Tapestries of Life: Women's Work, Women's Consciousness and the Meaning of Daily Life*. Amherst: University of Massachusetts Press, 1989.

Arendt, Hannah. *Between Past and Future: Eight Exercises in Political Thought*. 2d ed. New York: Viking, 1968.

——— . *The Human Condition*. Chicago: University of Chicago Press, 1958.

Axelrod, Robert. *The Evolution of Cooperation*. New York: Basic Books, 1984.

Bailey, Kenneth D. *Social Entropy Theory*. Albany: State University of New York Press, 1990.

Barash, David P. *The Hare and the Tortoise*. New York: Viking, 1986.

Barber, Bernard. "Introduction." In *L. J. Henderson on the Social System: Selected Writings*, ed. Bernard Barber, 1–53. Chicago: University of Chicago Press, 1970.

Bardo, Susan. "The Cartesian Masculinization of Thought." *Signs* 11 (Spring 1986): 439–56.

Barnes, Barry, and David Bloor. "Relativism, Rationalism and the Sociology of Knowledge." In *Rationality and Relativism*, ed. Martin Hollis and Steven Lukes, 21–47. Cambridge, Mass.: MIT Press, 1982.

Bashkar, Roy. *A Realist Theory of Science.* Sussex: Harvester Press, 1978.

Bataille, Georges. *Visions of Excess: Selected Writings, 1927–1939*, ed. and trans. Allan Stoekl. Minneapolis: University of Minnesota Press, 1985.

Bateman, John. "The Role of Language in the Maintenance of Intersubjectivity: A Computational Investigation." In *Social Action and Artificial Intelligence: Surrey Conferences on Sociological Theory and Method* 3, ed. C. Nigel Gilbert and Christian Heath, 40–81. Aldershot: Gower, 1985.

Bateson, Gregory. "A Theory of Play and Fantasy." *Psychiatric Research Reports* 2 (1955): 39–51.

Beck, Benjamin B. *Animal Tool Behavior.* New York: Garland STPM Press, 1980.

———. "Primate Tool Behavior." In *Socioecology and Psychology of Primates*, ed. Russell H. Tuttle, 413–47. The Hague: Mouton, 1977.

Becker, Gary. "Altruism, Egoism, and Genetic Fitness." *Journal of Economic Literature* 14 (September 1976): 817–26.

Becker, Howard S., et al. *Boys in White: Student Culture in Medical School.* Chicago: University of Chicago Press, 1961.

Beckstrom, John H. *Evolutionary Jurisprudence: Prospects and Limitations in the Use of Modern Darwinism Throughout the Legal Process.* Urbana: University of Illinois Press, 1989.

———. *Sociobiology and the Law: The Biology of Altruism in the Courtroom of the Future.* Urbana: University of Illinois Press, 1985.

Bell, Daniel. *The Cultural Contradictions of Capitalism.* New York: Basic Books, 1978.

Bellah, Robert N., et al. *The Good Society.* New York: Knopf, 1991.

———. *Habits of the Heart: Individualism and Commitment in American Life.* Berkeley: University of California Press, 1985.

Beniger, James R. *The Control Revolution.* Cambridge, Mass.: Harvard University Press, 1986.

Bennington, Geoffrey. "Aberrations: de Man (and) the Machine." In *Reading de Man Reading*, ed. Lindsay Waters and Wlad Godzich, 209–22. Minneapolis: University of Minnesota Press, 1989.

Berger, John. *Pig Earth.* New York: Pantheon Books, 1979.

Berger, Peter, and Thomas Luckmann. *The Social Construction of Reality: A Treatise in the Sociology of Knowledge.* Garden City, N.Y.: Doubleday, 1967.

Berklekamp, Elwyn R., John H. Conway, and Richard K. Guy. *Winning Ways (for Your Mathematical Plays).* New York: Academic Press, 1982.

Berlin, Isaiah. *The Crooked Timber of Humanity: Chapters in the History of Ideas.* New York: Knopf, 1991.

Bierstedt, Robert. "Introduction." In Florian Znaniecki, *On Humanistic Sociology: Selected Papers,* 1–34. Chicago: University of Chicago Press, 1969.

Blalock, Hubert M. "The Real and Unrealized Contributions of Quantitative Sociology." *American Sociological Review* 54 (June 1989): 447–60.

Blumer, Herbert. *Symbolic Interactionism: Perspective and Method.* Berkeley: University of California Press, 1969.

Bonner, John Tyler. *The Evolution of Culture in Animals.* Princeton, N.J.: Princeton University Press, 1980.

Booth, Wayne. *The Company We Keep: An Ethics of Fiction.* Berkeley: University of California Press, 1988.

Boskoff, Alvin. *The Mosaic of Sociological Theory.* New York: Crowell, 1972.

Bott, Elizabeth. *Family and Social Network: Roles, Norms, and External Relations in Ordinary Urban Families.* London: Tavistock, 1971.

Bottomore, Tom. *Sociology and Socialism.* New York: St. Martin's Press, 1984.

Boyd, Robert, and Peter J. Richardson. *Culture and the Evolutionary Process.* Chicago: University of Chicago Press, 1985.

Brent, Edward E. "Knowledge-Based Systems: A Qualitative Formalism." *Qualitative Sociology* 9 (Fall 1986): 256–82.

Brooke-Rose, Christine. "The Dissolution of Character in the Novel." In *Reconstructing Individualism: Autonomy, Individuality, and the Self in Western Thought,* ed. Thomas C. Heller, Morton Sosna, and David E. Wellbery, 184–96. Stanford, Calif.: Stanford University Press, 1986.

Brown, Norman O. *Life Against Death: The Psychoanalytic Meaning of History.* Middletown, Conn.: Wesleyan University Press, 1959.

Brown, Richard Harvey. *Society as Text: Essays on Rhetoric, Reason, and Reality.* Chicago: University of Chicago Press, 1987.

Bruner, Jerome. *Acts of Meaning.* Cambridge, Mass.: Harvard University Press, 1990.

Buckley, Kerry W. *Mechanical Man: John Broadus Watson and the Beginnings of Behaviorism*. New York: Guilford Press, 1989.

Cahan, Harley. "Against the Moral Considerability of Ecosystems." *Environmental Ethics* 10 (Fall 1988): 195–216.

Callicott, J. Baird. *In Defense of the Land Ethic: Essays in Environmental Philosophy*. Albany: State University of New York Press, 1989.

——— "Moral Considerability and Extraterrestrial Life." In *Beyond Spaceship Earth: Environmental Ethics and the Solar System*, ed. Eugene C. Hargrove, 227–59. San Francisco: Sierra Club Books, 1986.

Campbell, Jeremy. *The Improbable Machine: What the Upheavals in Artificial Intelligence Reveal About How the Mind Really Works*. New York: Simon and Schuster, 1989.

Catton, William R., Jr. "On the Dire Destiny of Human Lemmings." In *Deep Ecology*, ed. Michael Tobias, 74–89. San Marcos, Calif.: Avant Books, 1988.

——— *Overshoot: The Ecological Basis of Revolutionary Change*. Urbana: University of Illinois Press, 1980.

Cheney, Dorothy L., and Robert M. Seyfarth. *How Monkeys See the World: Inside the Mind of Another Species*. Chicago: University of Chicago Press, 1990.

Churchland, Patricia Smith. *Neurophilosophy: Toward a Unified Science of the Mind-Brain*. Cambridge, Mass.: MIT Press, 1986.

——— , and Terrence J. Sejnowski. "Perspectives on Cognitive Neuroscience." *Science* 242 (4 November 1988): 741–45.

Clancey, William J. "Use of MYCIN's Rules for Tutoring." In *Rule-Based Systems: The MYCIN Experiments of the Stanford Heuristic Programming Project*, ed. Bruce G. Buchanan and Edward H. Shortliffe, 464–89. Reading, Mass: Addison-Wesley, 1984.

Coleman, James S. *Foundations of Social Theory*. Cambridge, Mass.: Belknap Press of Harvard University Press, 1990.

Commoner, Barry. *The Closing Circle: Nature, Man, and Technology*. New York: Knopf, 1971.

Cooley, Charles Horton. *Human Nature and the Social Order*. New York: Schocken Books, 1964.

Coontz, Stephanie. *The Social Origins of Private Life: A History of the American Family, 1699–1900*. London: Verso, 1988.

Coulter, Jeff. "On Comprehension and 'Mental Representation.' " In *Social Action and Artificial Intelligence*, ed. C. Nigel Gilbert and Christian Heath, 8–23. Aldershot: Gower, 1985.

——— . *Rethinking Cognitive Theory*. New York: St. Martin's Press, 1983.

————. *The Social Construction of Mind.* London: Macmillan, 1979.

Daly, Herman E. "Economics and Sustainability: In Defense of a Steady-State Economy." In *Deep Ecology,* ed. Michael Tobias, 90–100. San Marcos, Calif.: Avant Books, 1988.

Dawkins, Richard. *The Blind Watchmaker.* New York: Norton, 1986.

————. *The Selfish Gene.* New York: Oxford University Press, 1976.

Degler, Carl. *In Search of Human Nature: The Decline and Revival of Darwinism in American Social Thought.* New York: Oxford University Press, 1991.

Deleuze, Gilles, and Félix Guattari. *Anti-Oedipus: Capitalism and Schizophrenia,* trans. Robert Hurley, Mark Seem, and Helen R. Lane. Minneapolis: University of Minnesota Press, 1983.

de Man, Paul. *Allegories of Reading: Figural Language in Rousseau, Nietzsche, Rilke, and Proust.* New Haven, Conn.: Yale University Press, 1979.

DeMott, Benjamin. "Rediscovering Complexity." *The Atlantic* 262 (1988): 67–74.

Dennett, Daniel C. *Brainstorms: Philosophical Essays on Mind and Psychology.* Montgomery, Vt.: Bradford, 1978.

———— *Consciousness Explained.* Boston: Little, Brown, 1991.

Derrida, Jacques. "Force of Law: The 'Mystical Foundation of Authority.' " *Cardozo Law Review* 11 (July/August 1990): 921–1045.

————. *The Post Card: From Socrates to Freud and Beyond,* trans. Alan Bass. Chicago: University of Chicago Press, 1987.

Devall, Bill. *Simple in Means, Rich in Ends: Practicing Deep Ecology.* Salt Lake City: Peregrine Smith Books, 1988.

————, and George Sessions. *Deep Ecology: Living as If Nature Mattered.* Salt Lake City: Peregrine Smith Books, 1985.

de Waal, Frans. *Chimpanzee Politics: Power and Sex Among Apes.* New York: Harper and Row, 1982.

————. *Peacemaking Among Primates.* Cambridge, Mass.: Harvard University Press, 1989.

Dilthey, Wilhelm. *Selected Works,* vol. 1: *Introduction to the Human Sciences,* ed. Rudolf A. Makkereel and Frithjof Rodi, 55–72. Princeton, N.J.: Princeton University Press, 1989.

Douglas, Mary. *Natural Symbols: Explorations in Cosmology.* New York: Pantheon Books, 1982.

Dreyfus, Hubert L. *What Computers Can't Do: The Limits of Artificial Intelligence.* Rev. ed. New York: Harper Colophon Books, 1979.

Durkheim, Emile. *The Division of Labor in Society,* trans. George Simpson. New York: Free Press, 1963. (Originally published in 1893.)

———— . "The Dualism of Human Nature and Its Social Conditions." In Durkheim, *On Morality and Society*, ed. Robert N. Bellah, 149–63. Chicago: University of Chicago Press, 1973.

———— . *The Elementary Forms of Religious Life*, trans. Joseph Ward Swain. New York: Free Press, 1965. (Originally published in 1912.)

———— , and Marcel Mauss. *Primitive Classification*, trans. Rodney Needham. Chicago: University of Chicago Press, 1963. (Originally published in 1903.)

Dworkin, Andrea. *Pornography: Men Possessing Women*. New York: Putnam, 1981.

Dyke, Charles. *The Evolutionary Dynamics of Complex Systems: A Study in Biological Complexity*. New York: Oxford University Press, 1988.

Edelman, Gerald M. *Neural Darwinism*. New York: Basic Books, 1987.

———— . *Topobiology*. New York: Basic Books, 1988.

———— , and Vernon B. Mountcastle. *The Mindful Brain: Cortical Organization and the Group-Selective Theory of Higher Brain Function*. Cambridge, Mass.: MIT Press, 1978.

Ehrenfeld, David. *The Arrogance of Humanism*. New York: Oxford University Press, 1978.

Elias, Norbert. *The Civilizing Process*. New York: Urizen Books, 1978.

Elster, Jon. *Nuts and Bolts for the Social Sciences*. Cambridge: Cambridge University Press, 1989.

Epstein, Cynthia Fuchs. *Deceptive Distinctions: Sex, Gender, and the Social Order*. New Haven, Conn.: Yale University Press, 1988.

Erikson, Kai. "On Sociological Prose." In *The Rhetoric of Social Research, Understood and Believed*, ed. Albert Hunter, 23–34. New Brunswick, N.J.: Rutgers University Press, 1990.

Feigenbaum, Edward A., and Julian Feldman, eds. *Computers and Thought*. New York: McGraw-Hill, 1963.

———— , and Pamela McCorduck. *The Fifth Generation: Artificial Intelligence and Japan's Computer Challenge to the World*. Reading, Mass.: Addison-Wesley, 1983.

Ferre, Frederick. "Obstacles in the Path to Organismic Ethics: Some Second Thoughts." *Environmental Ethics* 11 (Fall 1989): 231–41.

Ferry, Luc, and Alain Renaut. *French Philosophy of the Sixties: An Essay on Antihumanism*, trans. Mary Schnackenberg Cattani. Amherst: University of Massachusetts Press, 1990.

Fischer, Claude. *To Dwell Among Friends*. Chicago: University of Chicago Press, 1982.

Fish, Stanley. *Doing What Comes Naturally: Change, Rhetoric, and the Practice of Theory in Literary and Legal Studies*. Durham, N.C.: Duke University Press, 1989.

————. *Is There a Text in This Class? The Authority of Interpretative Communities*. Cambridge, Mass.: Harvard University Press, 1980.

Fiske, Alan Page. *Structures of Social Life: The Four Elementary Forms of Human Relations*. New York: Free Press, 1991.

Fiske, Donald W., and Richard Shweder, eds. *Metatheory in Social Science: Pluralisms and Subjectivities*. Chicago: University of Chicago Press, 1986.

Fodor, Jerry. *The Language of Thought*. New York: Crowell, 1975.

————. "Methodological Solipsism." In *Mind Design*, ed. John Haugland, 307–38. Montgomery, Vt.: Bradford, 1981.

————. *Representations: Philosophical Essays on the Foundations of Cognitive Science*. Cambridge, Mass.: MIT Press, 1981.

Foucault, Michel. *The Order of Things: An Archeology of the Human Sciences*. New York: Vintage, 1970.

Fox, Michael Allen. *The Case for Animal Experimentation: An Evolutionary and Ethical Perspective*. Berkeley: University of California Press, 1986.

Frank, Robert. *Passions Within Reason: The Strategic Role of the Emotions*. New York: Norton, 1988.

Frisby, David. *Sociological Impressionism*. London: Heinemann, 1981.

Gallup, Gordon. "Self Recognition in Primates: A Comparative Approach to the Bidirectional Properties of Consciousness." *American Psychologist* 32 (May 1977): 329–38.

————. "Towards on Operational Definition of Self-Awareness." In *Socioecology and Psychology of Primates*, ed. Russell H. Tuttle, 309–41. The Hague: Mouton, 1977.

Gans, Herbert J. *The Levittowners: Ways of Life and Politics in a New Suburban Community*. New York: Pantheon Books, 1967.

————. *Middle American Individualism: Political Participation and Liberal Democracy*. New York: Oxford University Press, 1988.

————. "Relativism, Equality, and Popular Culture." In *Authors of Their Own Lives: Intellectual Autobiographies by Twenty American Sociologists*, ed. Bennett M. Berger, 432–51. Berkeley: University of California Press, 1990.

————. *The Urban Villagers: Group and Class in the Life of Italian-Americans*. New York: Free Press, 1962.

Gardner, B. T., and R. A. Gardner. "Teaching Sign Language to a Chimpanzee." *Science* 165 (15 August 1960): 664–72.

Gardner, Howard. *Frames of Mind: The Theory of Multiple Intelligence*. New York: Basic Books, 1983.

——— . *The Mind's New Science: A History of the Cognitive Revolution*. New York: Basic Books, 1985.

Garfinkel, Harold. *Studies in Ethnomethodology*. Englewood Cliffs, N.J.: Prentice-Hall, 1967.

Gazzaniga, Michael S. *The Social Brain*. New York: Basic Books, 1985.

Geertz, Clifford. *The Interpretation of Cultures: Selected Essays*. New York: Basic Books, 1973.

Gehlen, Arnold. *Man: His Nature and Place in the World*, trans. Clare McMillan and Karl Pillemer. New York: Columbia University Press, 1988.

——— . *Man in the Age of Technology*, trans. Patricia Lipscomb. New York: Columbia University Press, 1980.

Gerson, Judith, and Kathy Peiss. "Boundaries, Negotiations and Consciousness: Reconceptualizing Gender Relations." *Social Problems* 32 (April 1985): 317–31.

Giddens, Anthony. *The Constitution of Society: Outline of the Theory of Structuration*. Berkeley: University of California Press, 1984.

——— . *New Rules of Sociological Method*. New York: Basic Books, 1976.

Gilbert, C. Nigel, and Christian Heath. "Introduction." In *Social Action and Artificial Intelligence*, ed. C. Nigel Gilbert and Christian Heath, 1–7. Aldershot: Gower, 1985.

Gilder, George. *Men and Marriage*. London: Pelican, 1986.

Glazer, Nathan. *The Limits of Social Policy*. Cambridge, Mass.: Harvard University Press, 1988.

Glenn, Evelyn Nakano. "Gender and the Family." In *Analyzing Gender: A Handbook of Social Science Research*, ed. Beth Hess and Myra Marx Ferree, 348–80. Newbury Park, Calif.: Sage, 1987.

Goffman, Erving. *Encounters: Two Studies in the Sociology of Interaction*. Indianapolis: Bobbs-Merrill, 1961.

——— . *Relations in Public: Microstudies of the Public Order*. New York: Harper Torchbooks, 1971.

Goldberg, Stephen. *The Inevitability of Patriarchy*. New York: Norton, 1973.

Goldman, Harvey. *Max Weber and Thomas Mann: Calling and the Shaping of the Self*. Berkeley: University of California Press, 1988.

Goldscheider, Frances K., and Linda J. Waite. *New Families, No Families? The Transformation of the American Home*. Berkeley: University of California Press, 1991.

Good, David. "Sociology and AI: The Lessons from Social Psychology." In *Social Action and Artificial Intelligence*, ed. C. Nigel Gilbert and Christian Heath, 82–103. Aldershot: Gower, 1985.

Goodall, Jane. *In the Shadow of Man*. Boston: Houghton Mifflin, 1971.
——— . *Through a Window: My Thirty Years with the Chimpanzees of Gombe*. Boston: Houghton Mifflin, 1990.
Goode, William J. *World Revolution and Family Patterns*. New York: Free Press, 1963.
Goody, Jack. *The Logic of Writing and the Organization of Society*. Cambridge: Cambridge University Press, 1986.
Gould, Stephen Jay. *Wonderful Life: The Burgess Shale and the Nature of History*. New York: Norton, 1989.
Gove, Walter R. "Sociobiology Misses the Mark: An Essay on Why Biology but Not Sociobiology Is Very Relevant to Sociology." *American Sociologist* 18 (Fall 1987): 258–77.
Greenberg, David. *The Construction of Homosexuality*. Chicago: University of Chicago Press, 1988.
Griffin, David R., ed. *Sacred Interconnections: Postmodern Spirituality, Political Economy, and Art*. Albany: State University of New York Press, 1990.
Griffin, Donald R. *Animal Thinking*. Cambridge, Mass.: Harvard University Press, 1984.
——— . *The Question of Animal Awareness: Evolutionary Continuity of Mental Experience*. Rev. ed. Los Altos, Calif.: William Kaufmann, 1981.
Griffin, Susan. *Woman and Nature*. New York: Harper and Row, 1978.
Grossberg, Stephen. *Neural Networks and Natural Intelligence*. Cambridge, Mass.: MIT Press, 1988.
Habermas, Jürgen. *The Theory of Communicative Action*, vol. 1: *Reason and the Rationalization of Society*, trans. Thomas McCarthy. Boston: Beacon Press, 1984.
——— . *The Theory of Communicative Action*, vol. 2: *Lifeworld and System: A Critique of Functionalist Reason*, trans. Thomas McCarthy. Boston: Beacon Press, 1987.
Hamilton, William D. "The Genetical Evolution of Social Behavior, I and II." *Journal of Theoretical Biology* 7 (July 1964): 1–52.
Hammond, Phillip E. *American Mosaic: Social Patterns of Religion in the United States*. New York: Random House, 1970.
Hannan, Michael T., and John Freeman. *Organizational Ecology*. Cambridge, Mass.: Harvard University Press, 1989.
Haraway, Donna. "A Manifesto for Cyborgs: Science, Technology, and Socialist Feminism in the 1980s." In *Feminism/Postmodernism*, ed. Linda J. Nicholson, 190–233. New York: Routledge, 1990.
——— . *Primate Visions: Gender, Race, and Nature in the World of Modern Science*. New York: Routledge, 1989.

Harding, Sandra. *The Science Question in Feminism*. Ithaca, N.Y.: Cornell University Press, 1986.

—. *Whose Science? Whose Knowledge? Thinking from Women's Lives*. Ithaca, N.Y.: Cornell University Press, 1991.

Hargrove, Eugene C., ed. *Religion and Environmental Crisis*. Athens: University of Georgia Press, 1986.

Harré, Rom, and Paul Secord. *The Explanation of Human Behavior*. Totowa, N.J.: Rowman and Littlefield, 1972.

Hawley, Amos H. *Human Ecology: A Theory of Community Structure*. New York: Ronald Press, 1950.

Hayles, N. Katherine. *Chaos Bound: Orderly Disorder in Contemporary Literature and Science*. Ithaca, N.Y.: Cornell University Press, 1990.

—, ed. *Chaos and Order: Complex Dynamics in Literature and Science*. Chicago: University of Chicago Press, 1991.

Heller, Thomas C. "Accounting for Law." In *Autopoietic Law: A New Approach to Law and Society*, ed. Gunther Teubner, 283–311. Berlin and New York: de Gruyter, 1988.

—, and David E. Wellbery. "Introduction." In *Reconstructing Individualism*, ed. Thomas C. Heller, Morton Sosna, and David E. Wellbery, 1–15. Stanford, Calif.: Stanford University Press, 1986.

Heritage, John. *Garfinkel and Ethnomethodology*. Cambridge, England: Polity Press, 1984.

Herrnstein Smith, Barbara. *Contingencies of Value: Alternative Perspectives for Critical Theory*. Cambridge, Mass.: Harvard University Press, 1988.

Hewlitt, Sylvia Ann. *When the Bough Breaks: The Cost of Neglecting Our Children*. New York: Basic Books, 1991.

Hinde, Robert A. *Individuals, Relationships, and Culture: Links Between Ethology and the Social Sciences*. Cambridge: Cambridge University Press, 1987.

Hinton, Geoffrey E., and James A. Anderson, eds. *Parallel Models of Associative Memory*. Hillsdale, N.J.: Erlbaum, 1982.

Hirschman, Albert O. *The Rhetoric of Reaction: Perversity, Futility, Jeopardy*. Cambridge, Mass.: Belknap Press of Harvard University Press, 1991.

Hobbs, Jerry R., and Robert C. Moore. *Formal Theories of the Commonsense World*. Norwood, N.J.: Ablex, 1985.

Hofstader, Douglas R. *Gödel, Escher, and Bach: An Eternal Golden Braid*. New York: Basic Books, 1979.

Hofstader, Richard. *Social Darwinism in American Thought, 1860–1915*. Philadelphia: University of Pennsylvania Press, 1945.

Honneth, Axel, and Hans Joas. *Social Action and Human Nature.* Cambridge: Cambridge University Press, 1988.

Horigan, Stephen. *Nature and Culture in Western Discourses.* London: Routledge, 1988.

Hubbard, Ruth. *The Politics of Woman's Biology.* New Brunswick, N.J.: Rutgers University Press, 1990.

Hunter, Albert. "Introduction: Rhetoric in Research, Networks of Knowledge." In *The Rhetoric of Social Research,* ed. Albert Hunter, 1–22. New Brunswick, N.J.: Rutgers University Press, 1990.

Hyde, Lewis. *The Gift: Imagination and the Erotic Life of Poetry.* New York: Vintage, 1983.

Jacob, François. *The Logic of Life: A History of Heredity,* trans. Betty E. Spillman. New York: Pantheon Books, 1973.

Jagger, Alison M. *Feminist Politics and Human Nature.* Totowa, N.J.: Rowman and Allanheld, 1983.

Jahoda, Marie. "Artificial Intelligence: An Outsider's Perspective." *Science and Public Policy* 13 (December 1986): 333–40.

Jamieson, Dale. "Against Zoos." In *In Defense of Animals,* ed. Peter Singer, 108–17. New York: Harper and Row, 1985.

Janik, Allan, and Stephen Toulmin. *Wittgenstein's Vienna.* New York: Simon and Schuster, 1973.

Janowitz, Morris. "The Social Ecology of Citizenship." In *Morris Janowitz on Social Organization and Social Control,* ed. James Burk, 251–71. Chicago: University of Chicago Press, 1991.

Jantsch, Erich. *The Self-Organizing Universe.* Oxford: Pergamon Press, 1980.

Jasper, James M., and Dorothy Nelkin. *Animal Rights: Dynamics of a Moral Crusade.* New York: Free Press, 1992.

Johnson-Laird, Philip N. *The Computer and the Mind: An Introduction to Cognitive Science.* Cambridge, Mass.: Harvard University Press, 1988.

Jones, Greta. *Social Darwinism and English Thought: The Interaction Between Biological and Social Theory.* Sussex: Harvester Press, 1980.

Jones, Nicholas Blurton, and Melvin J. Konner. "!Kung Knowledge of Animal Behavior." In *Kalahari Hunter Gatherers,* ed. Richard B. Lee and Irven Devore, 325–48. Cambridge, Mass.: Harvard University Press, 1976.

Karelis, Charles. "Reflections on the Turing Test." *Journal for the Theory of Social Behaviour* 16 (July 1986): 161–72.

Katz, Jack. *Seductions of Crime: Moral and Sensual Attractions of Doing Evil.* New York: Basic Books, 1988.

Kaye, Howard L. *The Social Meaning of Modern Biology: From Social Darwinism to Sociobiology.* New Haven, Conn.: Yale University Press, 1986.

Keller, Evelyn Fox. *Reflections on Gender and Science.* New Haven, Conn.: Yale University Press, 1985.

Kernan, Alvin. *The Death of Literature.* New Haven, Conn.: Yale University Press, 1990.

Kitcher, Philip. *Vaulting Ambition: Sociobiology and the Quest for Human Nature.* Cambridge, Mass.: MIT Press, 1985.

Koodsma, Donald E. "Aspects of Learning in the Ontogeny of Bird Song: Where, from Whom, When, How Many, Which, and How Accurately." In *The Development of Behavior: Comparative and Evolutionary Aspects,* ed. Gordon M. Burghardt and Marc Beckoff, 215–30. New York: Garland STPM Press, 1978.

Lamont, Michele, and Marcel Fournier, eds. *Cultivating Differences: Symbolic Boundaries and the Making of Inequality.* Chicago: University of Chicago Press, 1992.

Lasker, C. G. N., and G. W. Lasker, eds. *Biological Aspects of Human Migration.* Cambridge: Cambridge University Press, 1988.

Latour, Bruno. *Science in Action: How to Follow Scientists and Engineers Through Society.* Cambridge, Mass.: Harvard University Press, 1987.

Lepenies, Wolf. *Between Literature and Science: The Rise of Sociology,* trans. R. J. Hollingdale. Cambridge: Cambridge University Press, 1988.

Levine, Donald N. *The Flight from Ambiguity: Essays in Social and Cultural Theory.* Chicago: University of Chicago Press, 1985.

——— . "Simmel as a Resource for Sociological Metatheory." *Sociological Theory* 2 (Fall 1989): 161–73.

Levinson, Sanford. *Constitutional Faith.* Princeton, N.J.: Princeton University Press, 1988.

——— . "Law as Literature." In *Interpreting Law and Literature: A Hermeneutic Reader,* ed. Sanford Levinson and Steven Mailloux, 155–73. Evanston, Ill.: Northwestern University Press, 1988.

Lévi-Strauss, Claude. *The Elementary Structures of Kinship,* trans. James Harle Bell, John Richard von Sturmer, and Rodney Needham. Boston: Beacon Press, 1969. (Originally published in 1949.)

Lewontin, Richard C., Steven Rose, and Leon J. Kamin. *Not in Our Genes: Biology, Ideology, and Human Nature.* New York: Pantheon Books, 1984.

Lieberman, Philip. "The Phylogeny of Language." In *How Animals Communicate,* ed. Thomas Sebeok, 3–25. Bloomington: Indiana University Press, 1977.

———. *Uniquely Human: The Evolution of Speech, Thought, and Selfless Behavior.* Cambridge, Mass.: Harvard University Press, 1991.

Lindauer, Martin. *Communication Among Social Bees.* Rev. ed. Cambridge, Mass.: Harvard University Press, 1971.

———. "The Functional Significance of the Honey Bee Waggle Dance." *American Naturalist* 105 (March–April 1971): 89–96.

Lopreato, Joseph. *Human Nature and Biocultural Evolution.* Boston: Allen and Unwin, 1984.

Lovelock, James. *The Ages of Gaia: A Biography of Our Living Earth.* New York: Norton, 1988.

———. *Gaia: A New Look at Life on Earth.* New York: Oxford University Press, 1979.

Luhmann, Niklas. *The Differentiation of Society,* trans. Stephen Holmes and Charles Larmore. New York: Columbia University Press, 1982.

———. *Ecological Communication,* trans. John Bednarz, Jr. Chicago: University of Chicago Press, 1989.

———. *Essays on Self-Reference.* New York: Columbia University Press, 1990.

———. *Political Theory in the Welfare State,* trans. John Bednarz, Jr. Berlin and New York: de Gruyter, 1990.

———. "The Unity of the Legal System." In *Autopoietic Law: A New Approach to Law and Society,* ed. Gunther Teubner, 12–35. Berlin and New York: de Gruyter, 1988.

Luke, Tim. "The Dreams of Deep Ecology." *Telos* 76 (1988): 65–92.

Lukes, Steven. *Emile Durkheim: His Life and Work: A Critical Study.* London: Penguin Books, 1973.

Lumsden, Charles J., and Edward O. Wilson. *Genes, Mind, and Culture: The Coevolutionary Process.* Cambridge, Mass.: Harvard University Press, 1981.

———. *Promethean Fire: Reflections on the Origin of the Mind.* Cambridge, Mass.: Harvard University Press, 1983.

Lyotard, Jean-François. *The Postmodern Condition: A Report on Knowledge,* trans. Geoff Bennington and Brian Massumi. Minneapolis: University of Minnesota Press, 1984.

McAllister, Pam, ed. *Reweaving the Web of Life: Feminism and Nonviolence.* Philadelphia: New Society, 1982.

McClelland, J. L., D. E. Rumelhart, and G. E. Hinton. "A General Framework for Parallel Distributive Processing." In David E. Rumelhart, James L. McClelland, and the PDP Research Group, *Parallel Distributed Processing: Explorations in the Microstructure of*

Cognition, vol. 1: *Foundations*, 45–76. Cambridge, Mass.: MIT Press, 1986.

McCloskey, Donald. *The Rhetoric of Economics*. Madison: University of Wisconsin Press, 1985.

McCorduck, Pamela. *Machines Who Think*. San Francisco: Freeman, 1981.

MacIntyre, Alasdair. *After Virtue*. South Bend, Ind.: Notre Dame University Press, 1981.

MacIver, Robert. *The Web of Government*. New York: Free Press, 1965.

McKibben, Bill. *The End of Nature*. New York: Random House, 1989.

Macy, Joanna. "The Ecological Self: Postmodern Ground for Right Action." In *Sacred Interconnections*, ed. David R. Griffin, 35–48. Albany: State University of New York Press, 1990.

March, James G., and Johan P. Olson. *Rediscovering Institutions: The Organizational Bases of Politics*. New York: Free Press, 1989.

Marcus, Steven. *Engels, Manchester, and the Working Class*. New York: Random House, 1974.

Marx, Karl, and Frederick Engels. *The German Ideology*, ed. C. J. Arthur. New York: International Publishers, 1970.

Marx, Leo. *The Machine in the Garden: Technology and the Pastoral Ideal in America*. New York: Oxford University Press, 1964.

Matthews, Freya. "Conservation and Self-Realization: A Deep Ecology Perspective." *Environmental Ethics* 10 (1988): 347–55.

Maturana, Humberto R., and Francisco J. Varela. *The Tree of Knowledge: The Biological Roots of Human Understanding*. Boston: New Science Library, 1987.

Mauss, Marcel. *The Gift*. New York: Norton, 1967.

Mazlish, Bruce. *A New Science: The Breakdown of Connections and the Birth of Sociology*. New York: Oxford University Press, 1989.

Mead, Carver. *Analog VLSI and Neural Systems*. Reading, Mass.: Addison-Wesley, 1988.

Mead, George Herbert. *Mind, Self, and Society from the Standpoint of a Social Behaviorist*. Chicago: University of Chicago Press, 1962. (Originally published in 1934.)

Merchant, Carolyn. *The Death of Nature: Women, Ecology, and the Scientific Revolution*. New York: Harper and Row, 1980.

Merton, Robert K. *On Theoretical Sociology: Five Essays, Old and New*. New York: Free Press, 1967.

——— . *Sociological Ambivalence*. New York: Free Press, 1976.

Meyer, John W., and Brian Rowan. "Institutionalized Organizations:

Formal Structure as Myth and Ceremony." In *The New Institutionalism in Organizational Analysis*, ed. Walter W. Powell and Paul J. DiMaggio, 41–62. Chicago: University of Chicago Press, 1991.

Midgley, Mary. "Rival Fatalisms: The Hollowness of the Sociobiology Debate." In *Sociobiology Examined*, ed. Ashley Montague, 15–38. New York: Oxford University Press, 1980.

Mills, C. Wright. *The Sociological Imagination*. New York: Grove Press, 1959.

Minow, Martha. *Making All the Difference: Inclusion, Exclusion, and American Law*. Ithaca, N.Y.: Cornell University Press, 1990.

Minsky, Marvin. "A Framework for Representing Knowledge." In *Mind Design*, ed. John Haugland, 95–128. Montgomery, Vt.: Bradford, 1981.

———. *The Society of Mind*. New York: Simon and Schuster, 1986.

———, and Seymour Papert. *Perceptrons*. Cambridge, Mass.: MIT Press, 1969.

Mintz, Stephen, and Susan Kellogg. *Domestic Revolutions: A Social History of American Family Life*. New York: Free Press, 1988.

Mommsen, Wolfgang J. *Max Weber and German Politics, 1890–1920*, trans. Michael Steinberg. Chicago: University of Chicago Press, 1984.

Moravec, Hans. *Mind Children: The Future of Robot and Human Intelligence*. Cambridge, Mass.: Harvard University Press, 1988.

Morris, Charles W. "Introduction: George H. Mead as Social Psychologist and Social Philosopher." In G. H. Mead, *Mind, Self, and Society*, ix–xxxv. Chicago: University of Chicago Press, 1962.

———. *Signs, Language, and Behavior*. Englewood Cliffs, N.J.: Prentice-Hall, 1946.

Mortensen, Joseph. *Whale Songs and Wasp Maps: The Mystery of Animal Thinking*. New York: Dutton, 1987.

Myers, Norman. "Epilogue." In *Gaia: An Atlas of Planet Management*, 258. Garden City, N.Y.: Doubleday, 1984.

Naess, Arne. *Ecology, Community, and Lifestyle: Outline of an Ecosophy*, rev. ed., trans. David Rothenberg. Cambridge: Cambridge University Press, 1989.

———. "The Shallow and the Deep, Long-Range Ecology Movement: A Summary." *Inquiry* 16 (Spring 1973): 95–100.

Nash, Roderick Frazier. *The Rights of Nature: A History of Environmental Ethics*. Madison: University of Wisconsin Press, 1989.

Nehamas, Alexander. *Nietzsche: Life as Literature*. Cambridge, Mass.: Harvard University Press, 1985.

Nelson, John S., Allan Megill, and Donald McCloskey, eds. *The Rhetoric of the Human Sciences: Language and Argument in Scholarship and Public Affairs*. Madison: University of Wisconsin Press, 1987.

Newall, Allan, and Herbert A. Simon. *Human Problem Solving*. Englewood Cliffs, N.J.: Prentice-Hall, 1972.

Nicholson, Linda, ed. *Feminism/Postmodernism*. New York: Routledge, 1990.

Nietzsche, Friedrich. *Thus Spoke Zarathustra*, trans. Walter Kaufmann. In *The Portable Nietzsche*, ed. Walter Kaufmann, 103–439. New York: Viking, 1954.

Nisbet, Robert. *Sociology as an Art Form*. New York: Oxford University Press, 1976.

Norman, Donald A. "Reflections on Cognition and Parallel Distributive Processing." In David E. Rumelhart, James L. McClelland, and the PDP Research Group, *Parallel Distributed Processing*, vol. 2: *Psychological and Biological Models*, 531–52. Cambridge, Mass.: MIT Press, 1986.

Oldman, David, and Charles Drucker. "The Non-reducibility of Ethno-Methods: Can People and Computers Form a Society?" In *Social Action and Artificial Intelligence*, ed. C. Nigel Gilbert and Christian Heath, 144–59. Aldershot: Gower, 1985.

Pagels, Heinz. *The Dreams of Reason*. New York: Simon and Schuster, 1988.

Papert, Seymour. "One AI or Many?" *Daedalus* 117 (1988): 1–14.

Park, Robert Ezra. *Human Communities: The City and Human Ecology*. Glencoe, Ill.: Free Press, 1952.

———, and Ernest W. Burgess. *Introduction to the Science of Society*. 2d ed. Chicago: University of Chicago Press, 1924.

Parsons, Talcott. "The American Family: Its Relation to Personality and to the Social Structure." In Talcott Parsons and Robert F. Bales, *Family, Socialization and Interaction*, 3–33. New York: Free Press, 1955.

———. *The Social System*. Glencoe, Ill.: Free Press, 1951.

Paulson, William R. *The Noise of Culture: Literary Texts in a World of Information*. Ithaca, N.Y.: Cornell University Press, 1988.

Peirce, Charles. "How to Make Our Ideas Clear." In *Philosophical Writings of Peirce*, ed. Julius Buchler, 23–41. New York: Dover, 1955. (Originally published in 1878.)

Penley, Constance, and Andrew Ross, eds. *Technoculture*. Minneapolis: University of Minnesota Press, 1991.

Penrose, Roger. *The Emperor's New Mind: Concerning Computers, Minds, and the Laws of Physics*. New York: Oxford University Press, 1988.

Perrow, Charles. *Normal Accidents*. New York: Basic Books, 1984.

Phillips, Derek L. *Toward a Just Society*. Princeton, N.J.: Princeton University Press, 1986.

Pilisuk, Marc, and Susan Hillier Parks. *The Healing Web*. Hanover, N.H.: University Press of New England, 1986.

Plaskow, Judith, and Carol P. Christ, eds. *Weaving the Visions: New Patterns of Feminist Spirituality*. San Francisco: HarperCollins, 1989.

Popenoe, David. *Disturbing the Nest: Family Change and Decline in Modern Societies*. New York: Aldine de Gruyter, 1988.

Poster, Mark. *The Mode of Information: Poststructuralism and the Social Context*. Chicago: University of Chicago Press, 1990.

Poundstone, William. *The Recursive Universe: Cosmic Complexity and the Limits of Scientific Knowledge*. New York: Morrow, 1985.

Powell, Walter W., and Paul J. DiMaggio, eds. *The New Institutionalism in Organizational Analysis*. Chicago: University of Chicago Press, 1991.

Premack, David, and Guy Woodruff. "Does the Chimpanzee Have a Theory of Mind?" *Behavioral and Brain Sciences* 1 (December 1978): 515–26.

Pylyshyn, Zenon W. "Complexity and the Study of Artificial and Human Intelligence." In *Mind Design*, ed. John Haugland, 67–94. Montgomery, Vt.: Bradford, 1981.

Rabinow, Paul, and William M. Sullivan, eds. *Interpretive Social Science: A Second Look*. Berkeley: University of California Press, 1987.

Rapp, Rayna. "Family and Class in Contemporary America: Notes Toward an Understanding of Ideology." In *Rethinking the Family: Some Feminist Questions*, ed. Barrie Thorne and Marilyn Yalom, 168–87. New York: Longmans, 1982.

Reeke, George N., Jr., and Gerald M. Edelman. "Real Brains and Artificial Intelligence." *Daedalus* 117 (1988): 143–73.

Regan, Tom. *The Case for Animal Rights*. Berkeley: University of California Press, 1983.

Rehberg, Karl-Siegbert. " 'Anti-Sociology': A Conservative View on Social Sciences." *The History of Sociology* 5 (Spring 1985): 45–60.

Rhea, Buford, ed. *The Future of the Sociological Classics*. Boston: Allen and Unwin, 1981.

Rindos, David. "The Evolution of the Capacity for Culture: Sociobiology, Structuralism, and Cultural Selectiveness." *Current Anthropology* 27 (August–October 1986): 315–32.

Rollins, Bernard E. *The Unheeded Cry: Animal Consciousness, Animal Pain, and Society*. New York: Oxford University Press, 1990.

Rolston, Holmes, III. *Environmental Ethics: Duties to and Values in the Natural World*. Philadelphia: Temple University Press, 1988.

——— . *Philosophy Gone Wild: Essays in Environmental Ethics*. Buffalo, N.Y.: Prometheus Books, 1986.

Rorty, Richard. *Contingency, Irony, Solidarity*. New York: Cambridge University Press, 1989.

——— . *Philosophical Papers*, vol. 1: *Objectivity, Relativism, and Truth*. New York: Cambridge University Press, 1991.

Rosenau, Pauline Marie. *Post-modernism and the Social Sciences: Insights, Inroads, and Intrusions*. Princeton, N.J.: Princeton University Press, 1991.

Rosenblatt, Frank. *Principles of Neurodynamics*. New York: Spartan, 1962.

Rosenfield, Israel. *The Invention of Memory: A New View of the Brain*. New York: Basic Books, 1988.

Rossi, Alice. "A Biosocial Perspective on Parenting." *Daedalus* 106 (Spring 1977): 1–31.

——— . "Gender and Parenthood." *American Sociological Review* 49 (February 1984): 1–19.

Rumbaugh, Duane M. "Current and Future Research on Chimpanzee Intellect." In *Understanding Chimpanzees*, ed. Paul G. Heltne and Linda A. Marquardt, 296–310. Cambridge, Mass.: Harvard University Press, 1989.

——— , and Timothy V. Gill. "Lana's Acquisition of Language Skills." In *Language Learning by Chimpanzee: The LANA Project*, ed. Duane M. Rumbaugh, 165–92. New York: Academic Press, 1977.

Rumelhart, D. E., P. Smolensky, J. L. McClelland, and G. E. Hinton. "Schematic and Sequential Thought Processes in PDP Models." In David E. Rumelhart, James L. McClelland, and the PDP Research Group, *Parallel Distributed Processing*, vol. 2: *Psychological and Biological Models*, 7–57. Cambridge, Mass.: MIT Press, 1986.

Sagoff, Mark. "Animal Liberation and Environmental Ethics: Bad Marriage, Quick Divorce." *Osgoode Hall Law Journal* 22 (Summer 1984): 297–321.

——— . "What Is Environmentalism?" In *Three Essays on Ethics and the Environment*. Unpublished manuscript, 1990.

Sahlins, Marshall. *The Use and Abuse of Biology*. Ann Arbor: University of Michigan Press, 1976.

Sale, Kirkpatrick. "Deep Ecology and Its Critics." *The Nation*, 14 May 1988, 670–75.

Sallah, Ariel Kay. "Deeper Than Deep Ecology? The Eco-Feminist Connection." *Environmental Ethics* 6 (Winter 1984): 323–38.

Scaff, Lawrence A. *Fleeing the Iron Cage: Culture, Politics, and Modernity in the Thought of Max Weber.* Berkeley: University of California Press, 1989.

Schank, Roger C., and Robert P. Abelson. *Scripts, Plans, Goals, and Understanding.* Hillsdale, N.J.: Erlbaum, 1977.

Scheff, Thomas J. *Microsociology: Discourse, Emotion, and Social Structure.* Chicago: University of Chicago Press, 1990.

Schegloff, Emmanuel, and Harvey Sacks. "Opening Up Closings." In *Ethnomethodology: Selected Readings*, ed. Ray Turner, 233–64. Baltimore: Penguin Books, 1979.

Schotter, Andrew. *The Economic Theory of Social Institutions.* New York: Cambridge University Press, 1981.

Schrödinger, Erwin. *"What Is Life? The Physical Aspect of the Living Cell" and "Mind and Matter."* Cambridge: Cambridge University Press, 1967.

Scott, Joan Wallach. *Gender and the Politics of History.* New York: Columbia University Press, 1988.

Searle, John R. "Minds, Brains, and Programs." In *Mind Design*, ed. John Haugland, 282–306. Montgomery, Vt.: Bradford, 1981.

Sebeok, Thomas A., ed. *How Animals Communicate.* Bloomington: Indiana University Press, 1977.

Serres, Michel. "The Origin of Language: Biology, Information Theory, and Thermodynamics." In *Hermes: Literature, Science, Philosophy*, ed. Josue V. Harari and David F. Bell, 71–83. Baltimore: Johns Hopkins University Press, 1982.

Shannon, Benny. "A Simple Comment Regarding the Turing Test." *Journal for the Theory of Social Behaviour* 19 (July 1989): 249–56.

Shepsle, Kenneth. "Studying Institutions: Some Lessons from the Rational Choice Approach." *Journal of Theoretical Politics* 1 (April 1989): 131–47.

Shils, Edward. *Tradition.* Chicago: University of Chicago Press, 1981.

Shklar, Judith. *Ordinary Vices.* Cambridge, Mass.: Harvard University Press, 1984.

Short, James F., Jr. *The Social Fabric.* Beverly Hills, Calif.: Sage, 1985.

——— , ed. *The Social Fabric of the Metropolis: Contributions of the Chicago School of Urban Sociology.* Chicago: University of Chicago Press, 1971.

Shweder, Richard A. *Thinking Through Cultures: Explorations in Cultural Psychology.* Cambridge, Mass.: Harvard University Press, 1991.

Sica, Alan. *Weber, Irrationality, and Social Order.* Berkeley: University of California Press, 1988.

Simmel, Georg. *Conflict and the Web of Group Affiliations.* New York: Free Press, 1955.

Simon, Herbert A. *Sciences of the Artificial.* Cambridge, Mass.: MIT Press, 1969.

Simons, Herbert W., ed. *The Rhetorical Turn: Invention and Persuasion in the Conduct of Inquiry.* Chicago: University of Chicago Press, 1990.

Singer, Peter. *Animal Liberation: A New Ethics for Our Treatment of Animals.* New York: Avon Books, 1975.

Skolnick, Arlene. *Embattled Paradise: The American Family in an Age of Uncertainty.* New York: Basic Books, 1992.

Sleeman, Derek. "Inferring Student Models for Intelligent Computer-Aided Instruction." In *Machine Learning: An Artificial Intelligence Approach,* ed. Ryszard S. Michaelski, Jaime G. Carbonell, and Tom M. Mitchell, 483–509. Palo Alto, Calif.: Tioga, 1983.

———, and John Seely Brown. "Intelligent Tutoring Systems: An Overview." In Derek Sleeman and John Seely Brown, *Intelligent Tutoring Systems,* 1–11. New York: Academic Press, 1982.

Smith, Dorothy E. *The Everyday World as Problematic: A Feminist Sociology.* Boston: Northeastern University Press, 1987.

Smith, Maynard J. "The Concepts of Sociobiology." In *Morality as a Biological Phenomenon: The Presuppositions of Sociobiological Research,* ed. Gunther S. Stent, 21–30. Berkeley: University of California Press, 1980.

Smith, W. John. "Communication in Birds." In *How Animals Communicate,* ed. Thomas A. Sebeok, 545–74. Bloomington: Indiana University Press, 1977.

Somit, Albert, ed. *Biology and Politics: Recent Explorations.* The Hague: Mouton, 1976.

Sperling, Susan. *Animal Liberators: Research and Morality.* Berkeley: University of California Press, 1988.

Stacey, Judith. "Are Feminists Afraid to Leave Home? The Challenge of Profamily Feminism." In *What Is Feminism?* ed. Juliet Mitchell and Ann Oakley, 208–37. New York: Pantheon Books, 1986.

———. *Brave New Families: Stories of Domestic Upheaval in Late Twentieth Century America.* New York: Basic Books, 1990.

Stent, Gunther S. "Introduction." In *Morality as a Biological Phenomenon,* ed. Gunther S. Stent, 1–18. Berkeley: University of California Press, 1980.

Stone, Christopher. *Earth and Other Ethics: The Case for Moral Pluralism.* New York: Harper and Row, 1987.

———. "Should Trees Have Standing? Toward Legal Rights for Natural Objects." *Southern California Law Review* 45 (Spring 1972): 450–501.

Sullivan, Roger. *Immanuel Kant's Moral Theory.* Cambridge: Cambridge University Press, 1989.

Tarde, Gabriel de. *The Laws of Imitation,* trans. Elsie Clews Parsons. New York: Holt, 1903.

Taylor, Charles. *Philosophical Papers,* vol. 1: *Human Agency and Language.* Cambridge: Cambridge University Press, 1985.

———. *Sources of the Self: The Making of Modern Identity.* Cambridge, Mass.: Harvard University Press, 1989.

Taylor, Paul W. "In Defense of Biocentrism." *Environmental Ethics* 5 (Fall 1983): 337–43.

———. *Respect for Nature: A Theory of Environmental Ethics.* Princeton, N.J.: Princeton University Press, 1986.

Thomas, Keith. *Man and the Natural World: Changing Attitudes in England, 1500–1800.* New York: Penguin Books, 1984.

Thorson, Thomas Landon. *Biopolitics.* New York: Holt, Rinehart and Winston, 1970.

Tobias, Michael, ed. *Deep Ecology.* San Marcos, Calif.: Avant Books, 1988.

Tompkins, Jane, ed. *Reader-Response Criticism from Formalism to Post-structuralism.* Baltimore: Johns Hopkins University Press, 1980.

Trivers, R. L. "The Evolution of Reciprocal Altruism." *Quarterly Review of Biology* 46 (March 1971): 35–57.

Turing, Alan. "Computing Machines and Intelligence." *Mind* 49 (1950): 433–60.

Turkle, Sherry. *The Second Self: Computers and the Human Spirit.* New York: Touchstone Books, 1984.

Vidich, Arthur, and Stanford Lyman. *American Sociology: Worldly Rejections of Religion and Their Directions.* New Haven, Conn.: Yale University Press, 1985.

Wagman, Morton. *Artificial Intelligence and Human Cognition: A Theoretical Comparison of Two Realms of Intellect.* New York: Praeger, 1991.

Wagner, Peter. "Science of Society Lost: On the Failure to Establish Sociology in Europe During the Classical Period." In *Discourses on Society,* vol. 15, ed. Peter Wagner, Bjorn Wittrock, and R. Whitley, 219–45. Amsterdam: Kluwer, 1990.

Waldrop, M. Mitchell. "Soar: A Unified Theory of Cognition?" *Science* 241 (15 July 1988): 296–98.

———. "Toward a Unified Theory of Cognition." *Science* 241 (1 July 1988): 27–29.

Walker, Stephen. *Animal Thought*. London: Routledge and Kegan Paul, 1983.

Wallace, Walter L. *Principles of Scientific Sociology*. New York: Aldine, 1983.

Wasserman, Harry, and Holly E. Danforth. *The Human Bond: Support Groups and Mutual Aid*. New York: Springer, 1988.

Watt, Ian. *The Rise of the Novel: Studies in Defoe, Richardson, and Fielding*. Berkeley: University of California Press, 1957.

Weaver, Robert R. "Some Implications of the Emergence and Diffusion of Medical Expert Systems." *Qualitative Sociology* 9 (Fall 1986): 237–57.

Weber, Max. "Politics as a Vocation" and "Religious Rejections of the World and Their Directions." In *From Max Weber: Essays in Sociology*, ed. Hans Gerth and C. Wright Mills, 77–128, 323–59. New York: Oxford University Press, 1958.

Weizenbaum, Joseph. *Computer Power and Human Reason*. San Francisco: Freeman, 1976.

Wenger, Etienne. *Artificial Intelligence and Tutoring Systems*. Los Altos, Calif.: William Kaufmann, 1987.

Wertsch, James V. *Voices of the Mind: A Sociocultural Approach to Mediated Action*. Cambridge, Mass.: Harvard University Press, 1991.

Westra, Laura. "Let It Be: Heidegger and Future Generations." *Environmental Ethics* 7 (Winter 1985): 341–50.

Willhoite, Fred H., Jr. "Primates and Political Authority: A Biobehavioral Perspective." *American Political Science Review* 70 (December 1976): 1110–26.

Williamson, Oliver E. *Markets and Hierarchies*. New York: Free Press, 1975.

Wilson, Edward O. *The Insect Societies*. Cambridge, Mass.: Belknap Press of Harvard University Press, 1971.

———. *On Human Nature*. Cambridge, Mass.: Harvard University Press, 1978.

———. *Sociobiology: The New Synthesis*. Cambridge, Mass.: Harvard University Press, 1975.

Wirth, Louis. *On Cities and Social Life: Selected Essays*, ed. Albert J. Riess, Jr. Chicago: University of Chicago Press, 1964.

Wolfe, Alan. "Books Versus Articles: Two Ways of Publishing Sociology." *Sociological Forum* 5 (September 1990): 477–89.

———. "Democracy Versus Sociology: Boundaries and Their Political Consequences." In *Cultivating Differences*, ed. Michel Lamont and Marcel Fournier, 309–25. Chicago: University of Chicago Press, 1992.

———. "Sociology as a Vocation." *American Sociologist* 21 (Summer 1990): 136–48.

———. *Whose Keeper? Social Science and Moral Obligation*. Berkeley: University of California Press, 1989.

Woolger, Steve. "Why Not a Sociology of Machines? The Case of Sociology and Artificial Intelligence." *Sociology* 19 (November 1985): 557–72.

Worster, Donald. *Nature's Economy: The Roots of Ecology*. San Francisco: Sierra Club Books, 1977.

Wozniak, Paul R. "Making Sociobiological Sense out of Sociology." *Sociological Quarterly* 25 (Spring 1984): 191–204.

Wright, Robert. *Three Scientists and Their Gods: Looking for Meaning in an Age of Information*. New York: Times Books, 1988.

Zeleny, Milan. *Autopoeisis: A Theory of Living Organisms*. New York: North-Holland, 1981.

Zerubavel, Eviatar. *The Fine Line: Boundaries and Distinctions in Everyday Life*. New York: Free Press, 1991.

Zimmerman, Michael F. *Eclipse of the Self: The Development of Heidegger's Concept of Authenticity*. Athens: Ohio University Press, 1981.

———. "Toward a Heideggerian *Ethos* for Radical Environmentalism." *Environmental Ethics* 5 (Summer 1983): 99–132.

Index

Abbey, Edward, 97
Actors: natural and corporate, 152–53
Adorno, Theodor, 7
AI (artificial intelligence): as computational, 18–19; hardware approach to, 69–73, 74–75; and human intelligence, 55–57, 76–81; meaning for, 80; modeled on mind, 71–72, 78; post-modernism awed by, 119; reality represented by, 62–64, 69, 78; rule-relating by, 77–78; and social sciences, 75–76; sociobiology linked to, 56, 108; software approach to, 62–65, 68–69, 77–78; solving Humean homunculi, 71; and Turing test, 57. *See also* Computers.
Altmann, Stuart A., 32
American Sign Language, 31
Ammerman, Albert J., 46
Animal rights: and ecology movement, 83, 92, 96; imaginative life conflicting with, 87–88, 89, 90, 91, 198n.11; as passive, 17–18; reflecting rationalism, 16; and scientific experimentation, 85–86; utilitarian view of, 84–85, 91. *See also* Nonhuman species
Animals. *See* Nonhuman species
Anthropocentrism: challenges to, 6–8, 11, 81, 82–83, 161; of sociological theory, 3–4, 22–23. *See also* Human species
Ants, 39
Ardrey, Robert, 40
Arendt, Hannah, 24, 86, 168
Artificial intelligence. *See* AI (artificial intelligence)

Autopoietic systems: applied to literary theory, 122–25, 132; complexity controlled by, 130–31; language as, 128–29; life as, 121–22. *See also* Systems theory

Bardo, Susan, 11
Bateman, John, 66
Bateson, Gregory, 104
Beck, Benjamin, 36, 37
Becker, Gary, 14
Behaviorism, 12–13, 33–34. *See also* Natural sciences
Bennington, Geoffrey, 119–20
Bentham, Jeremy, 84
Berger, John, 86–87
Berger, Peter, 22
Biology: culture defined by, 37–38; ecology's shift from, 94, 95; as limiting social model, 166–68, 173–74; literary theory linked to, 124; revolution in, 29–30, 40; social theory influenced by, 22–23, 28, 105, 106, 178; speech affected by, 31; as young science, 167–68. *See also* Natural sciences
"Biotic community," 92, 93. *See also* Ecology; Nature; Nonhuman species
Bird communication, 31. *See also* Communication
Blumer, Herbert, 146
Bonner, John Tyler, 37
Brain: AI modeled on, 62–63, 69–70, 74–75; mind distinguished from, 50, 58, 60–61, 65, 67–68, 76; reality represented by, 64, 65

Compositor: Impressions
Text: 11/13 Caledonia
Display: Caledonia
Printer: Edwards Brothers, Inc.
Binder: Edwards Brothers, Inc.